Graffiti Art Coloring Book

Kenneth Andre Brown Sr.© 2017

In 1986 I began doing graffiti art under the tag name "Search". This is some of my latest works. Maybe not my greatest works. This was done when I was in the Linc program in Wilmington. I was in a rush to get published. I may have placed some of the drawings in twice. This was my first book.

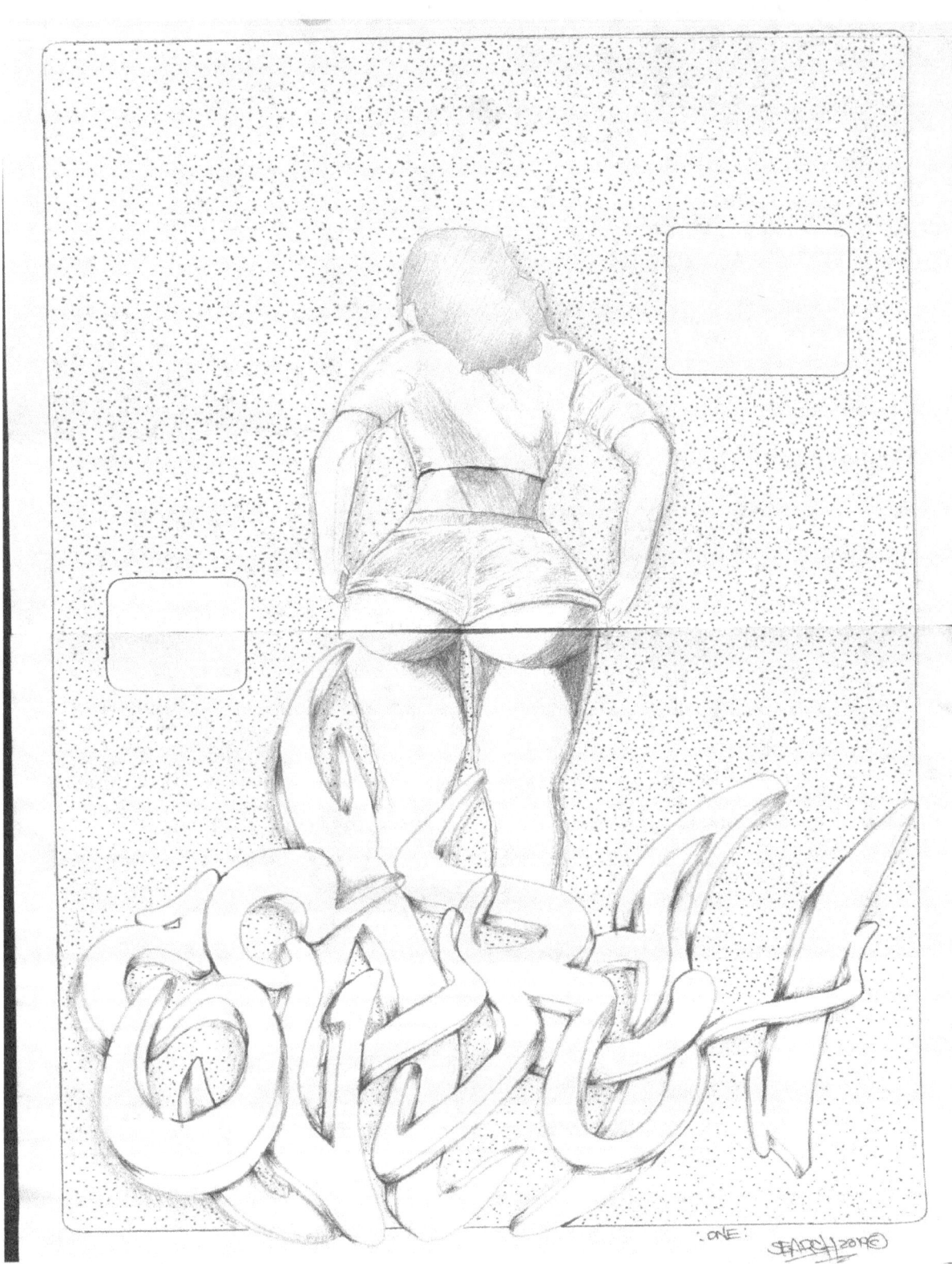

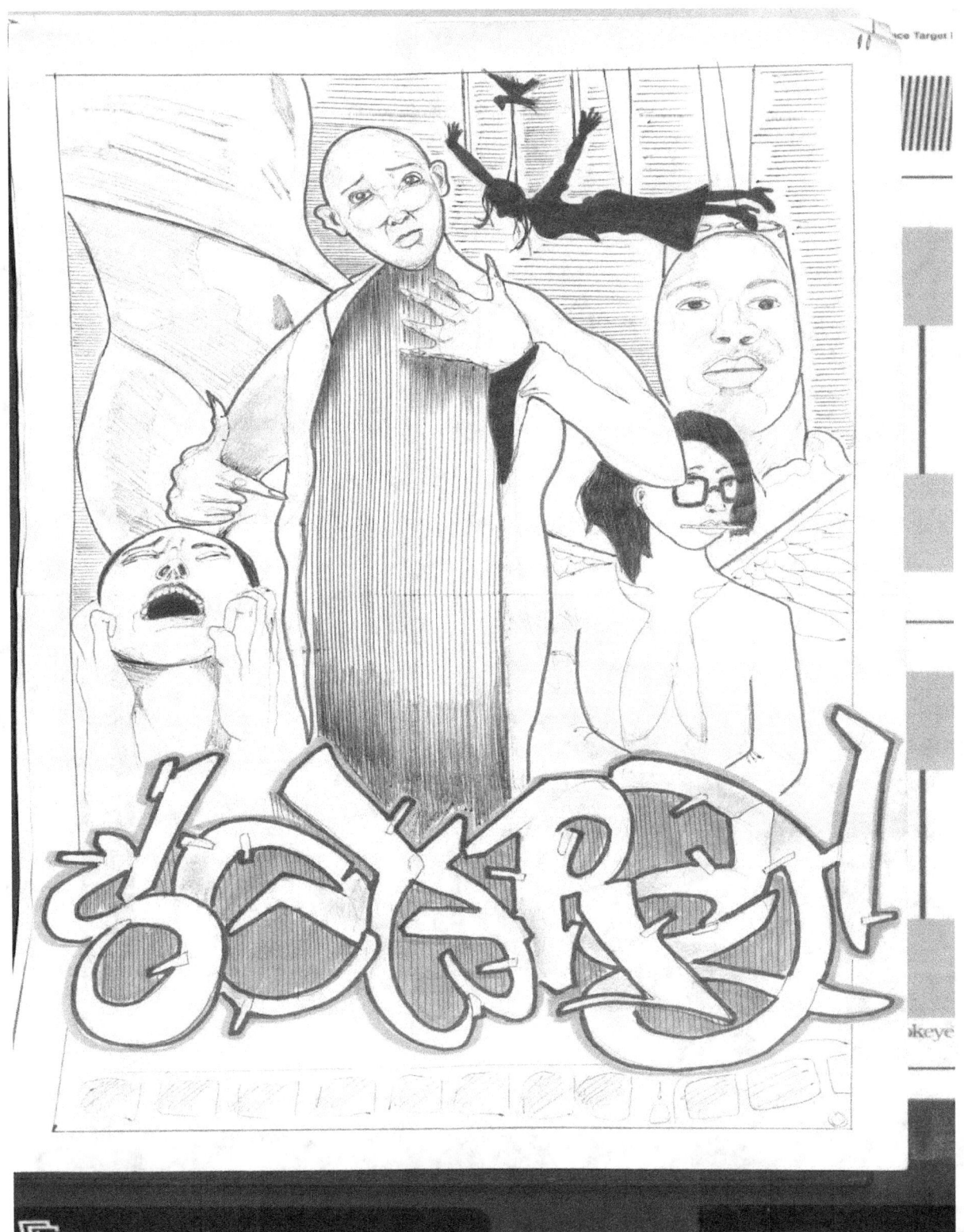

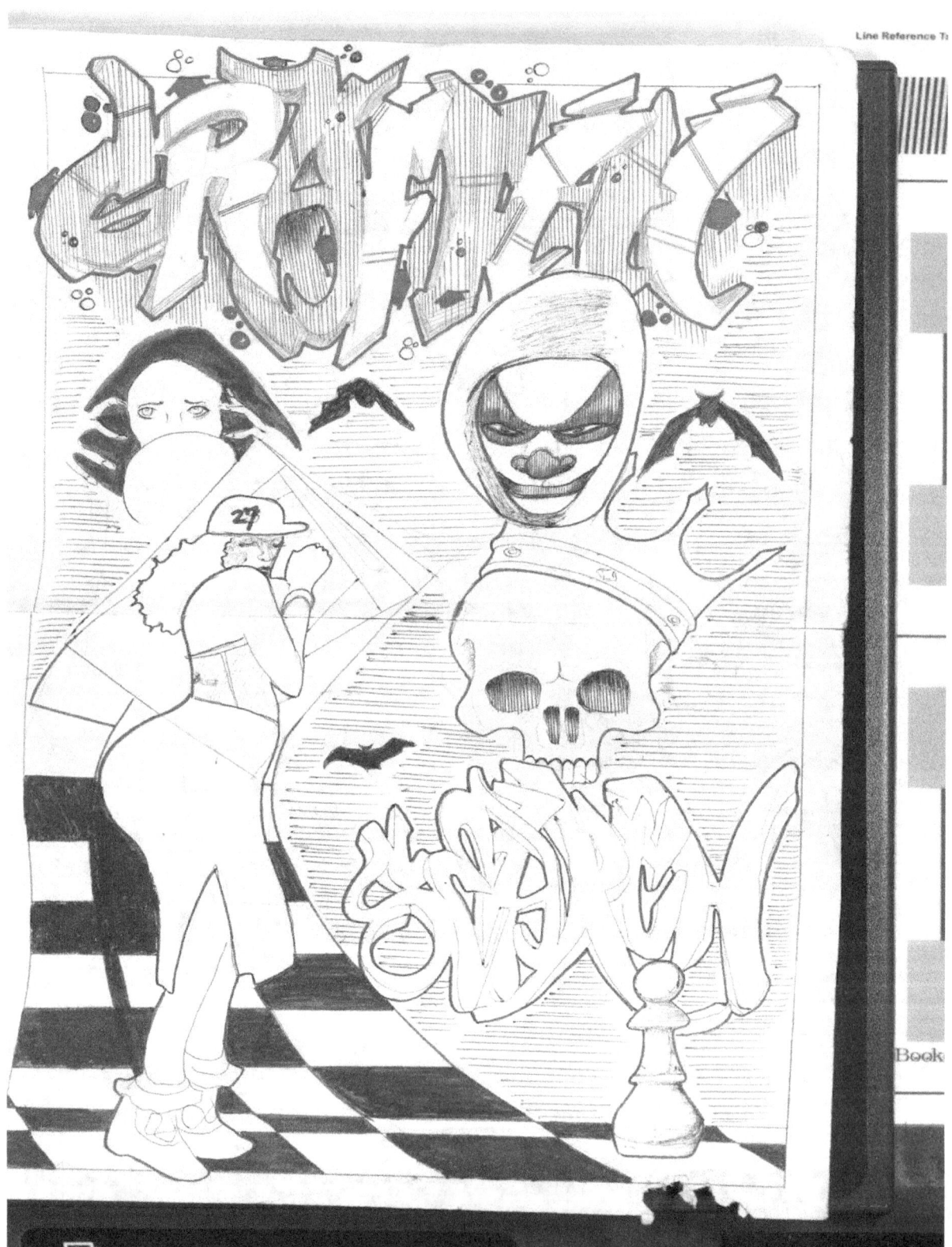

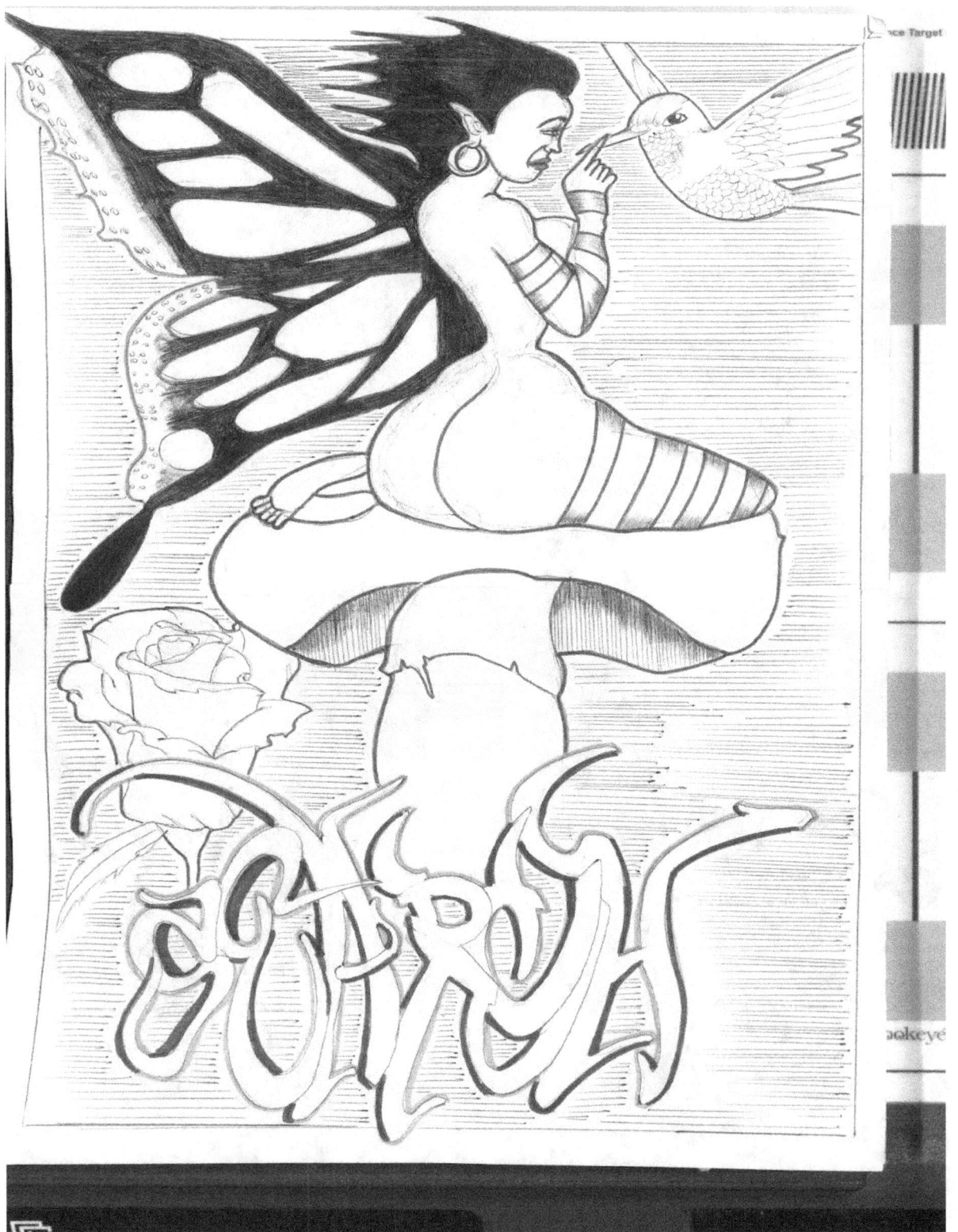

4

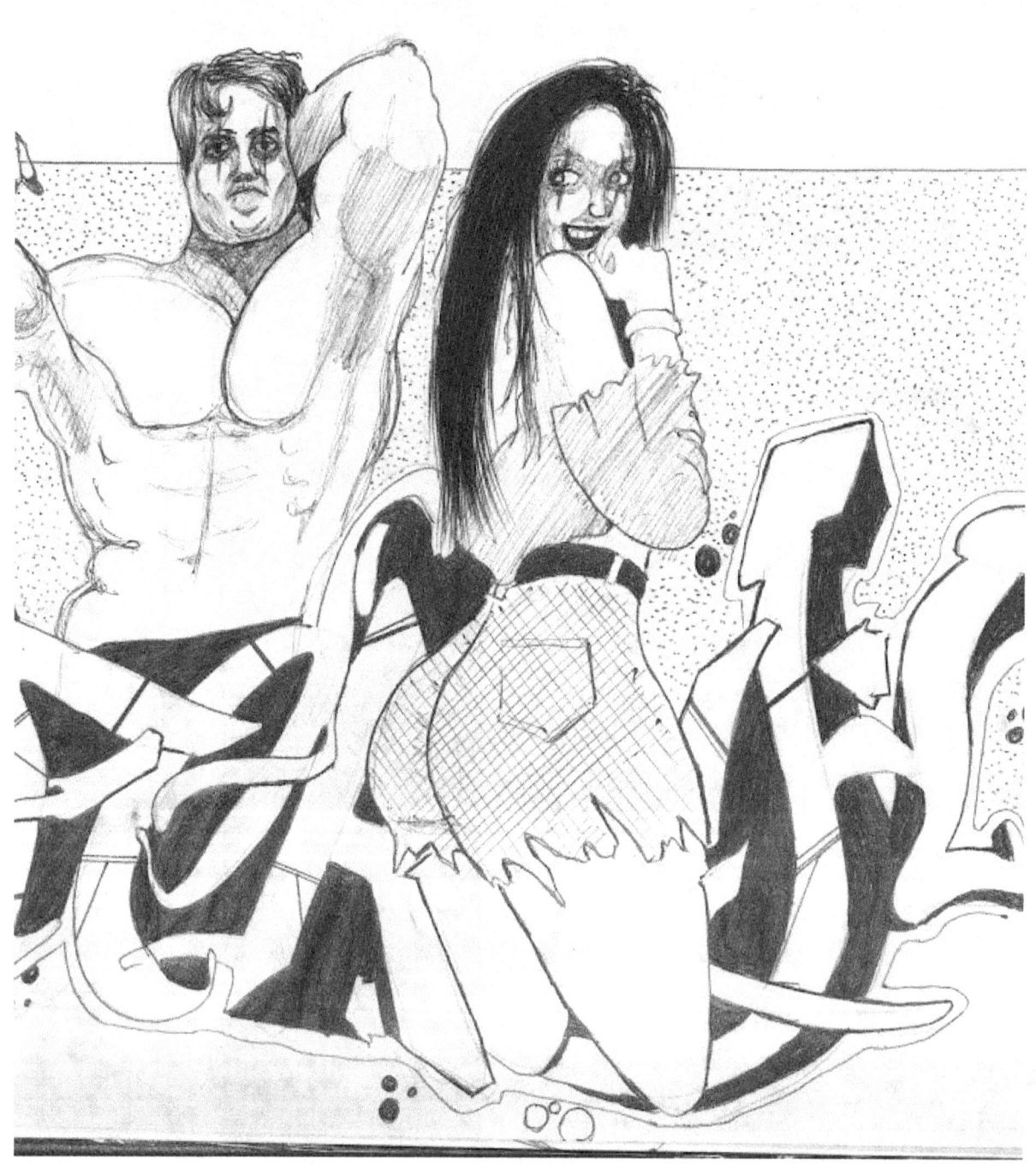

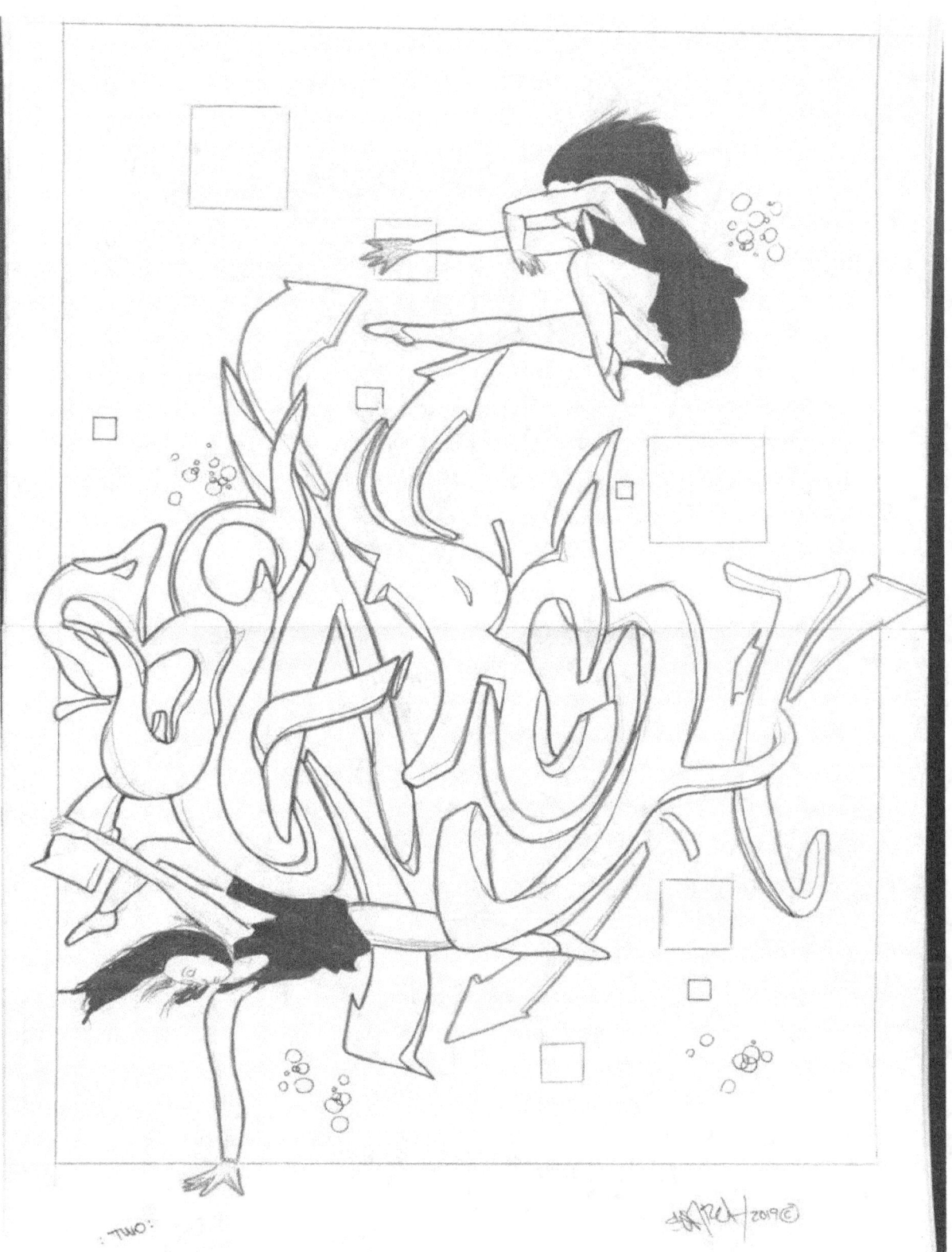

:TWO:

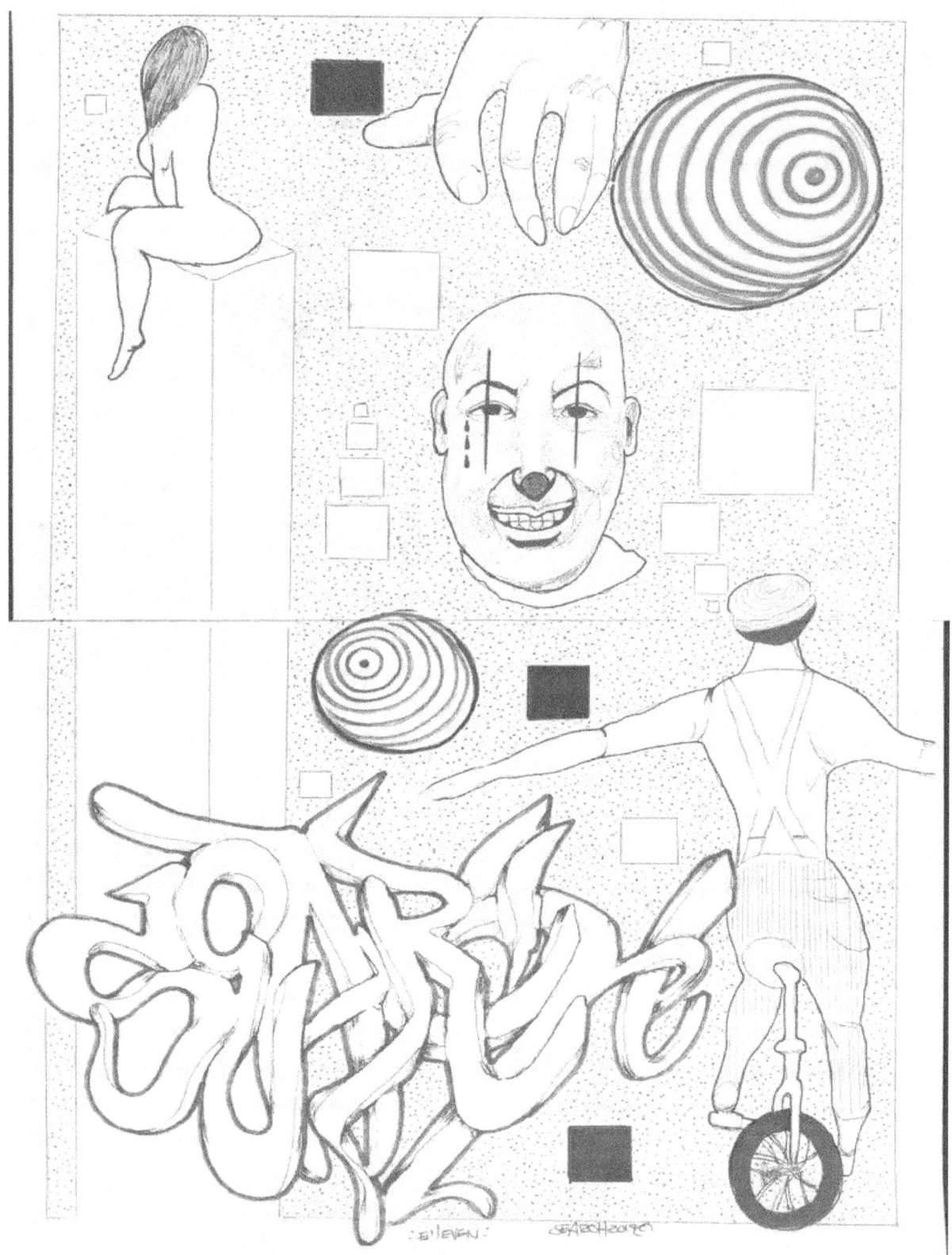

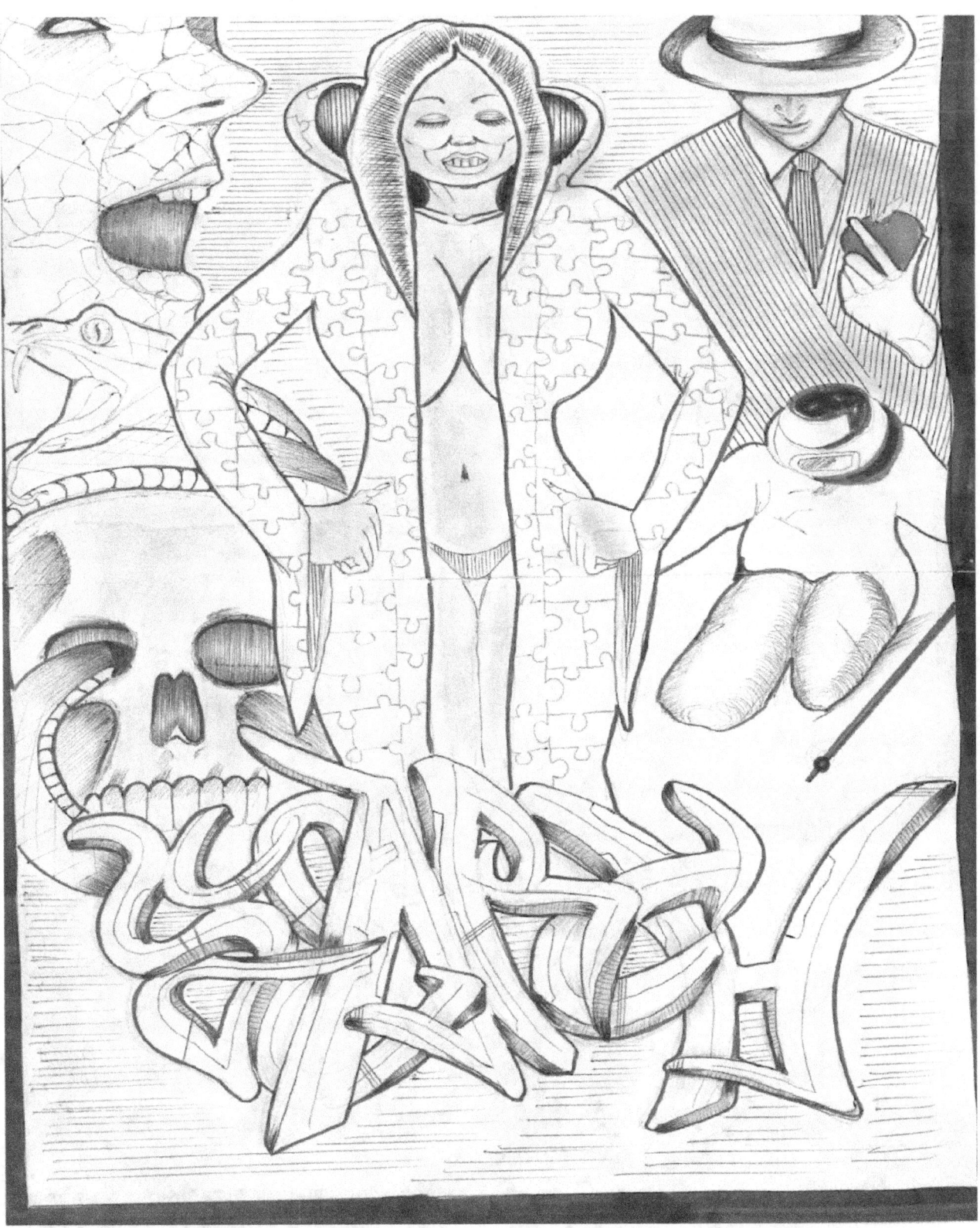

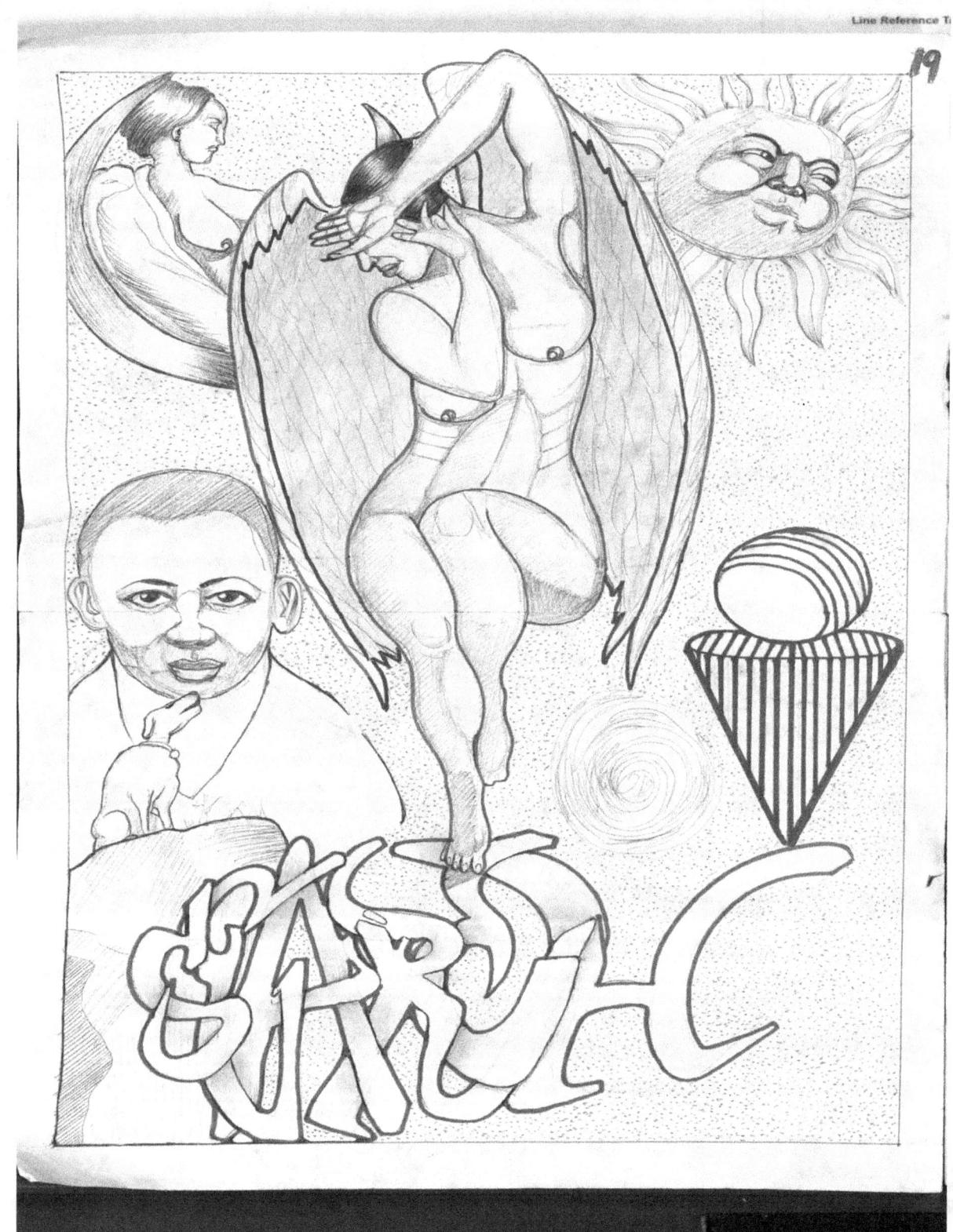

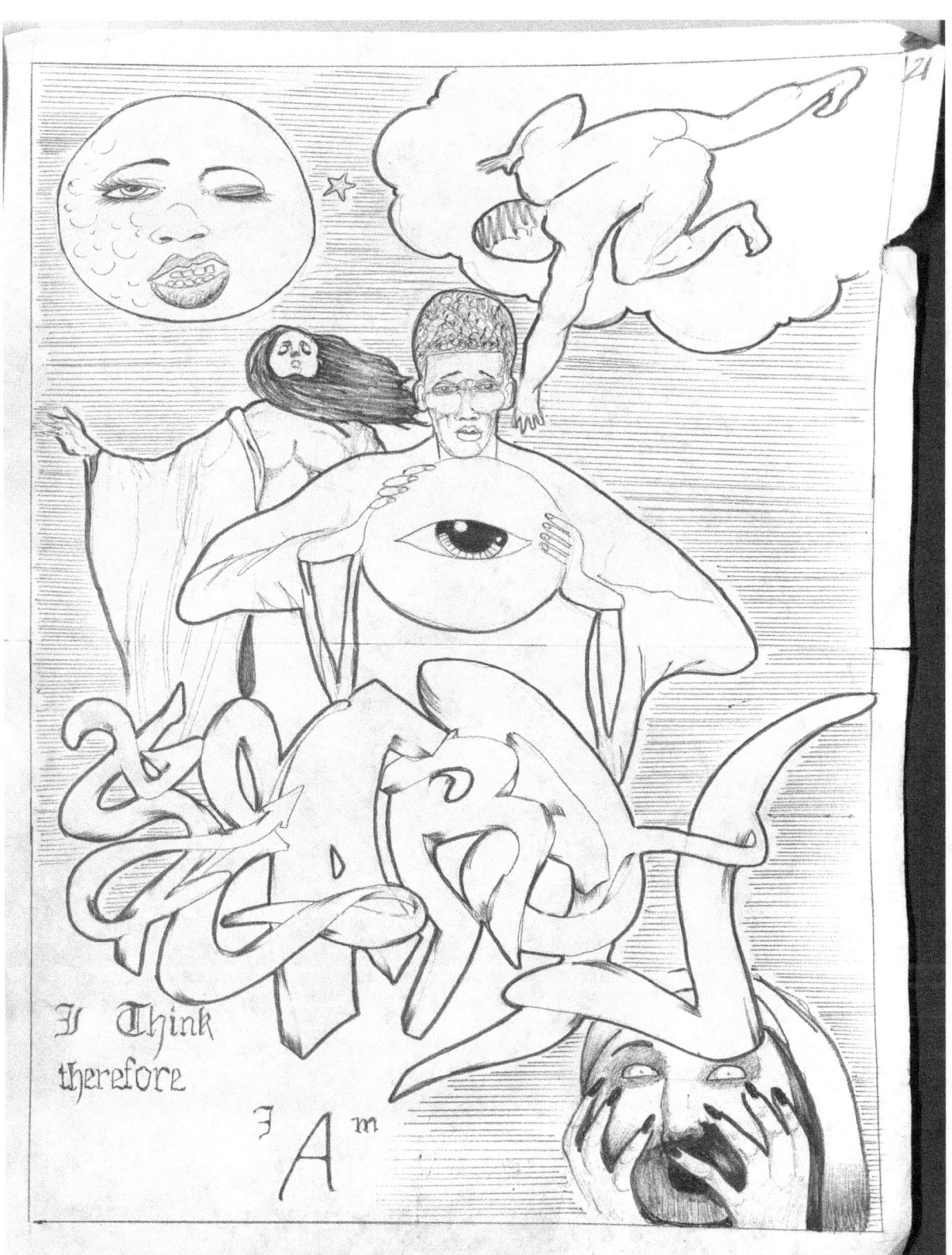

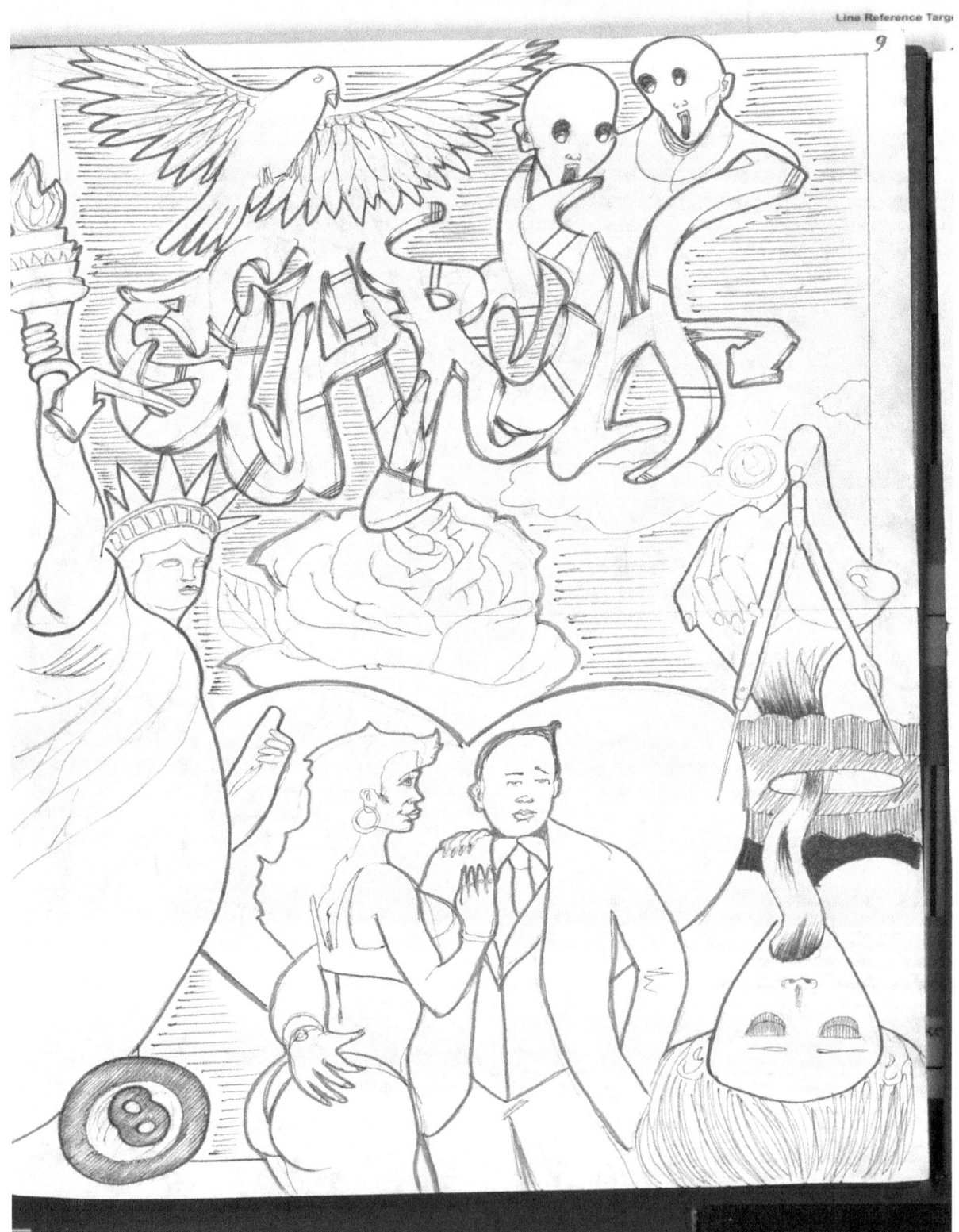

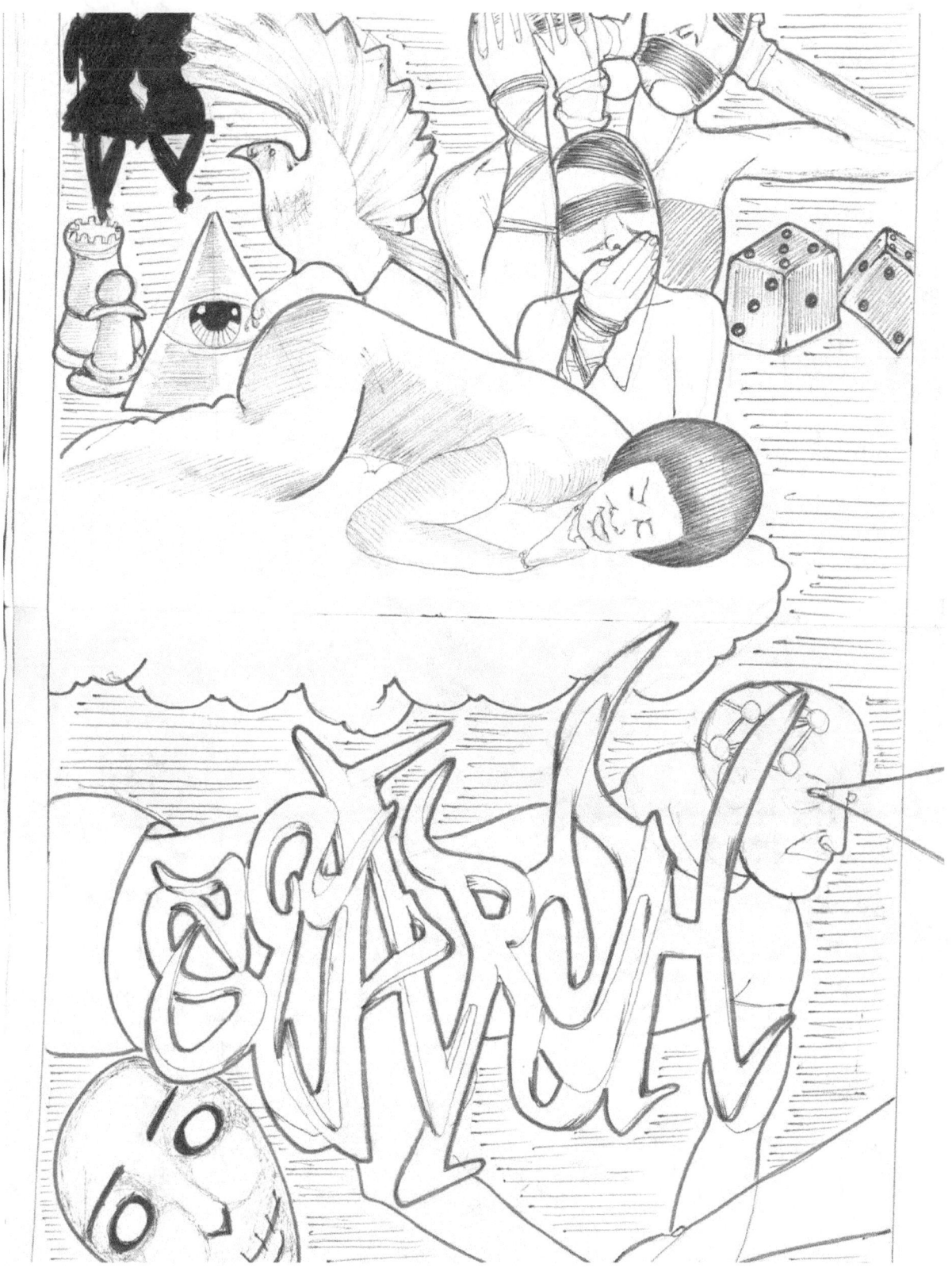

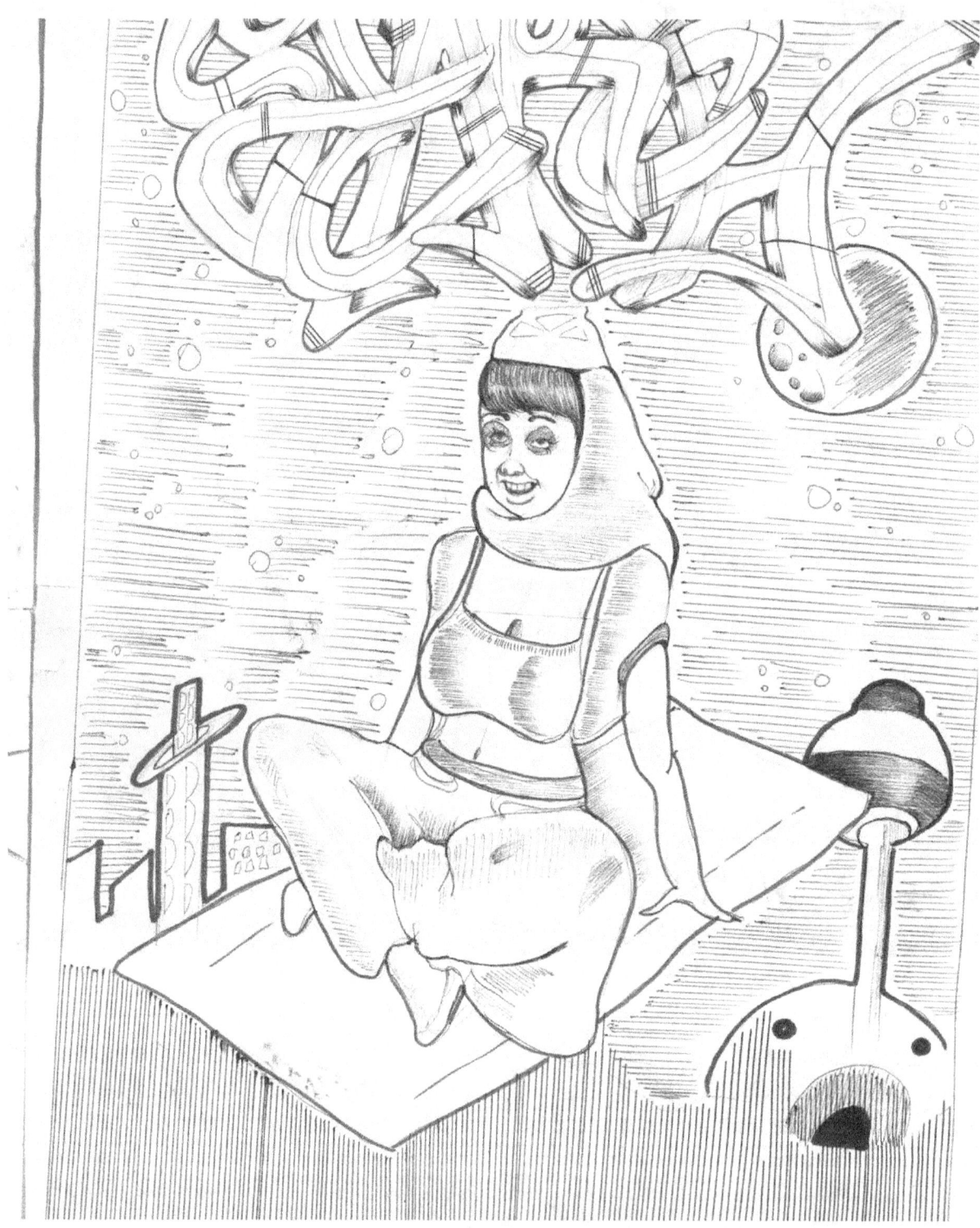

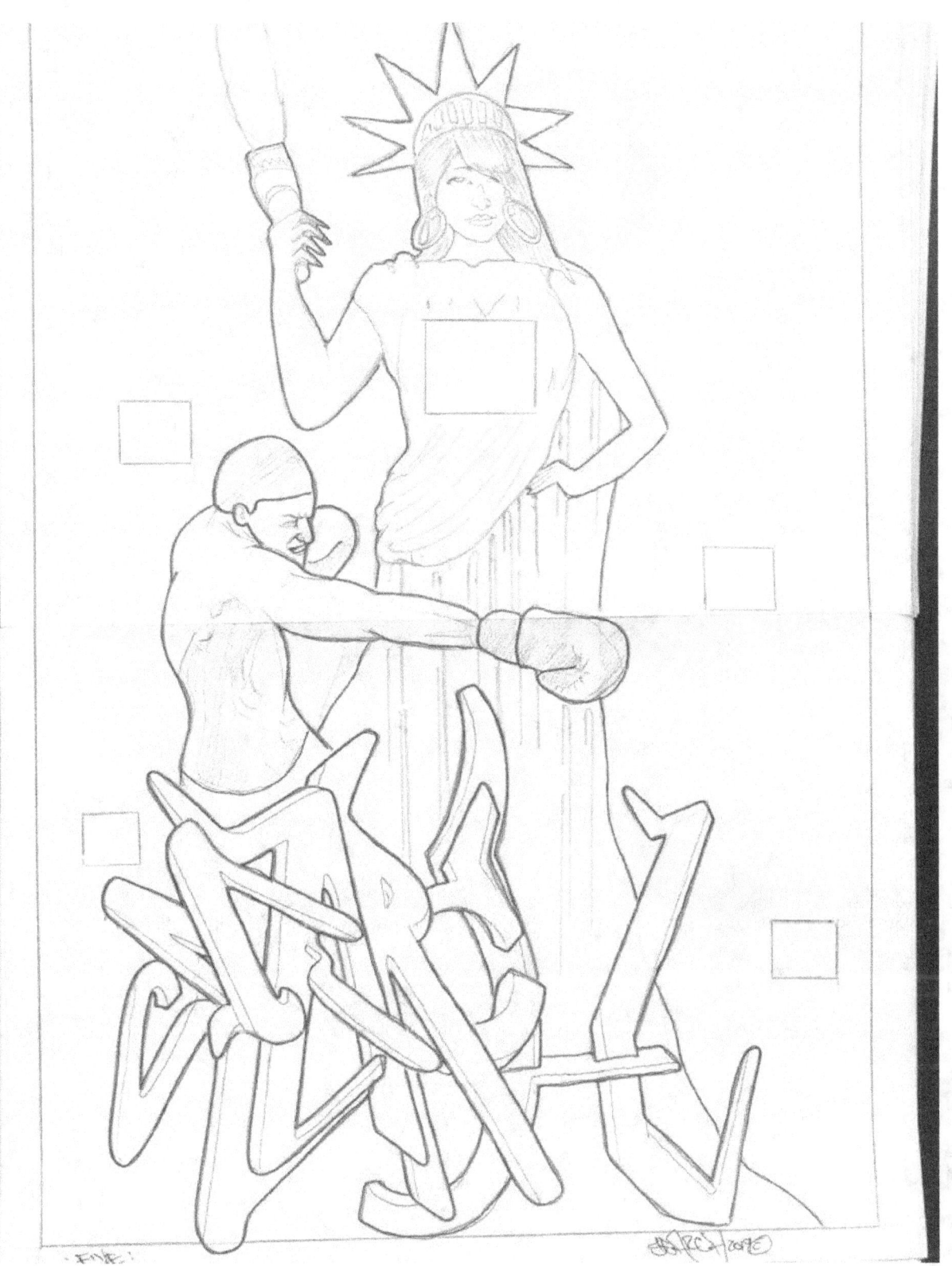

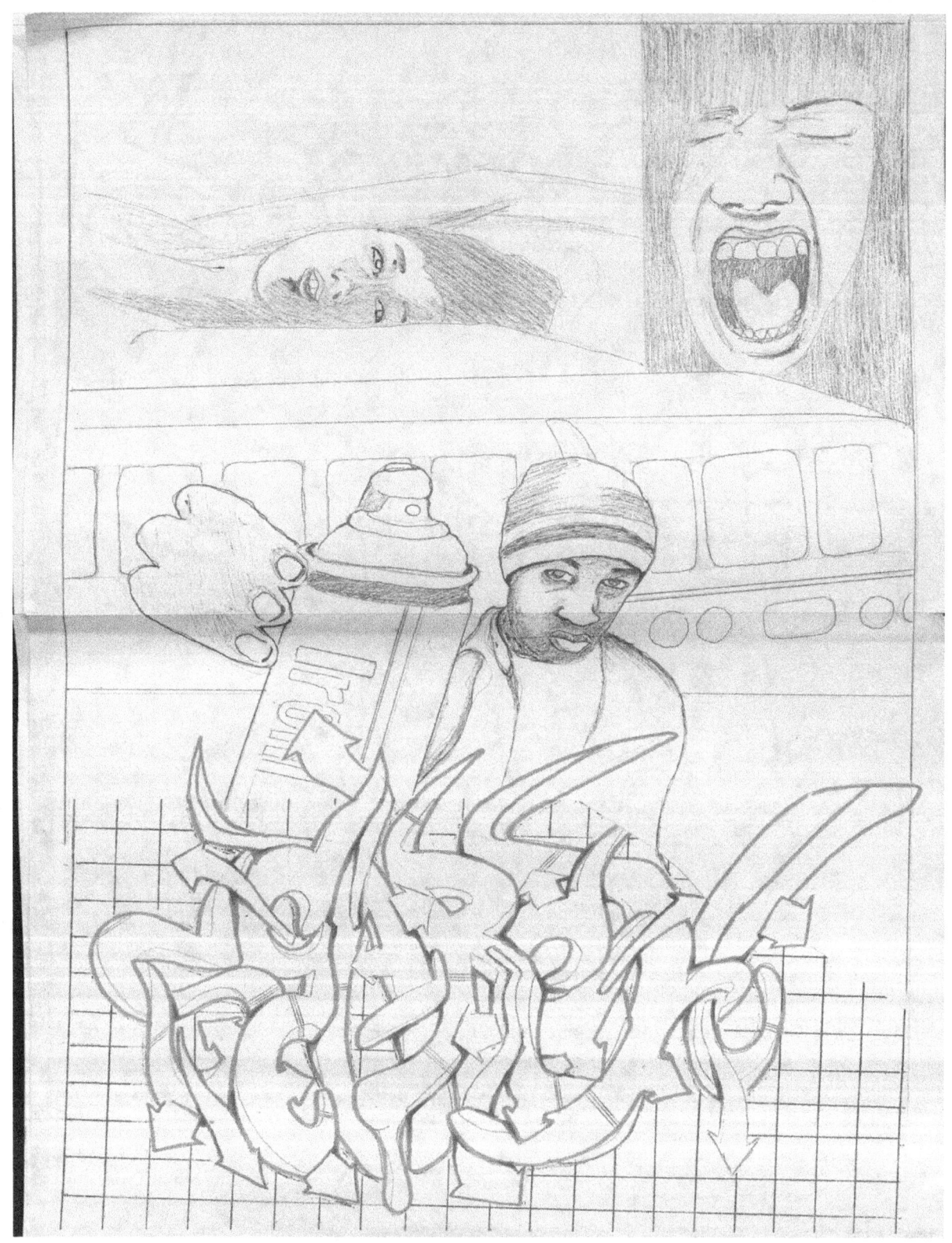

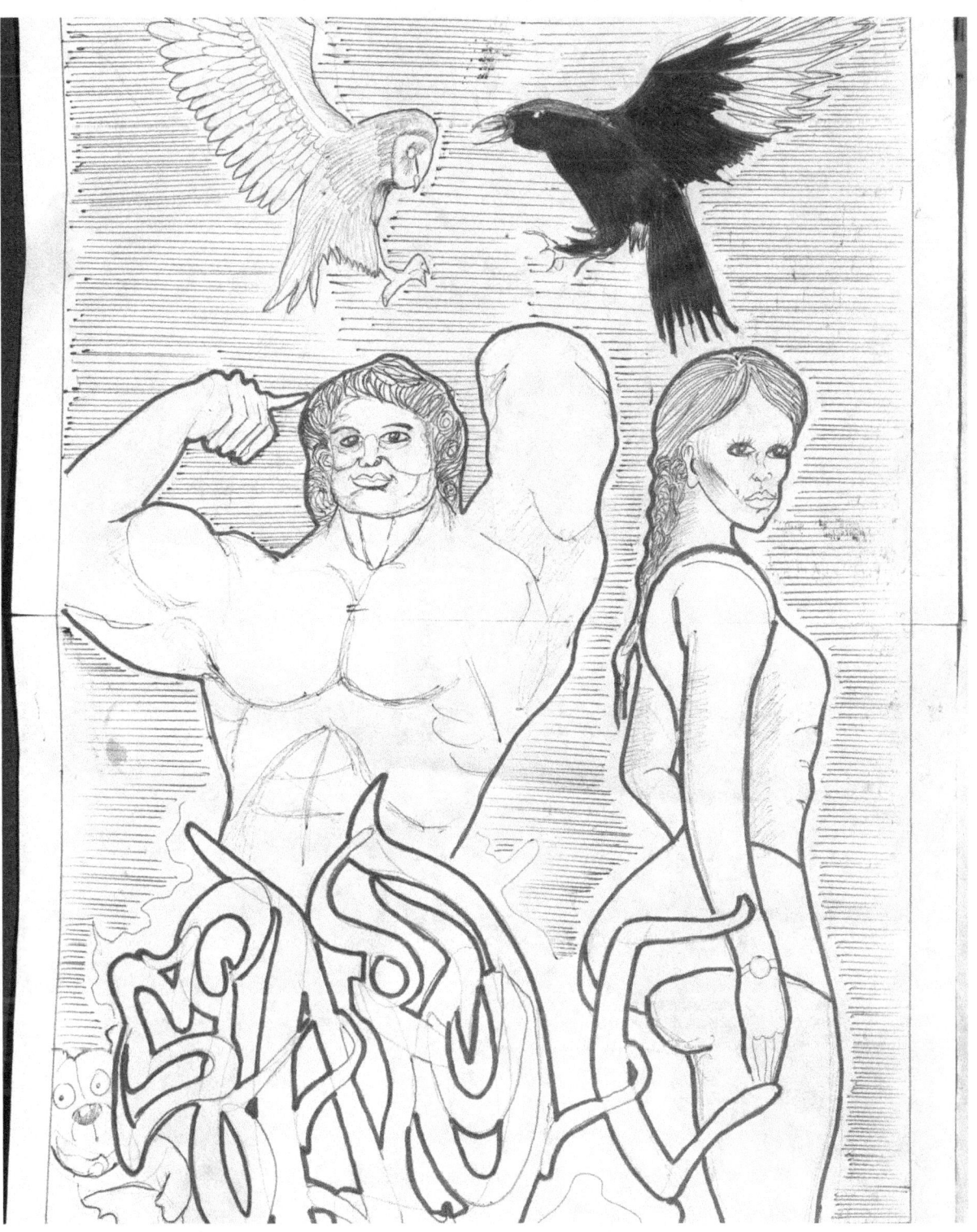

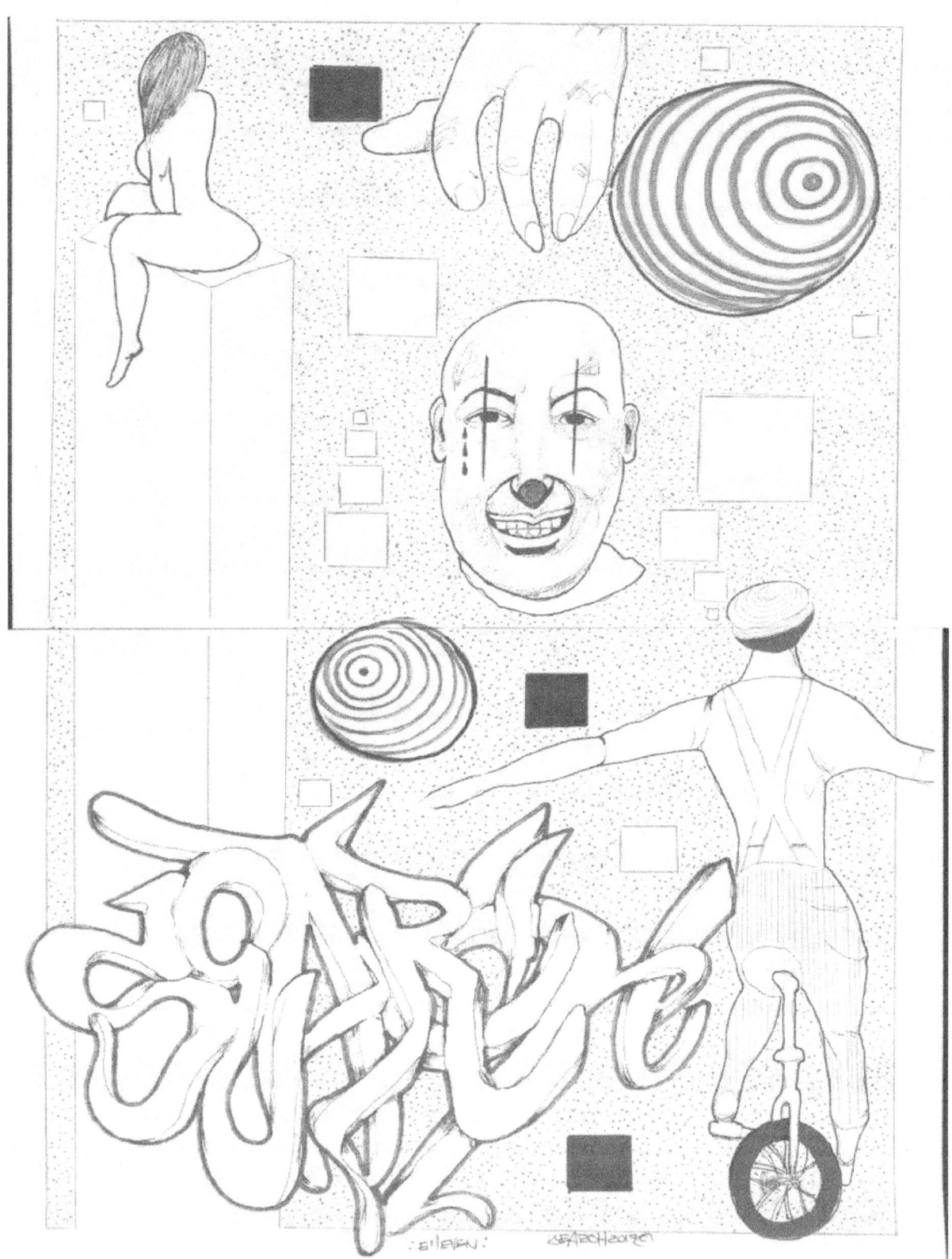

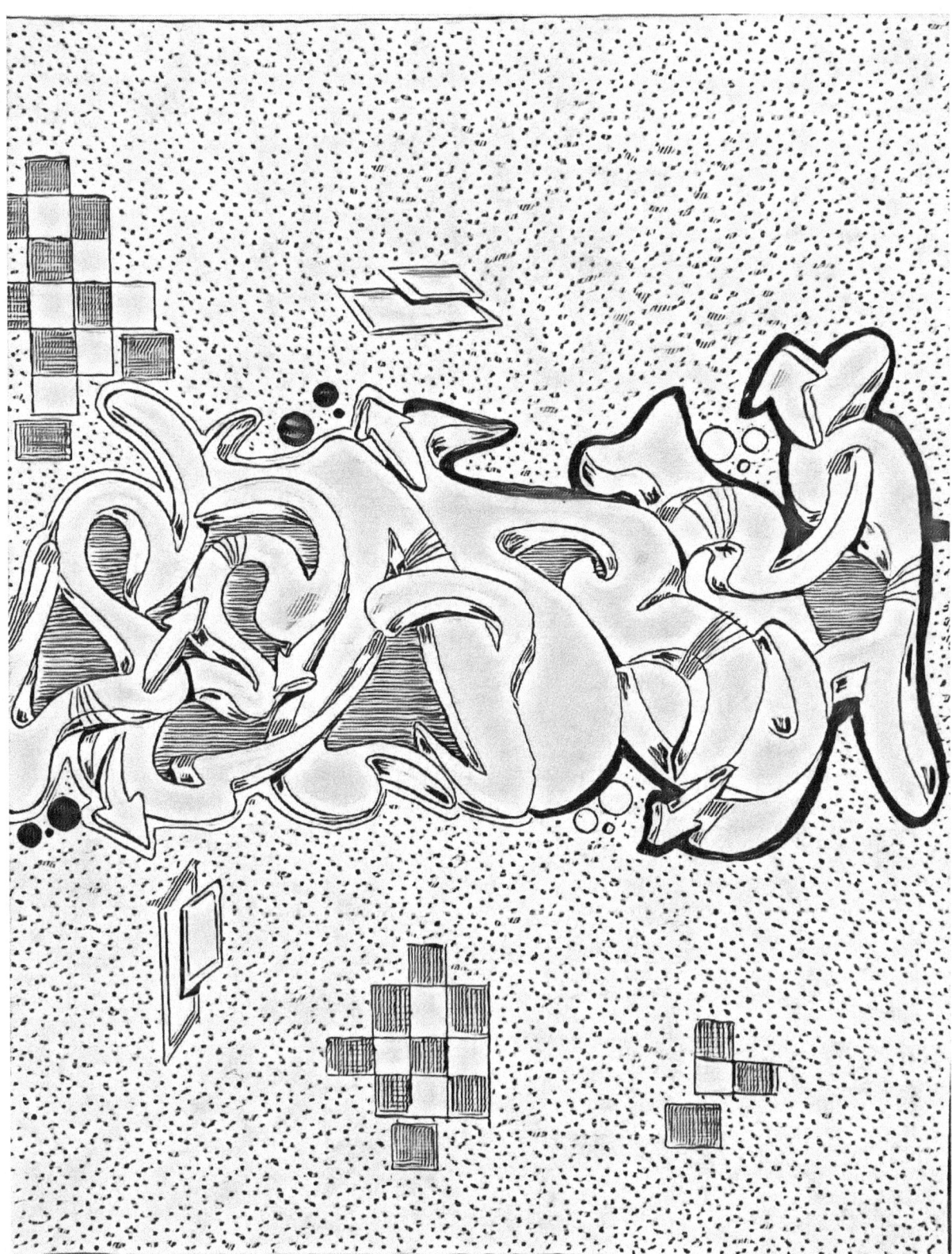

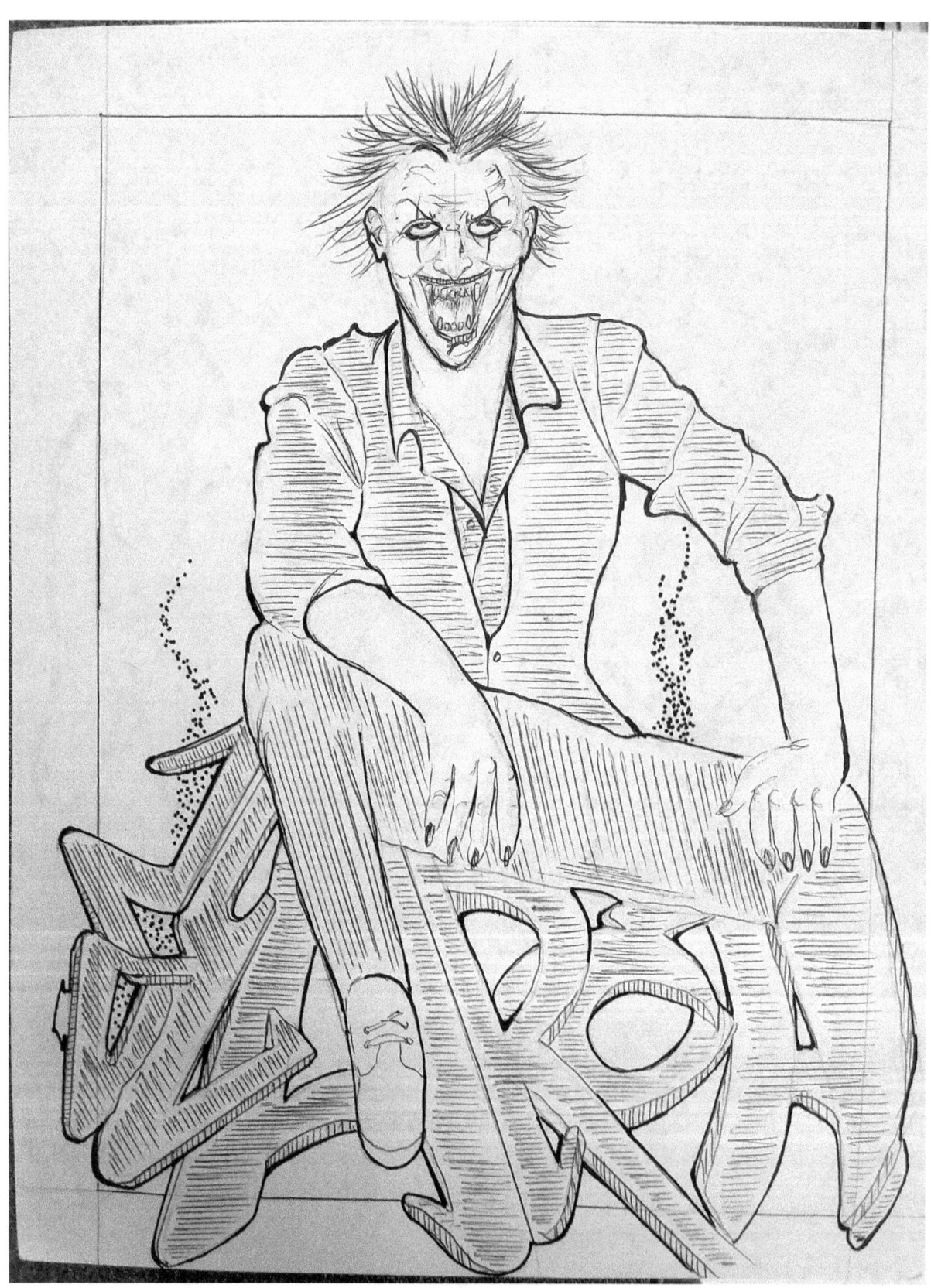

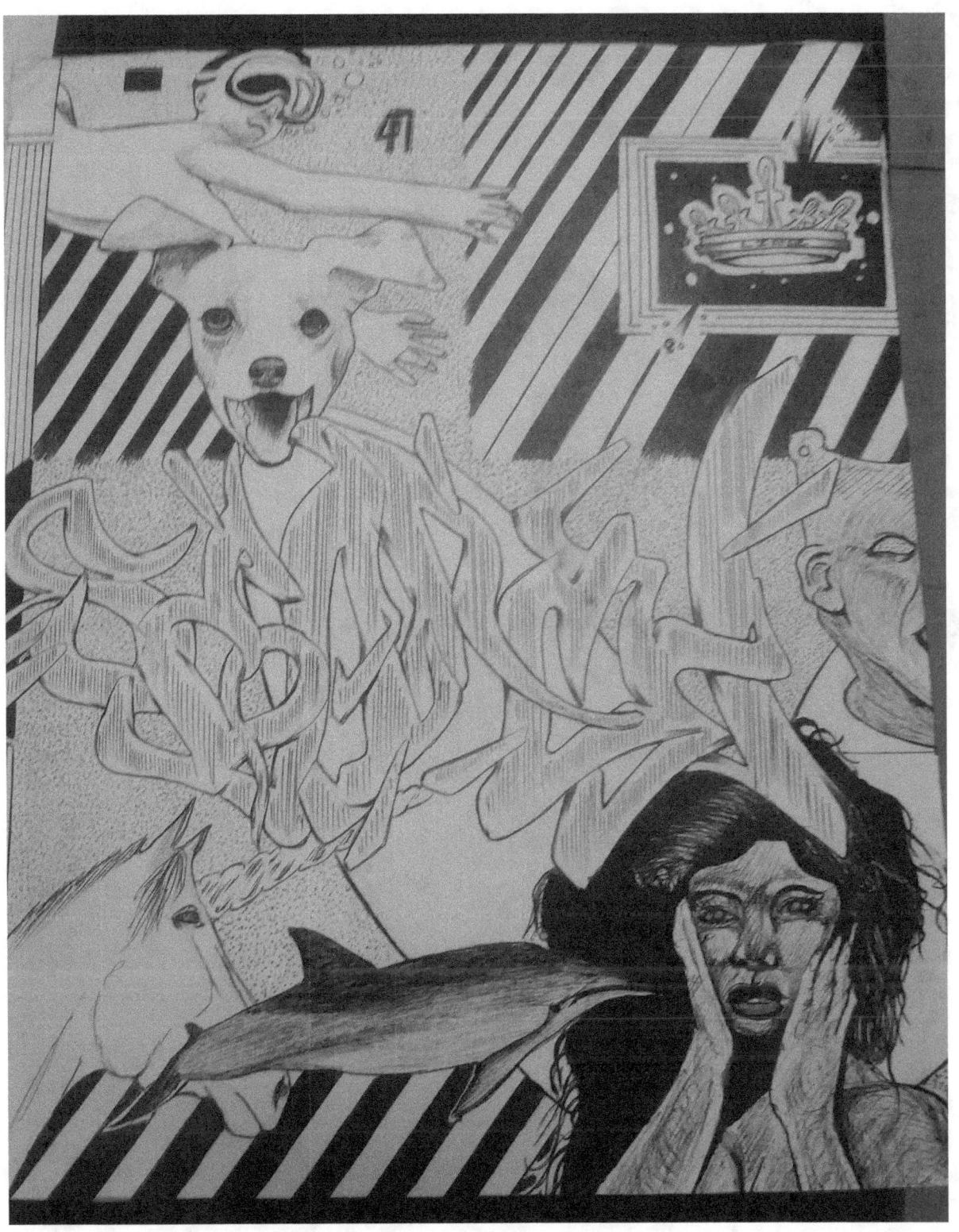

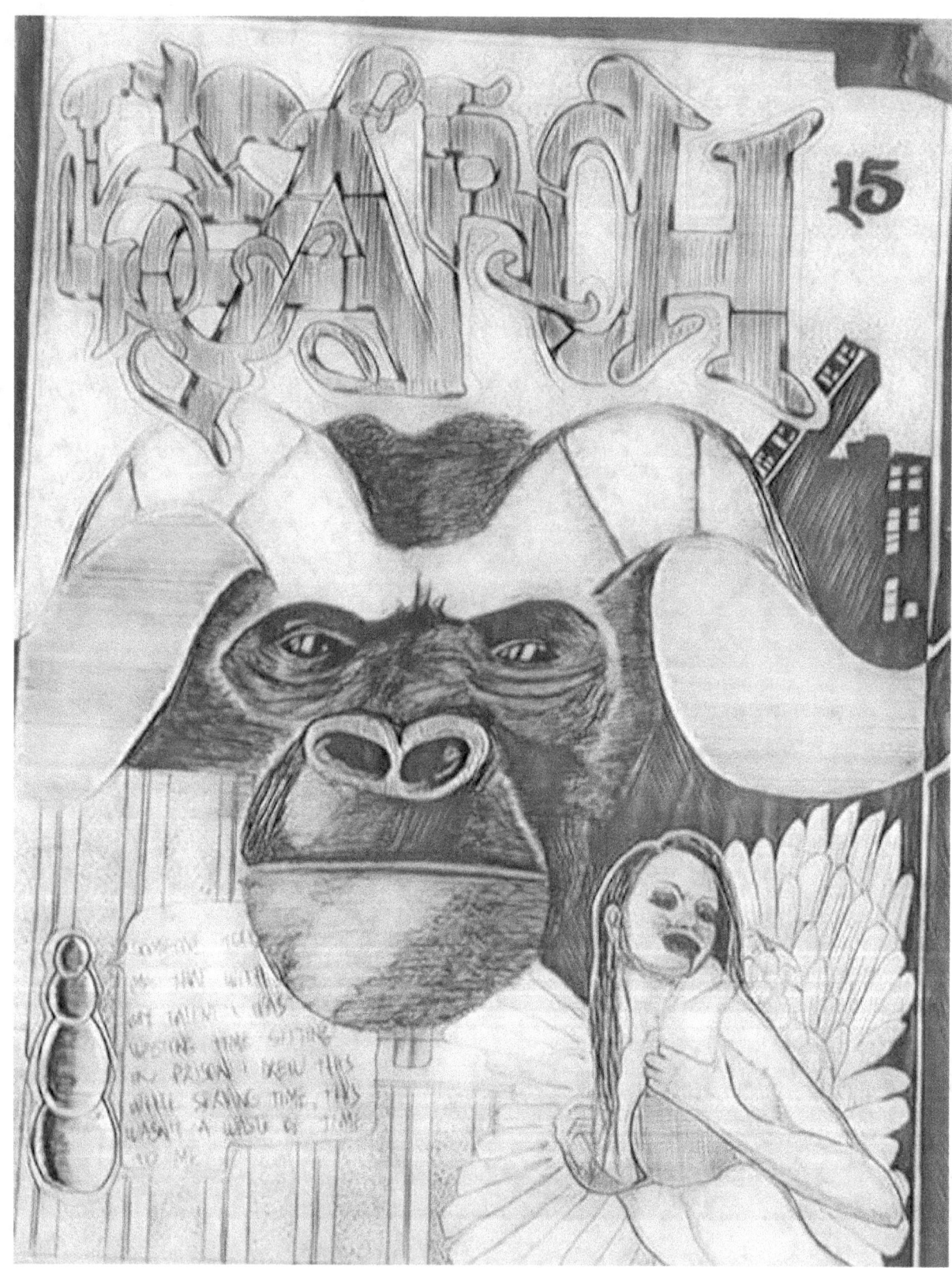

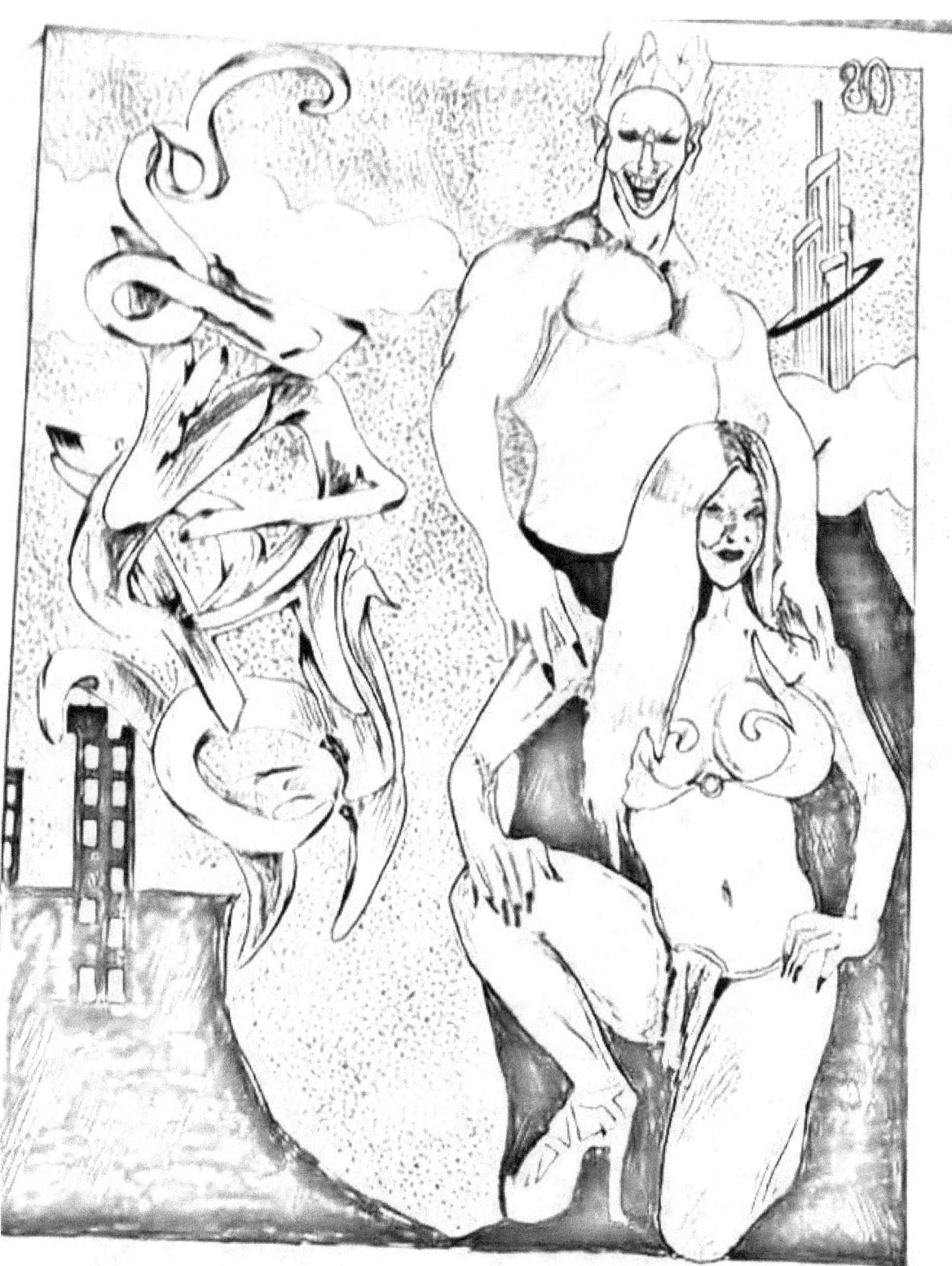

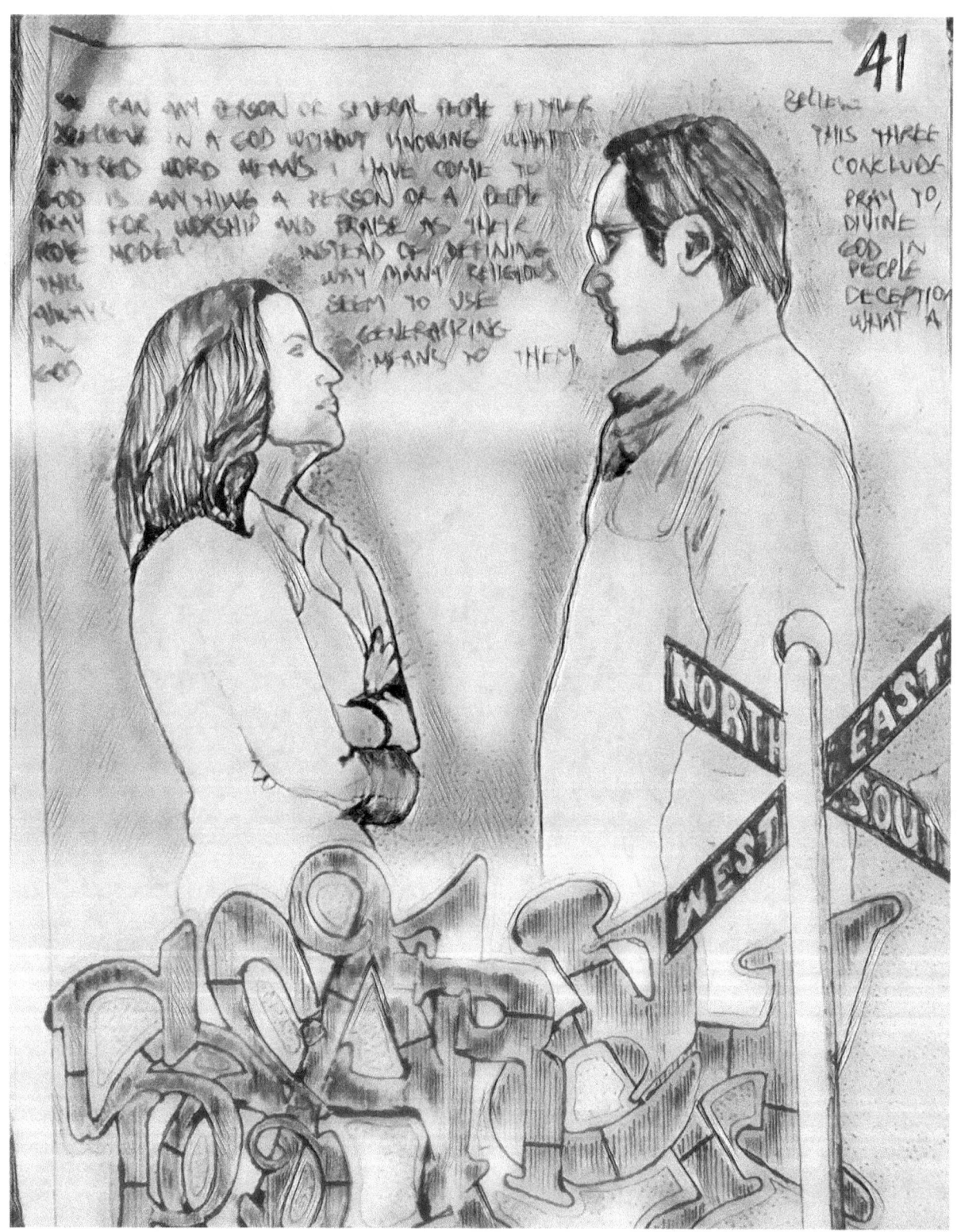

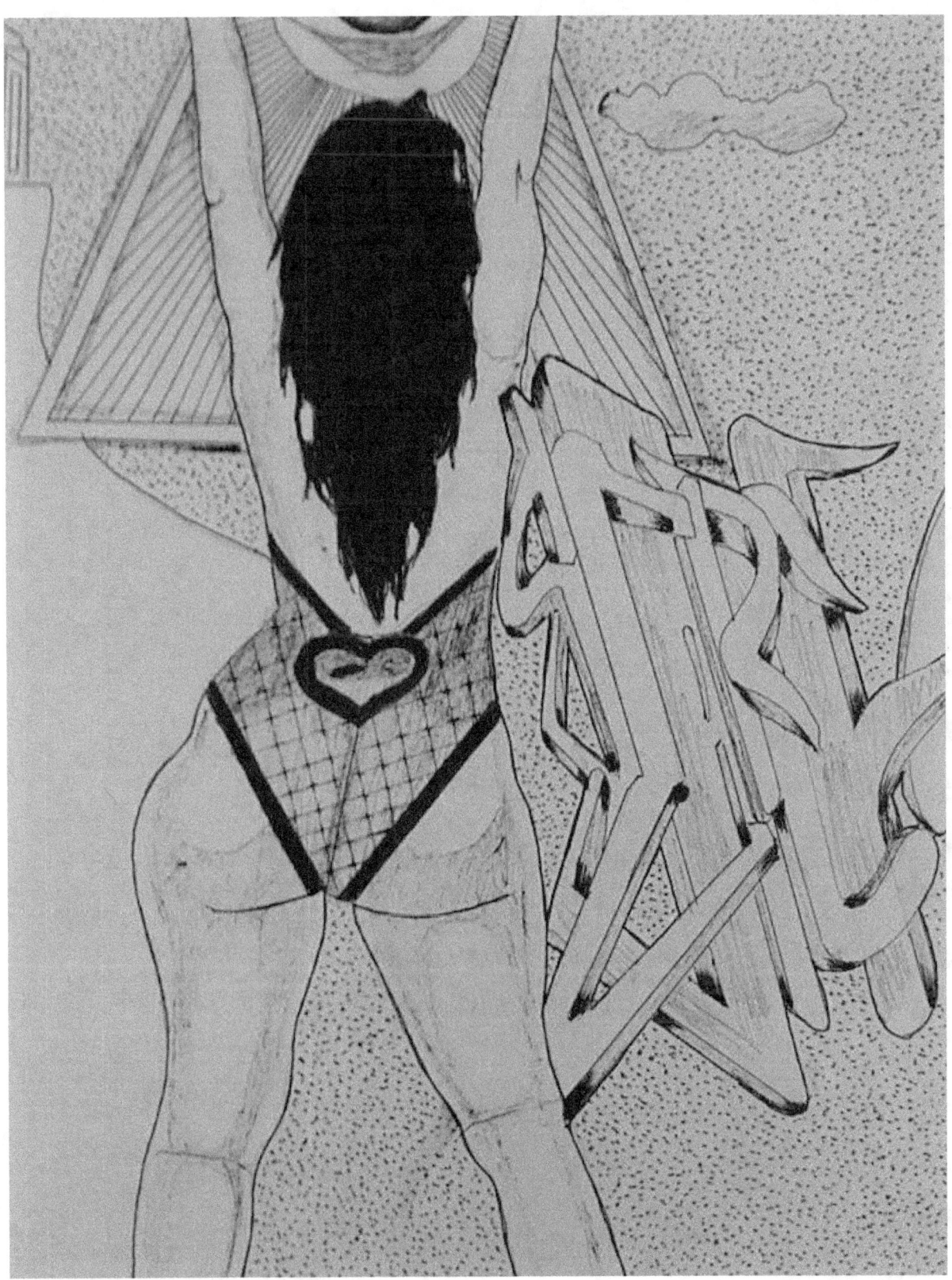

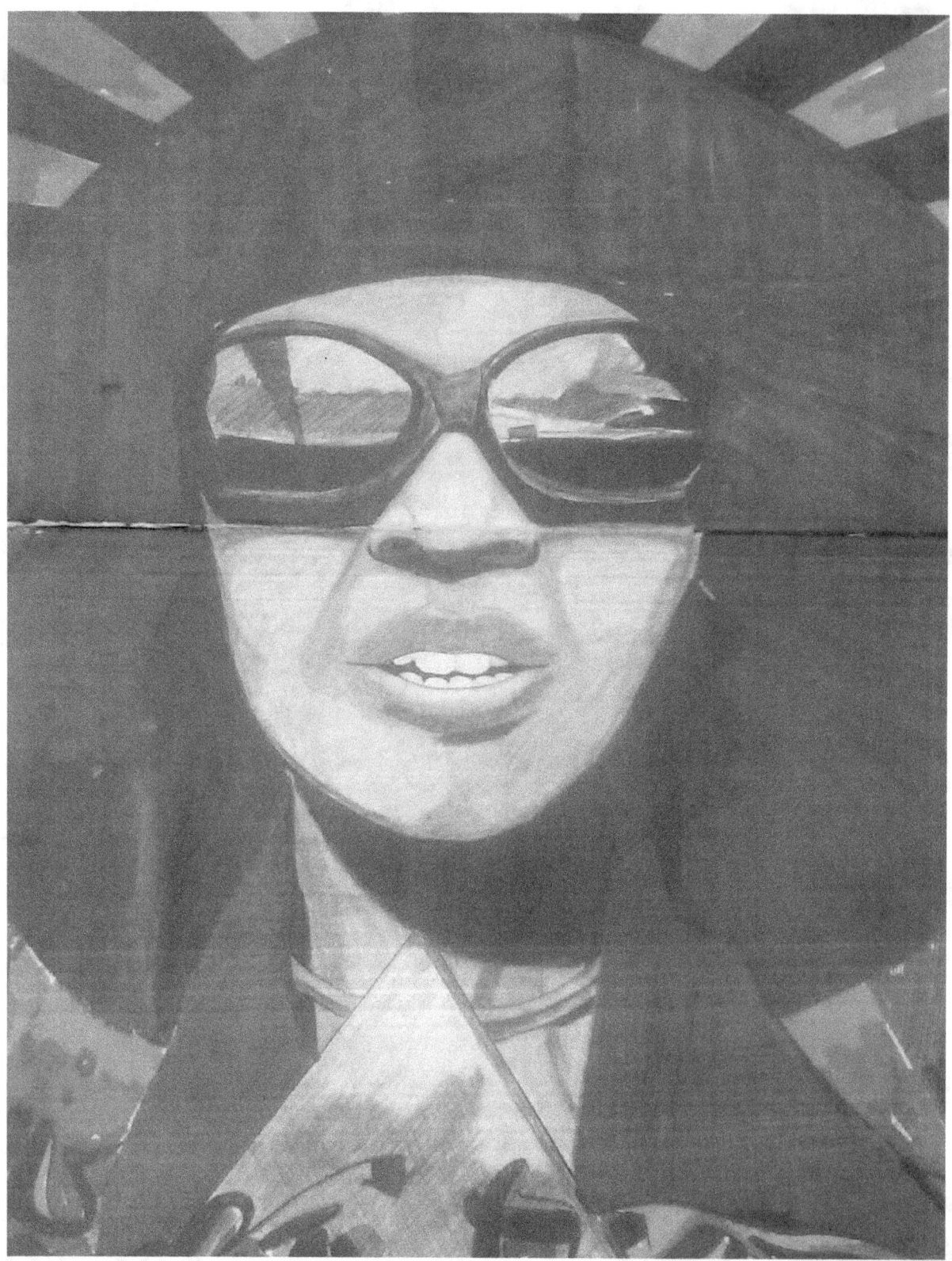

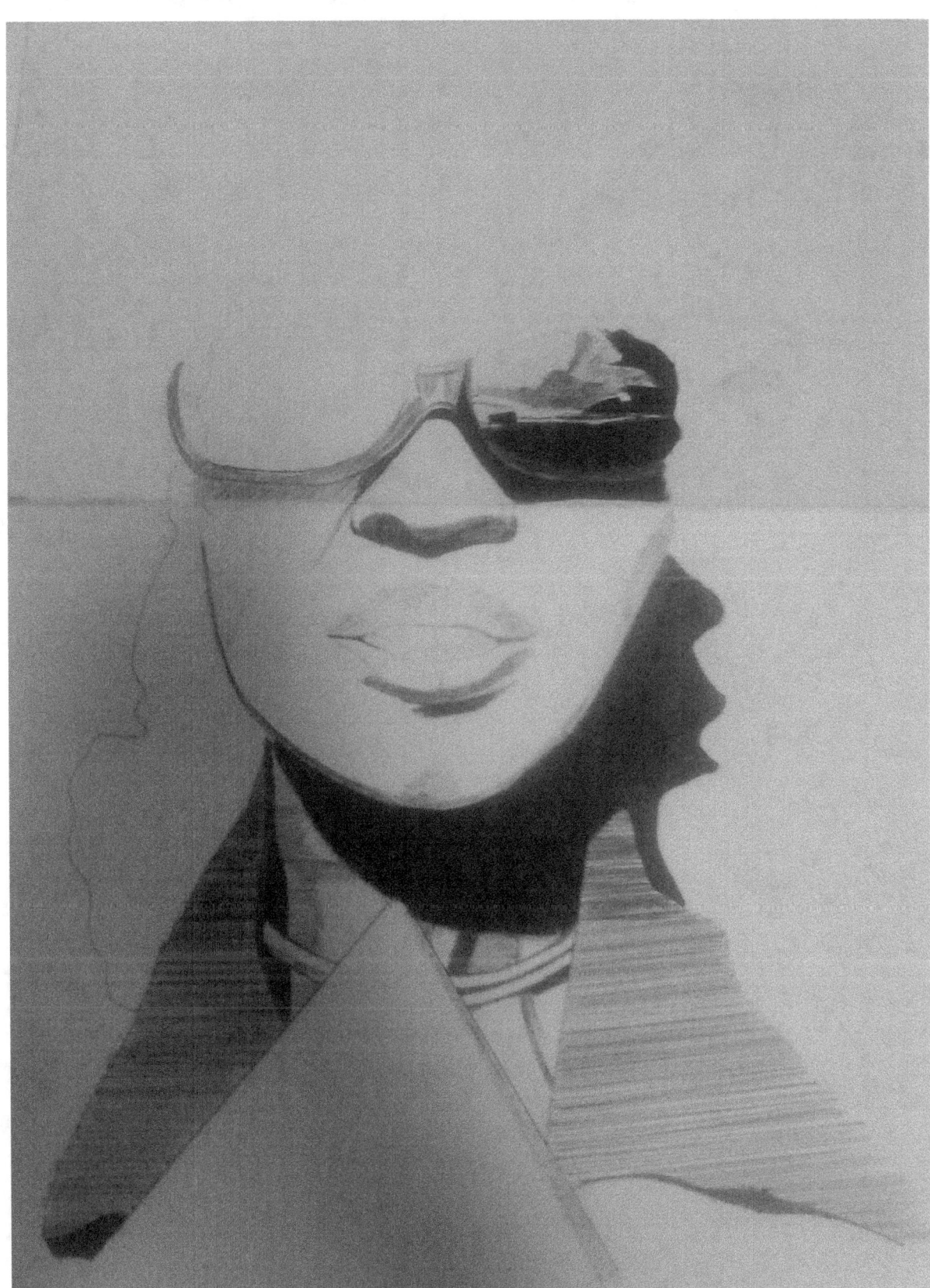

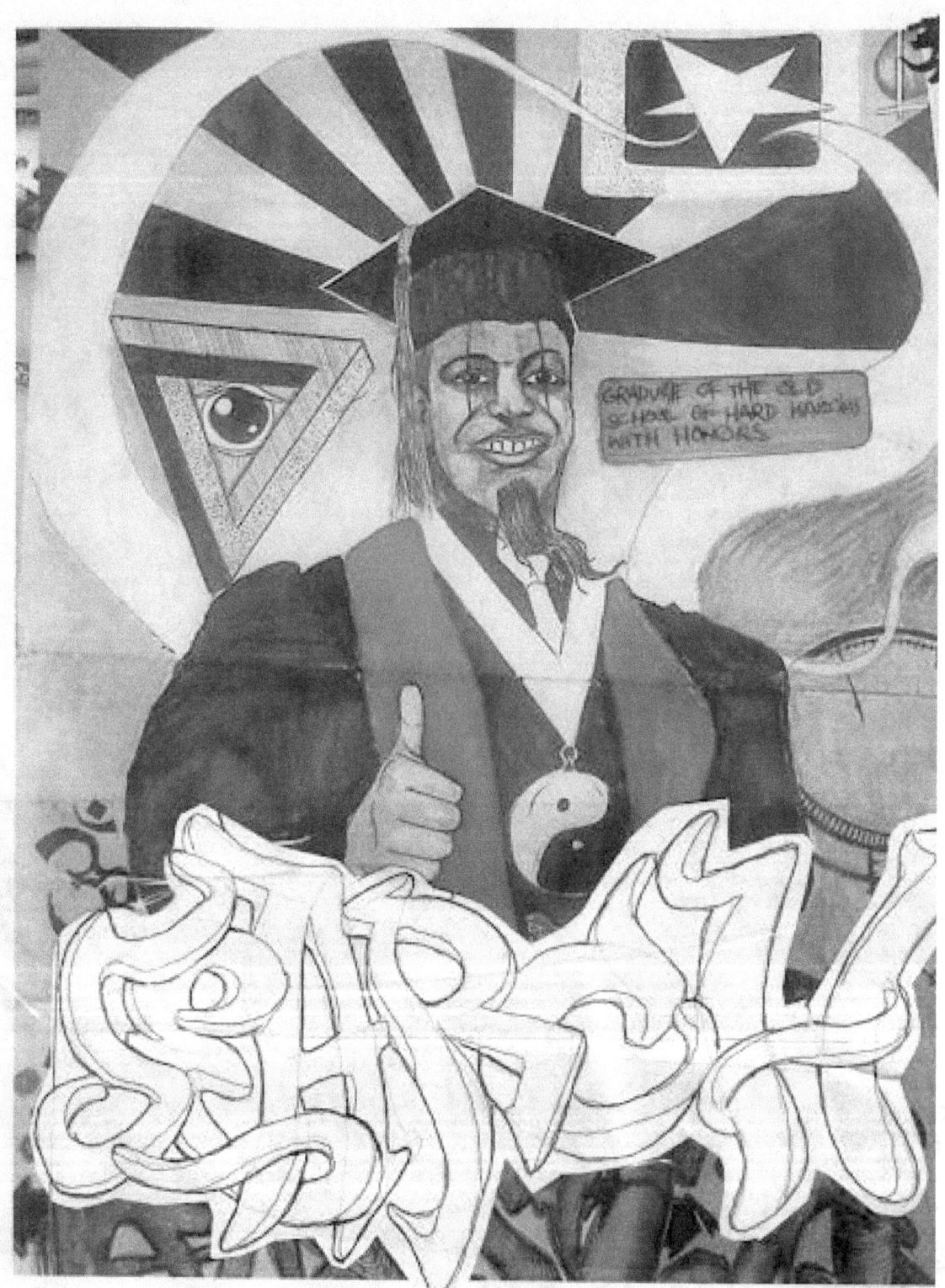

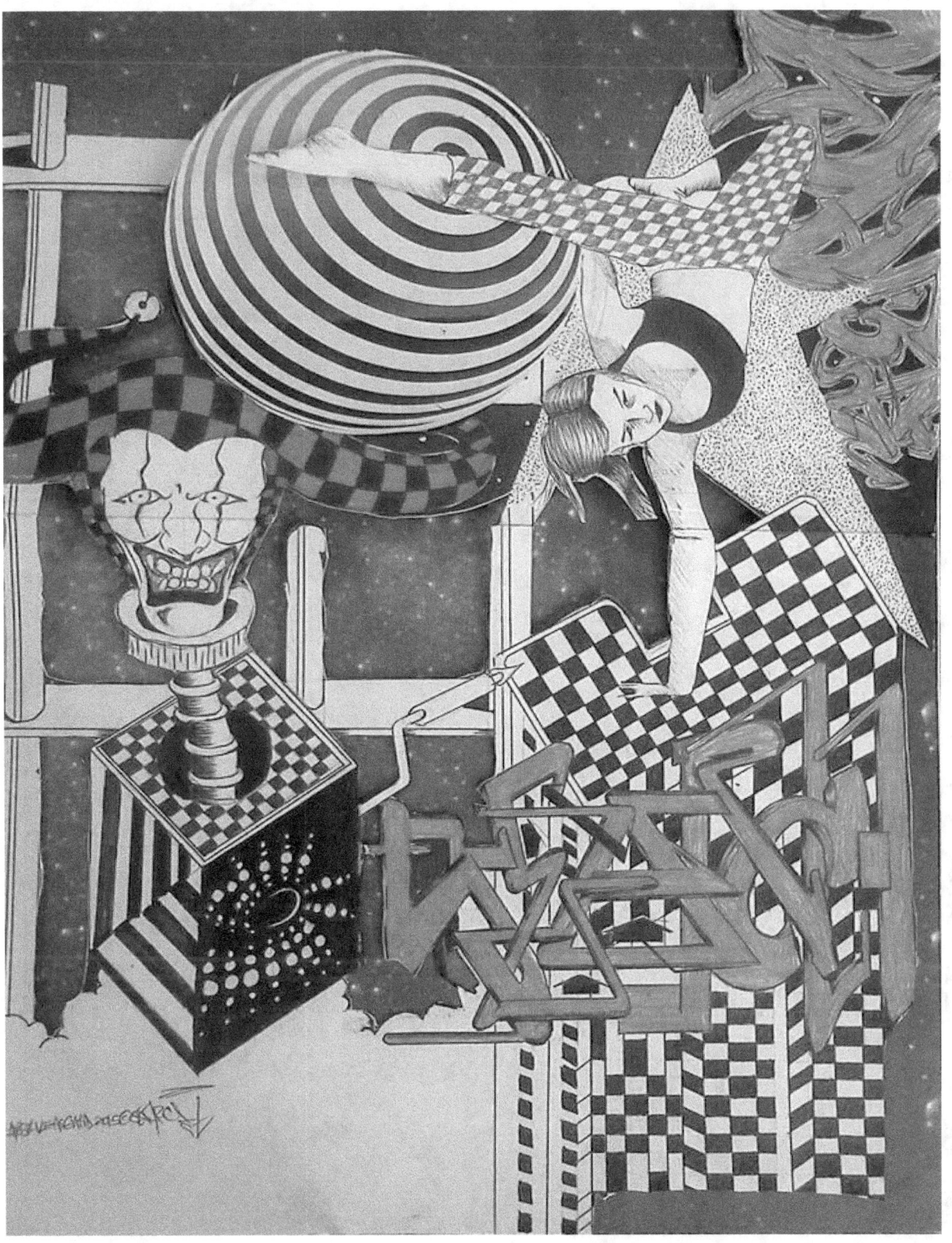

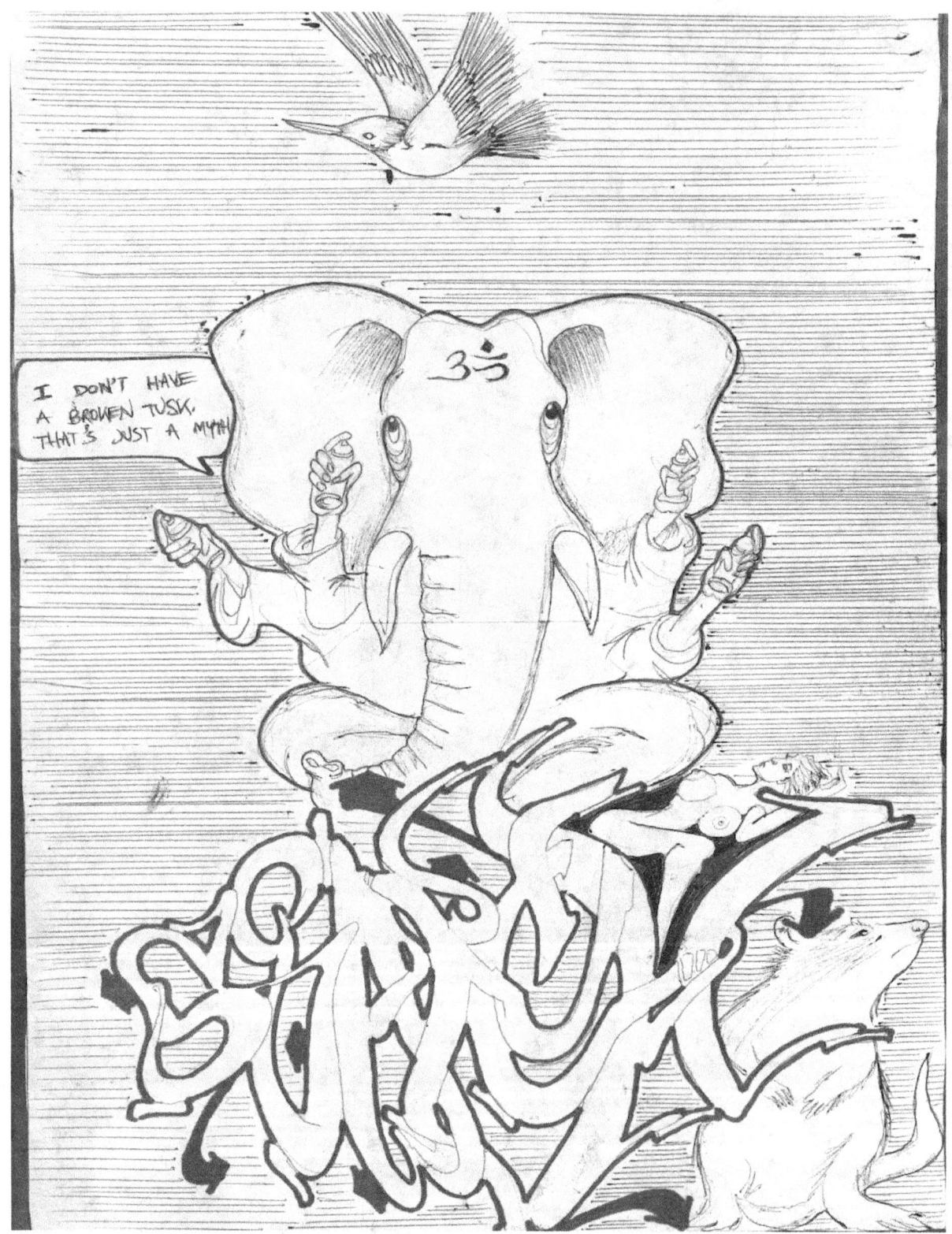

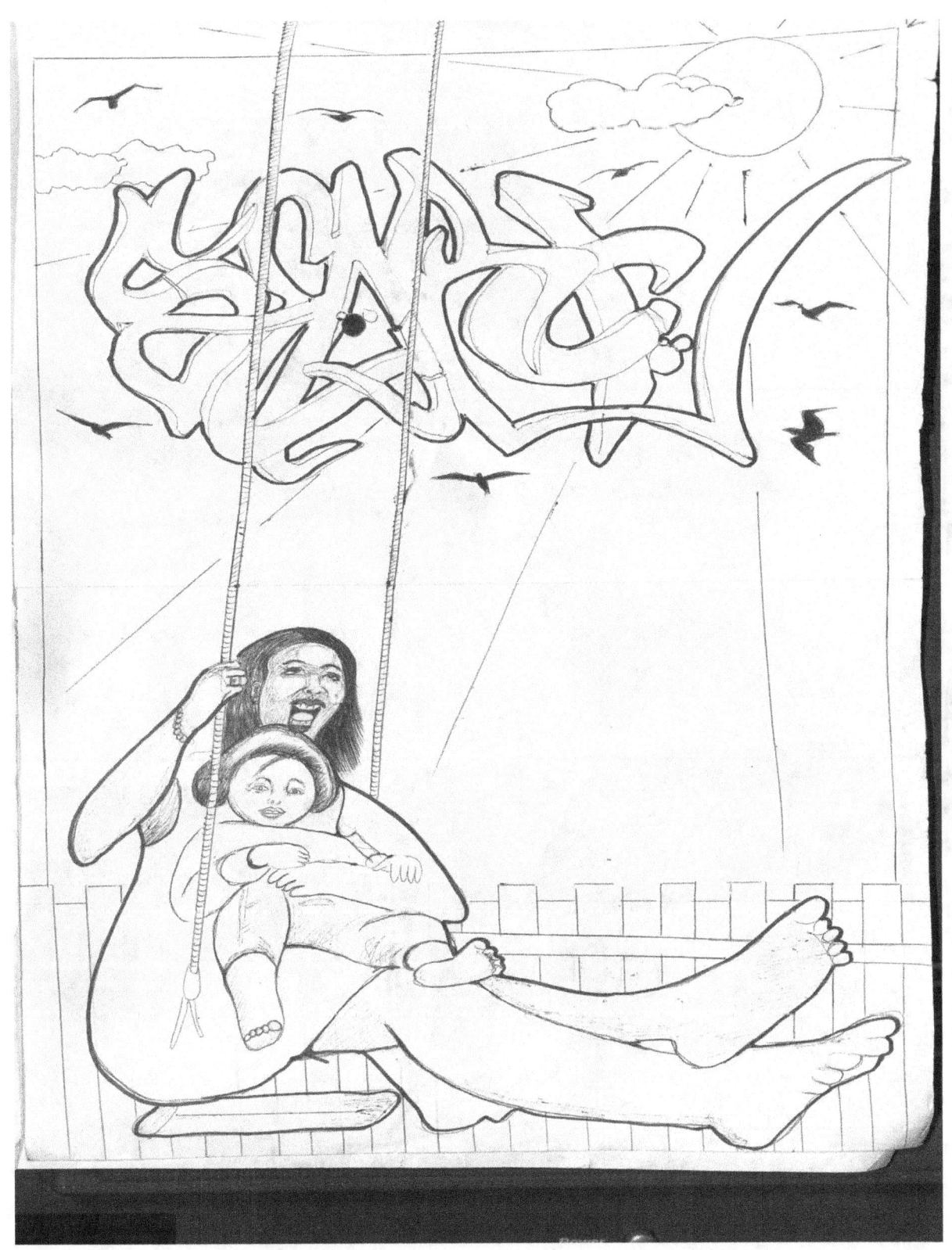

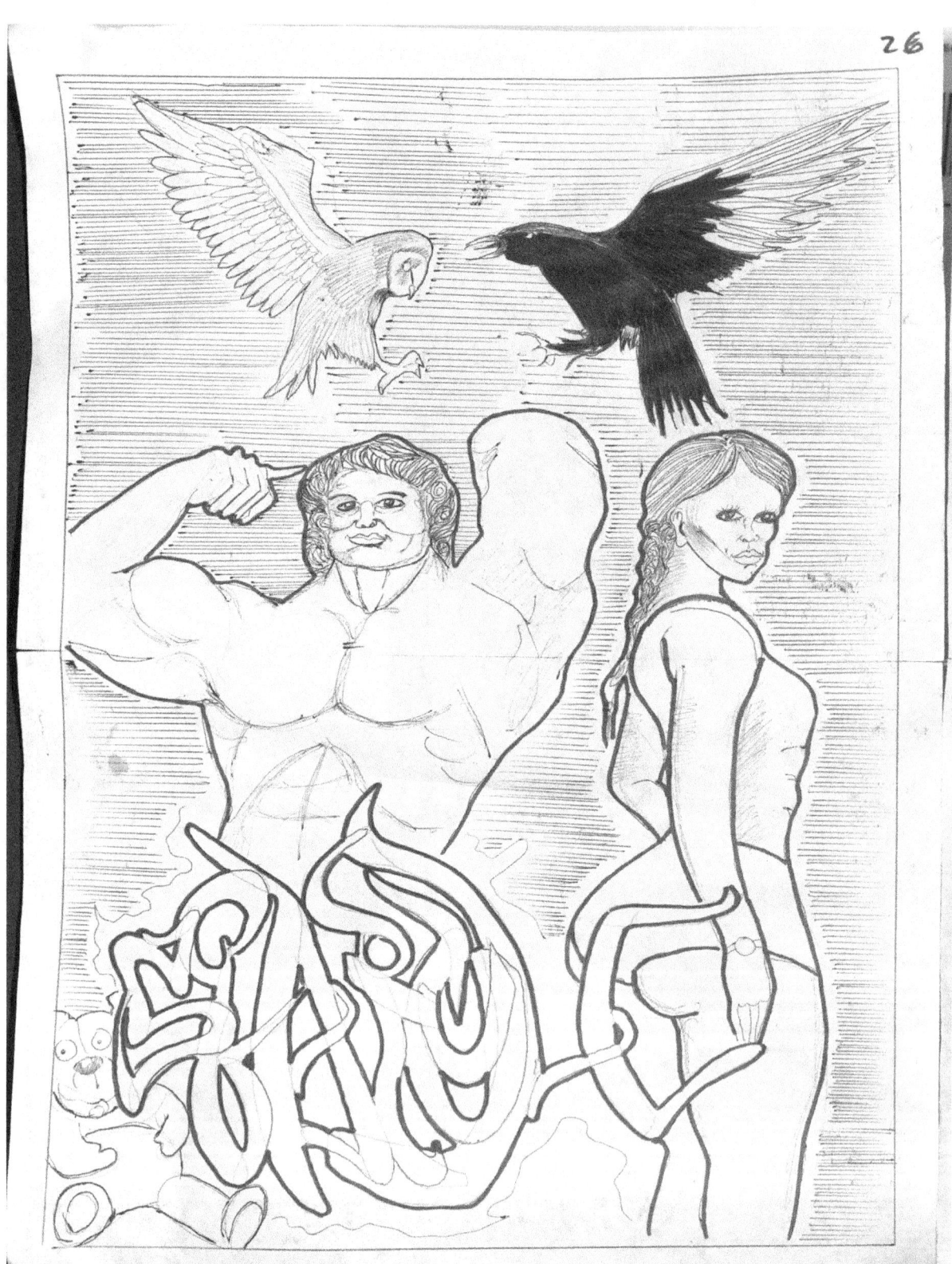

26

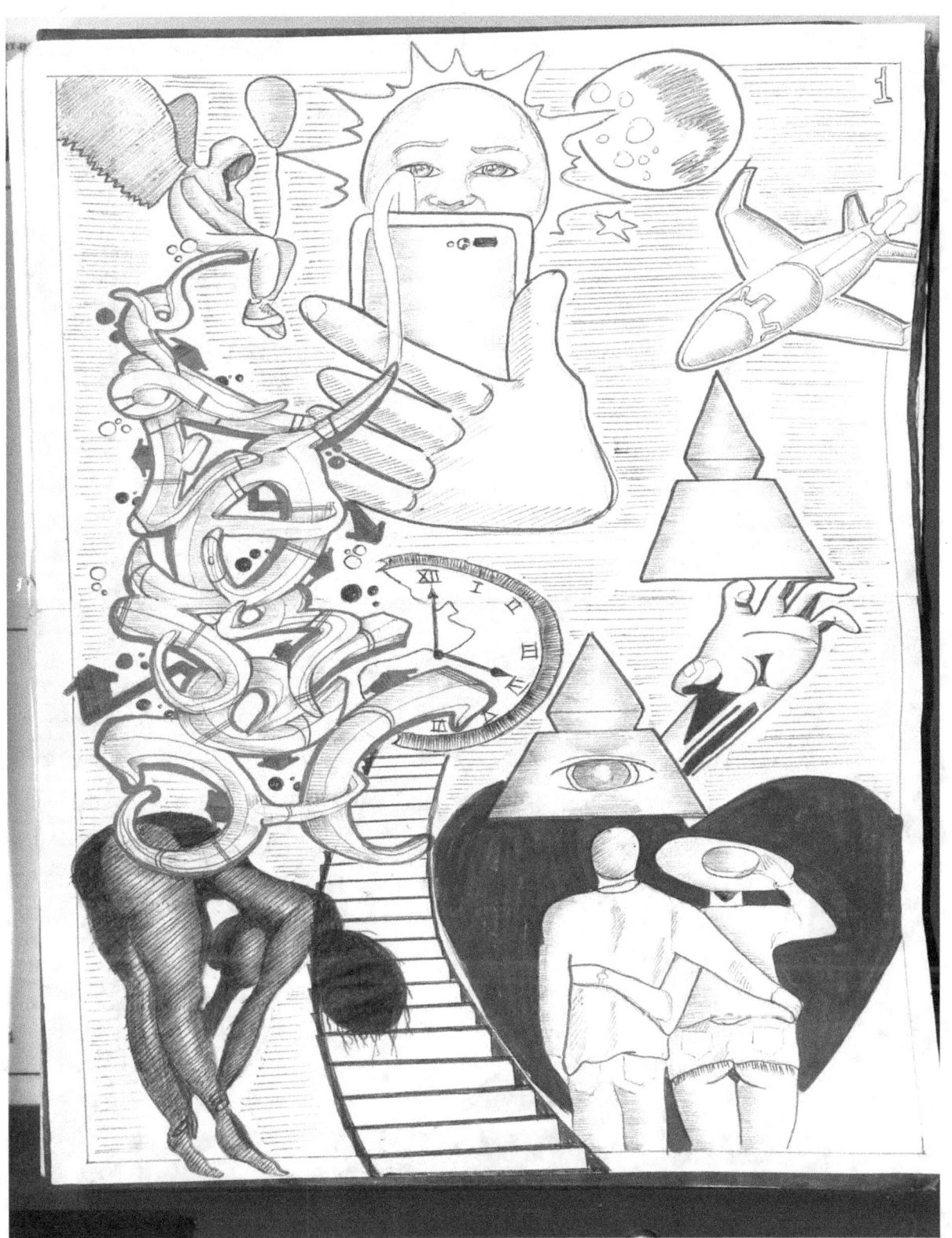

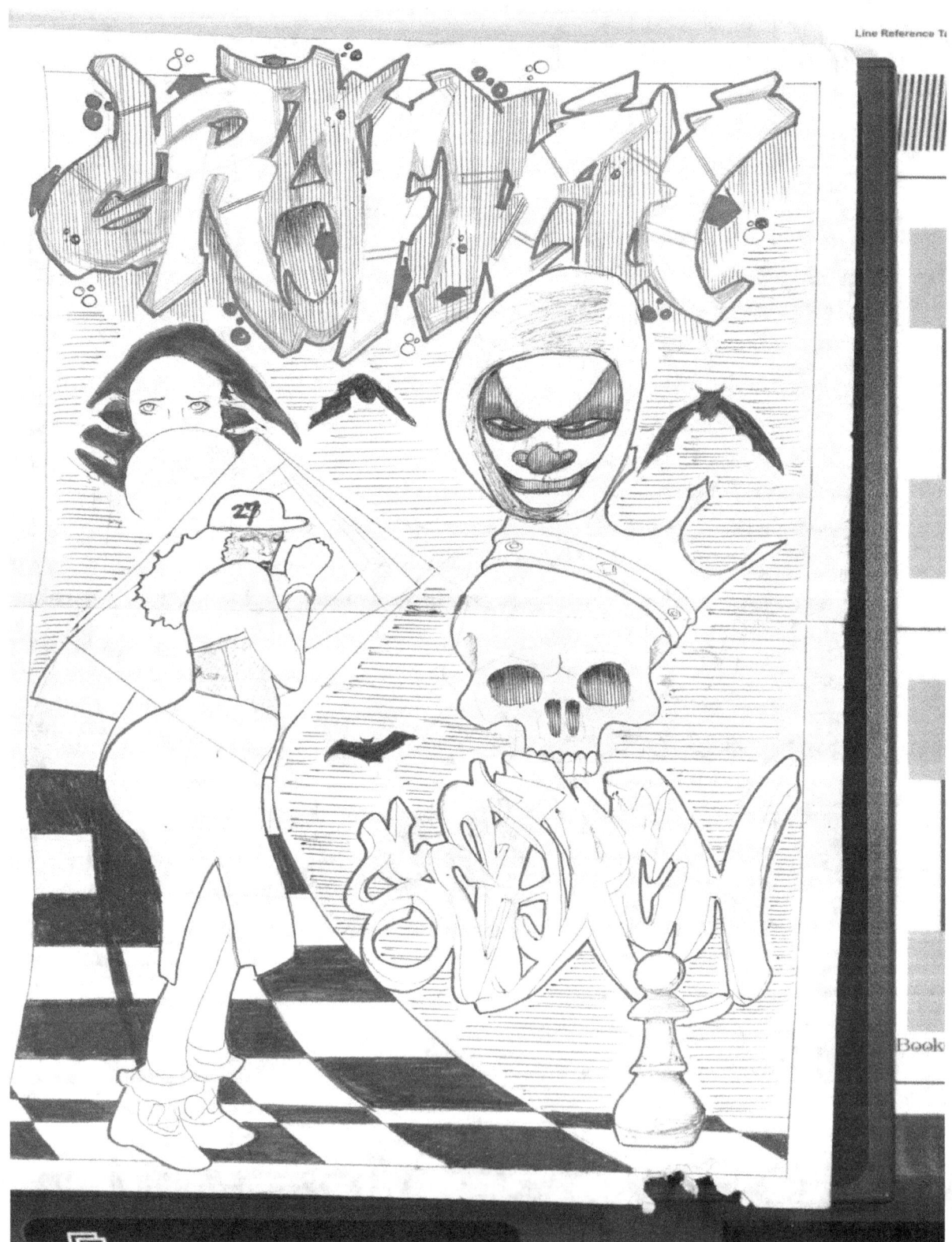

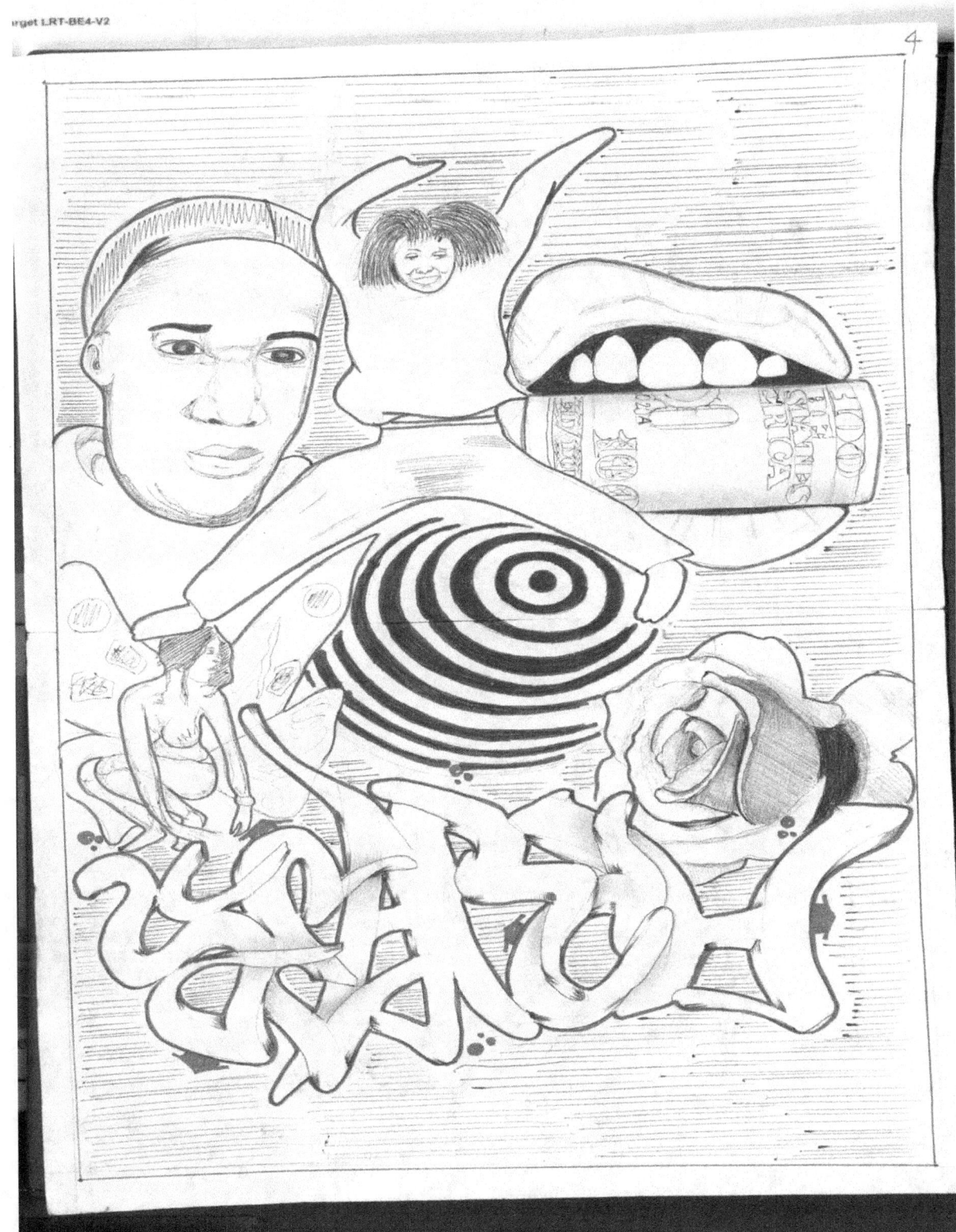

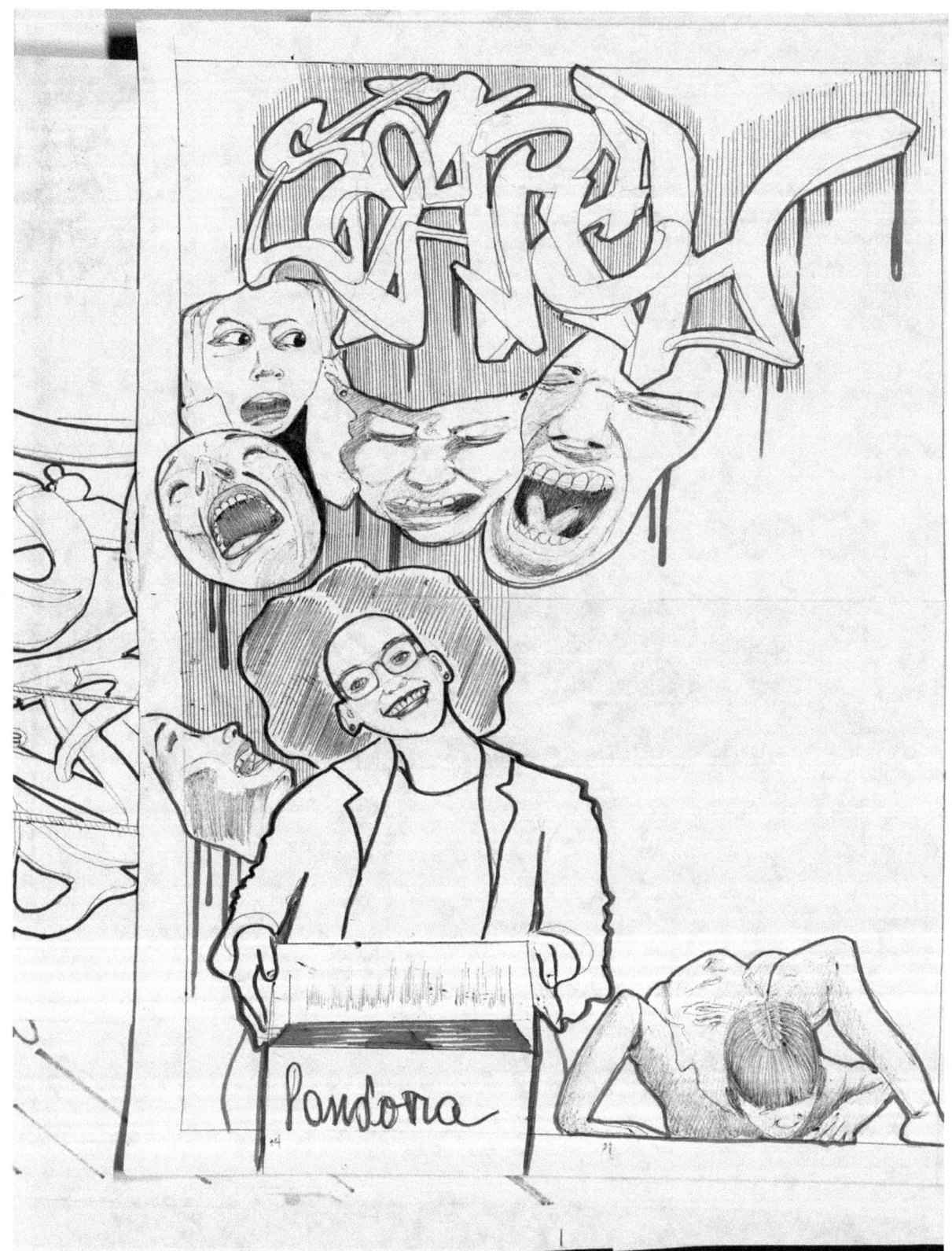

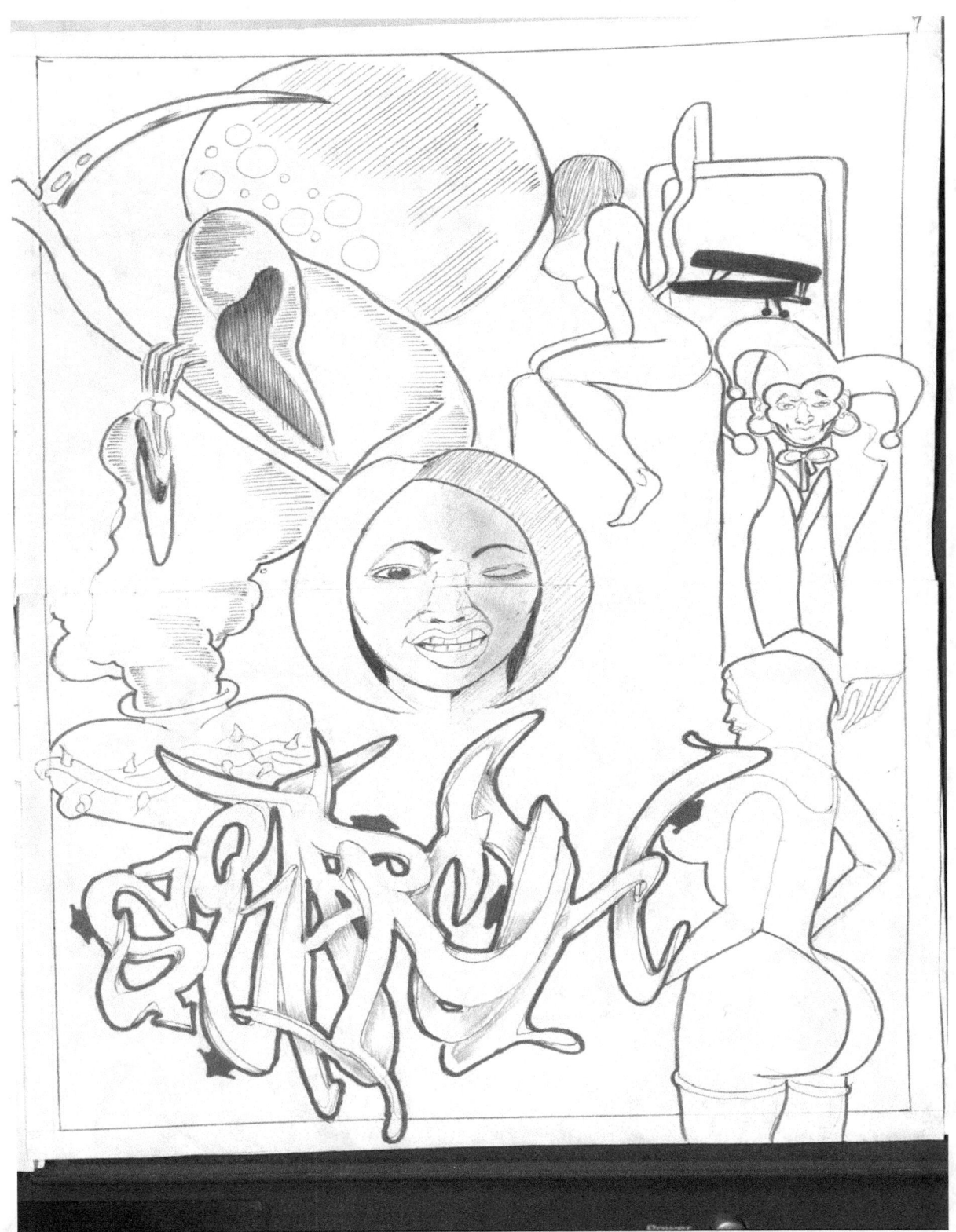

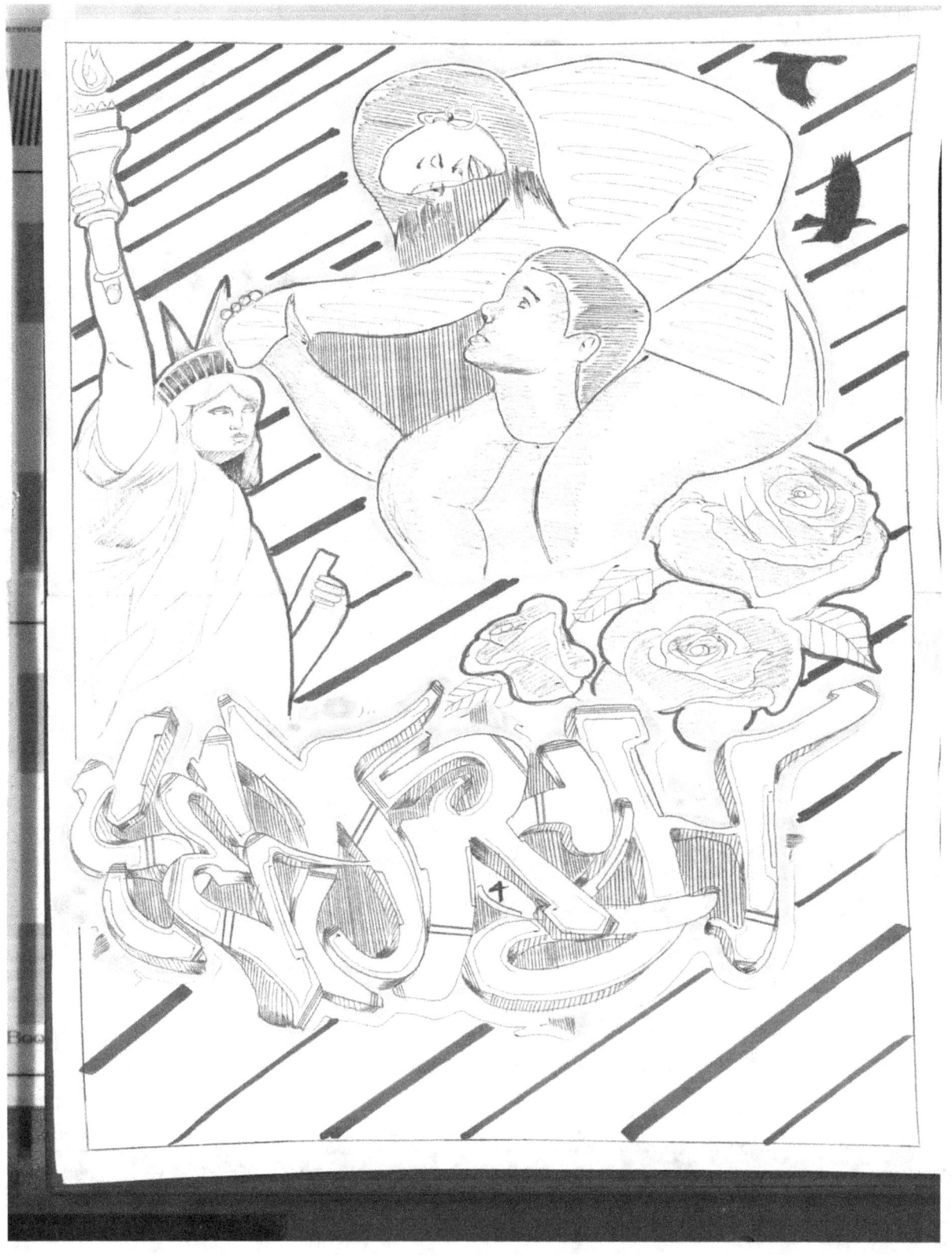

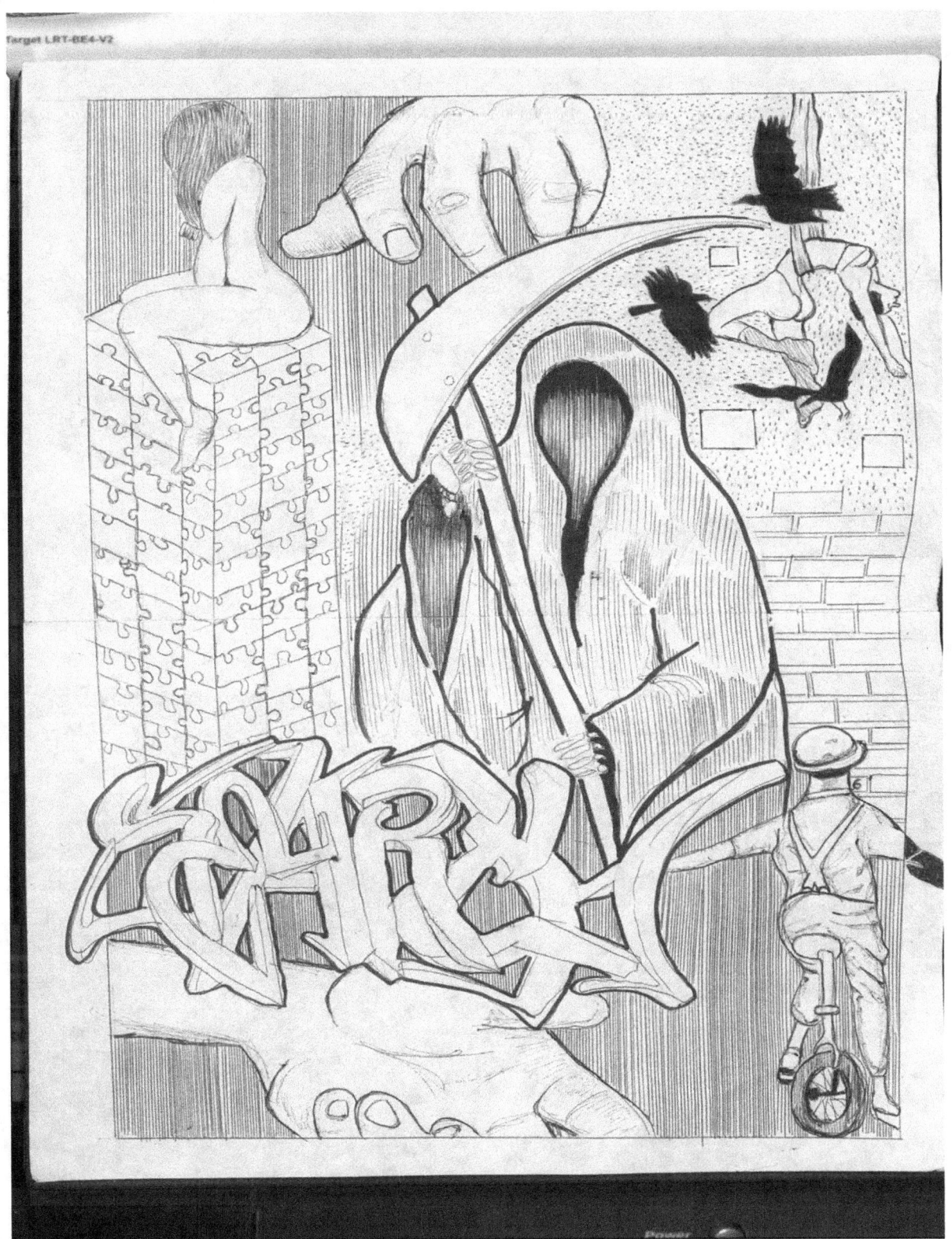

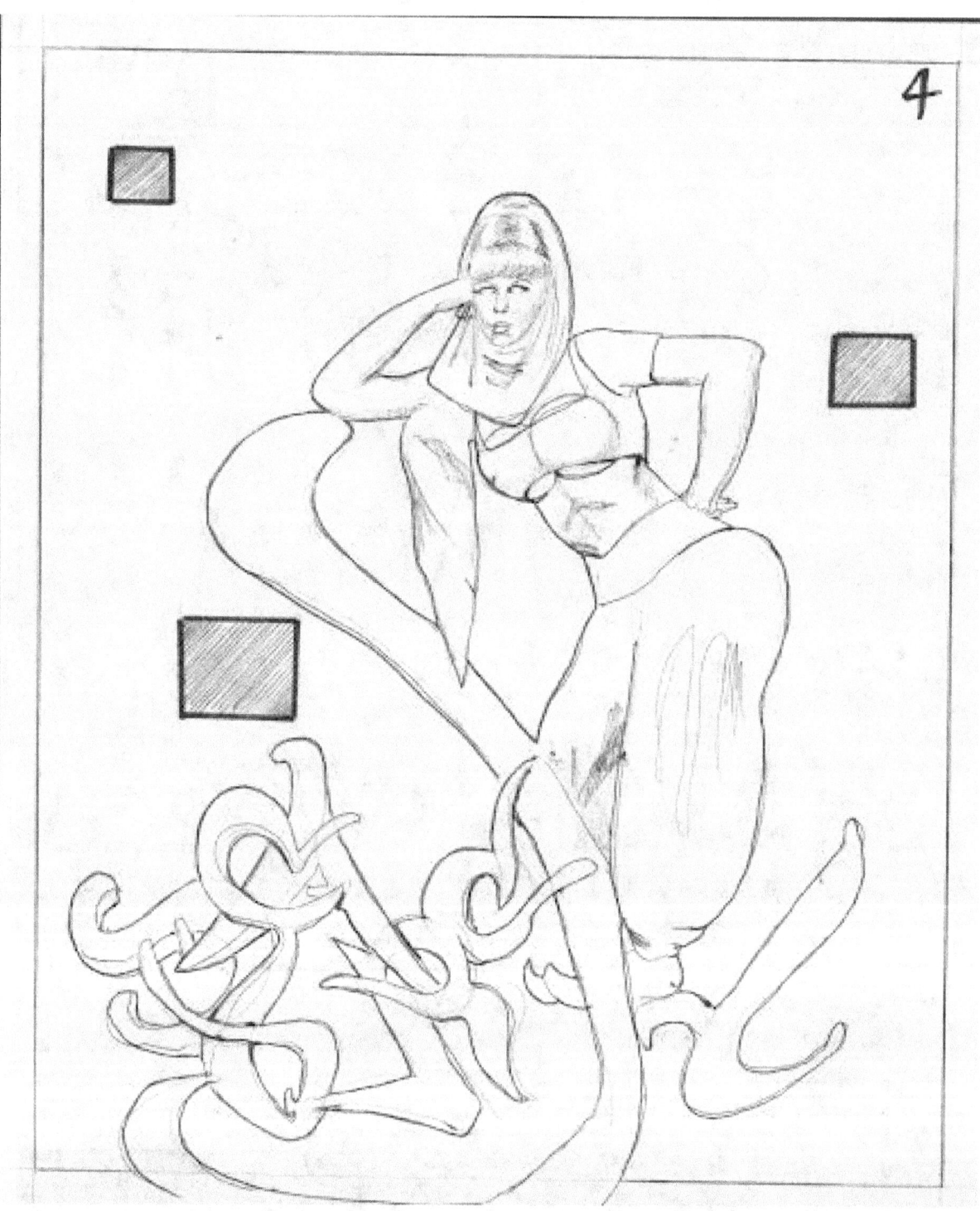

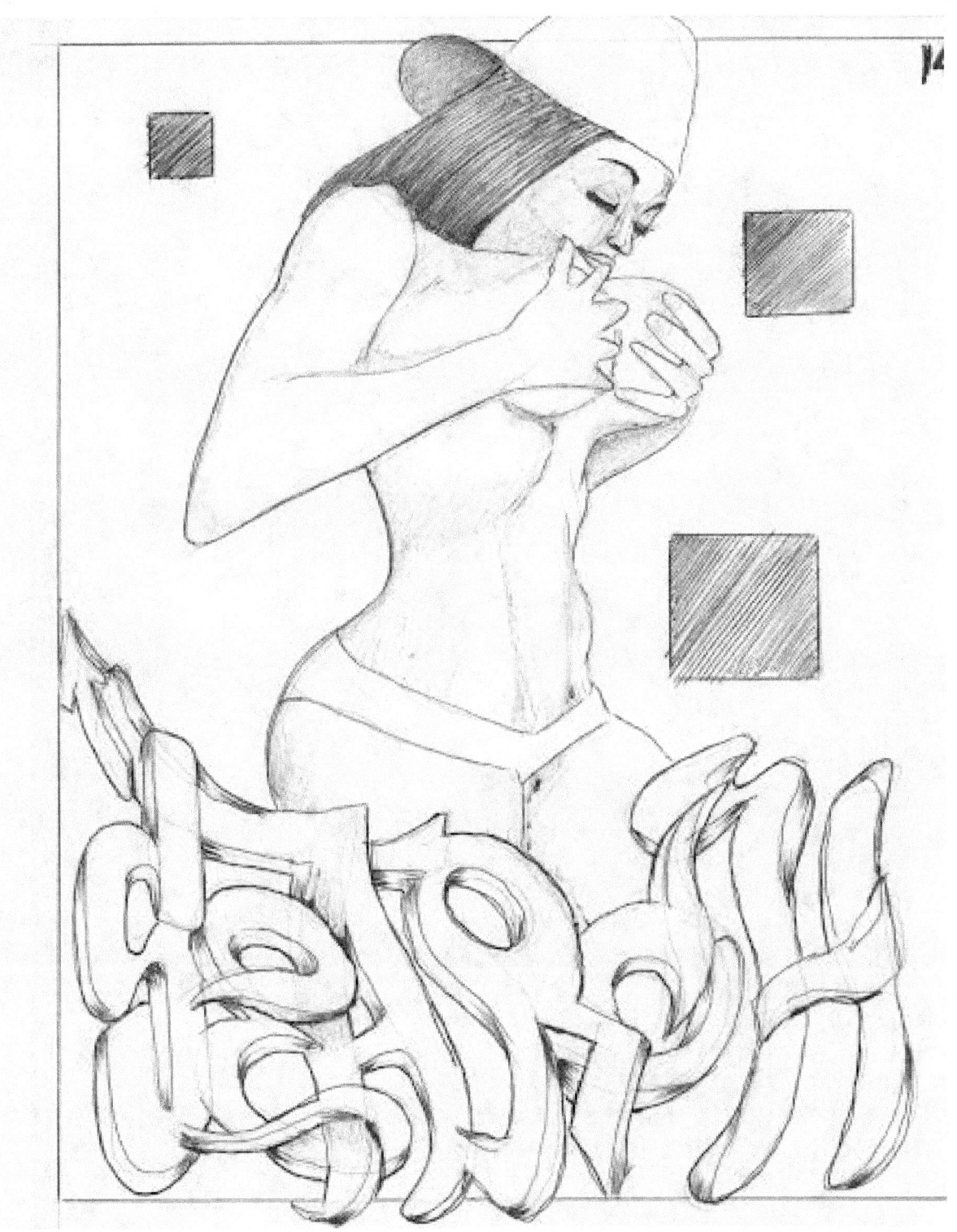

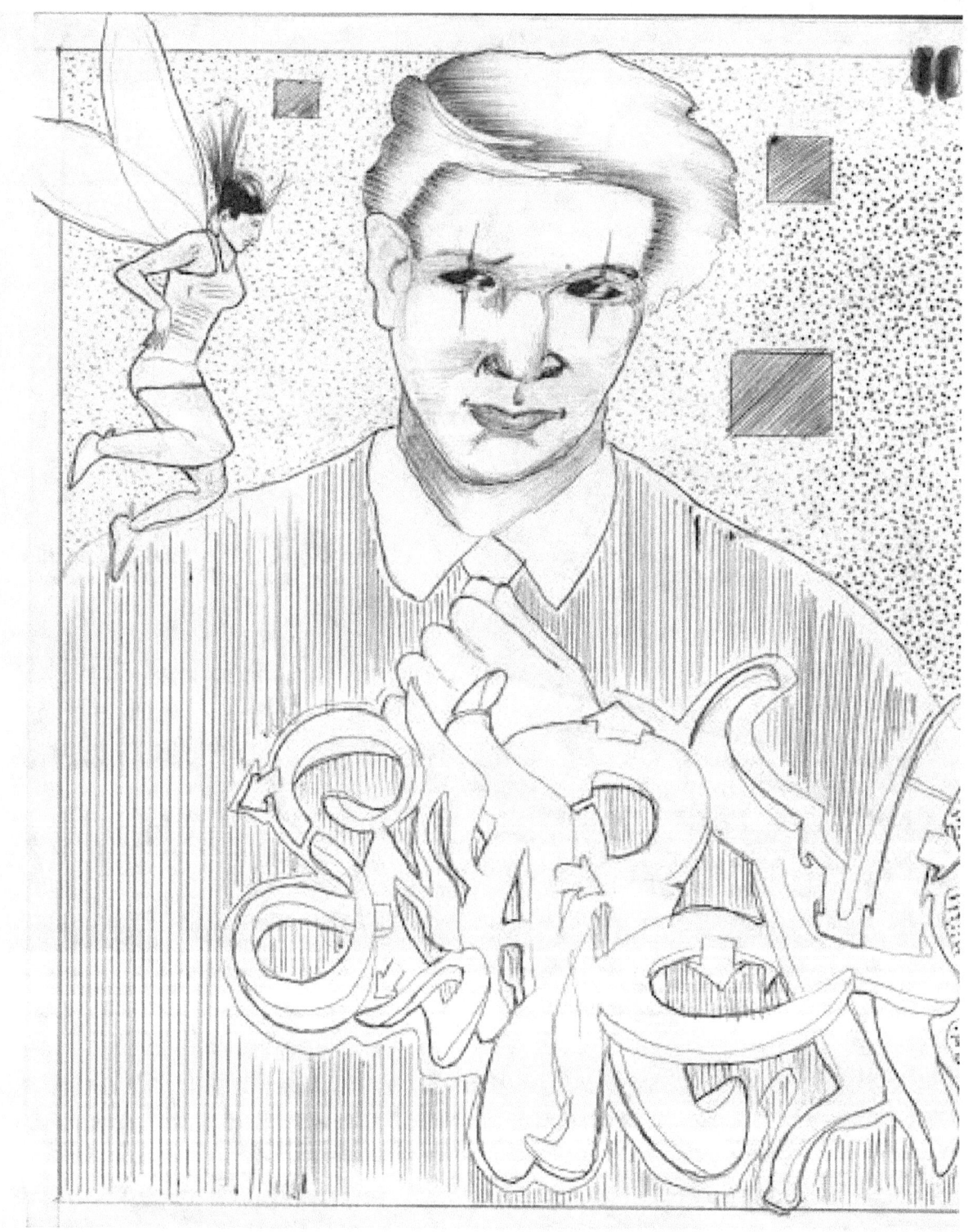

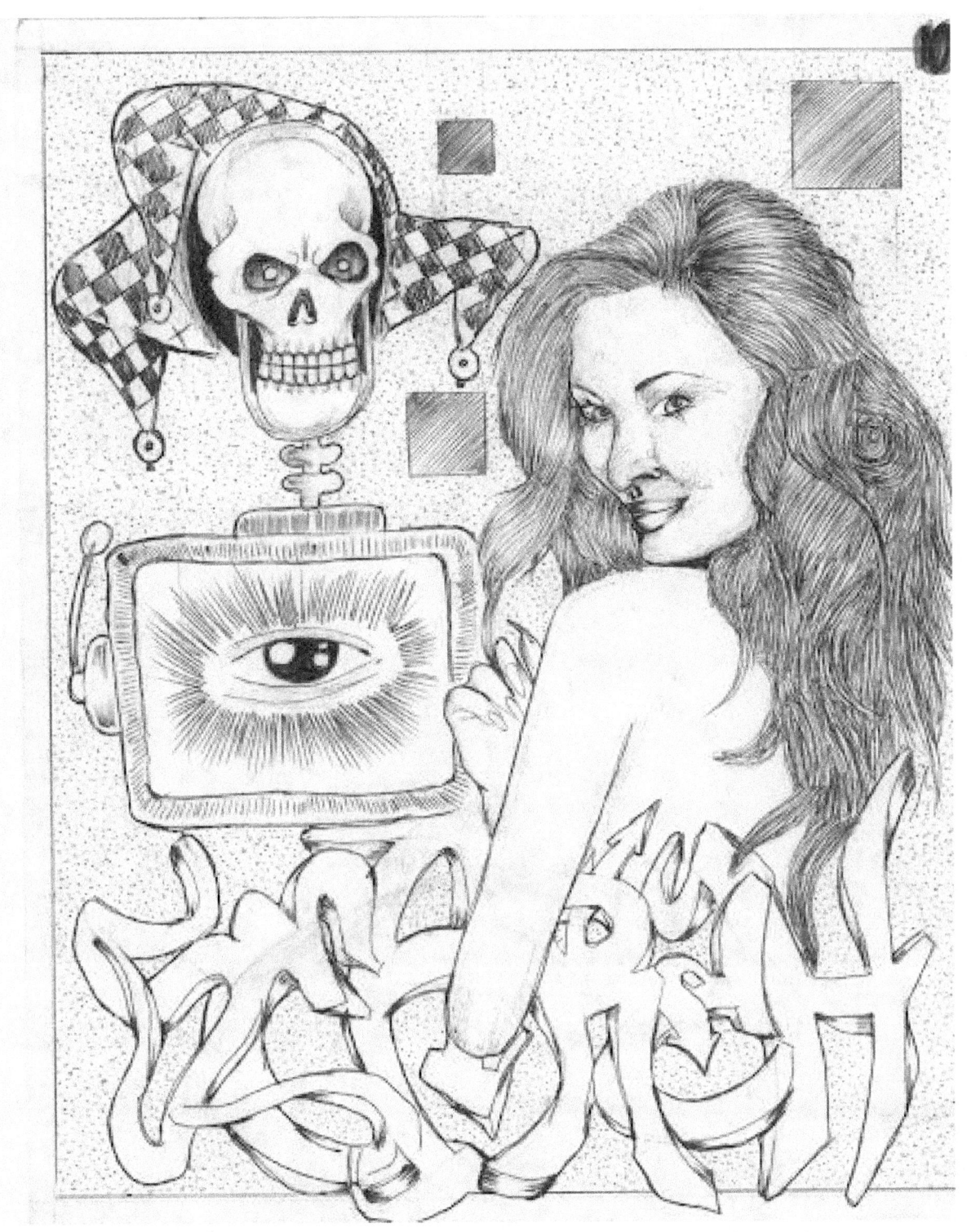

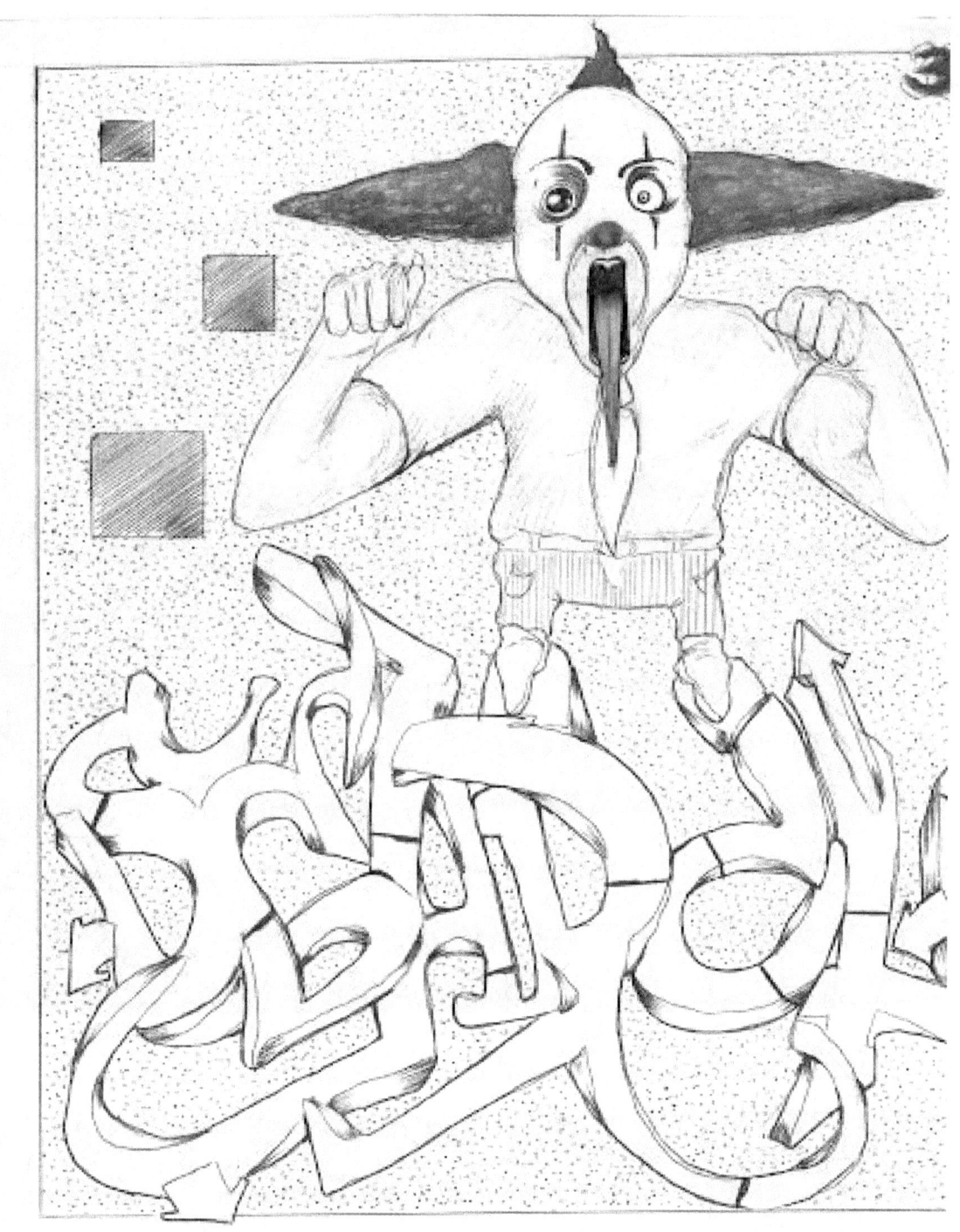

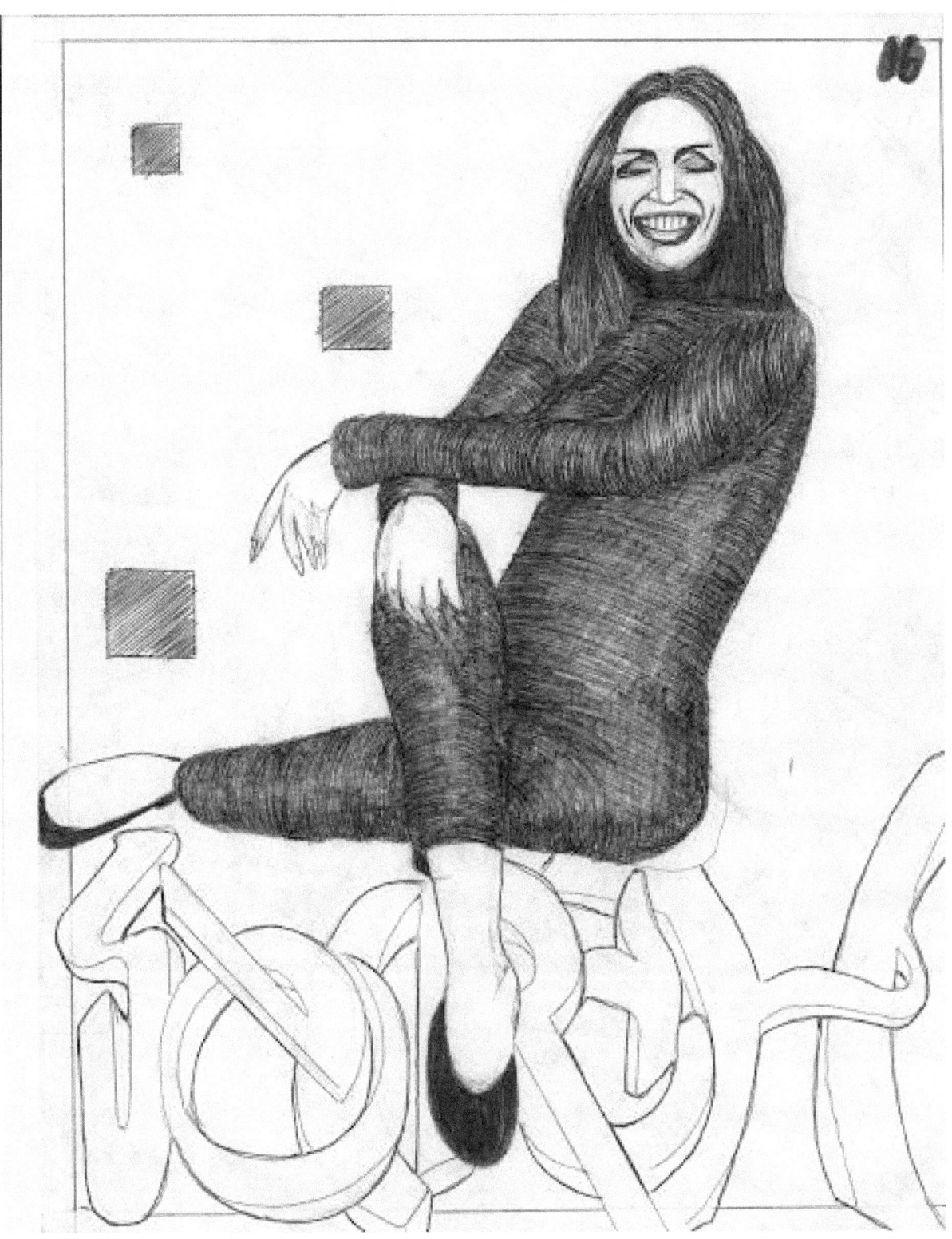

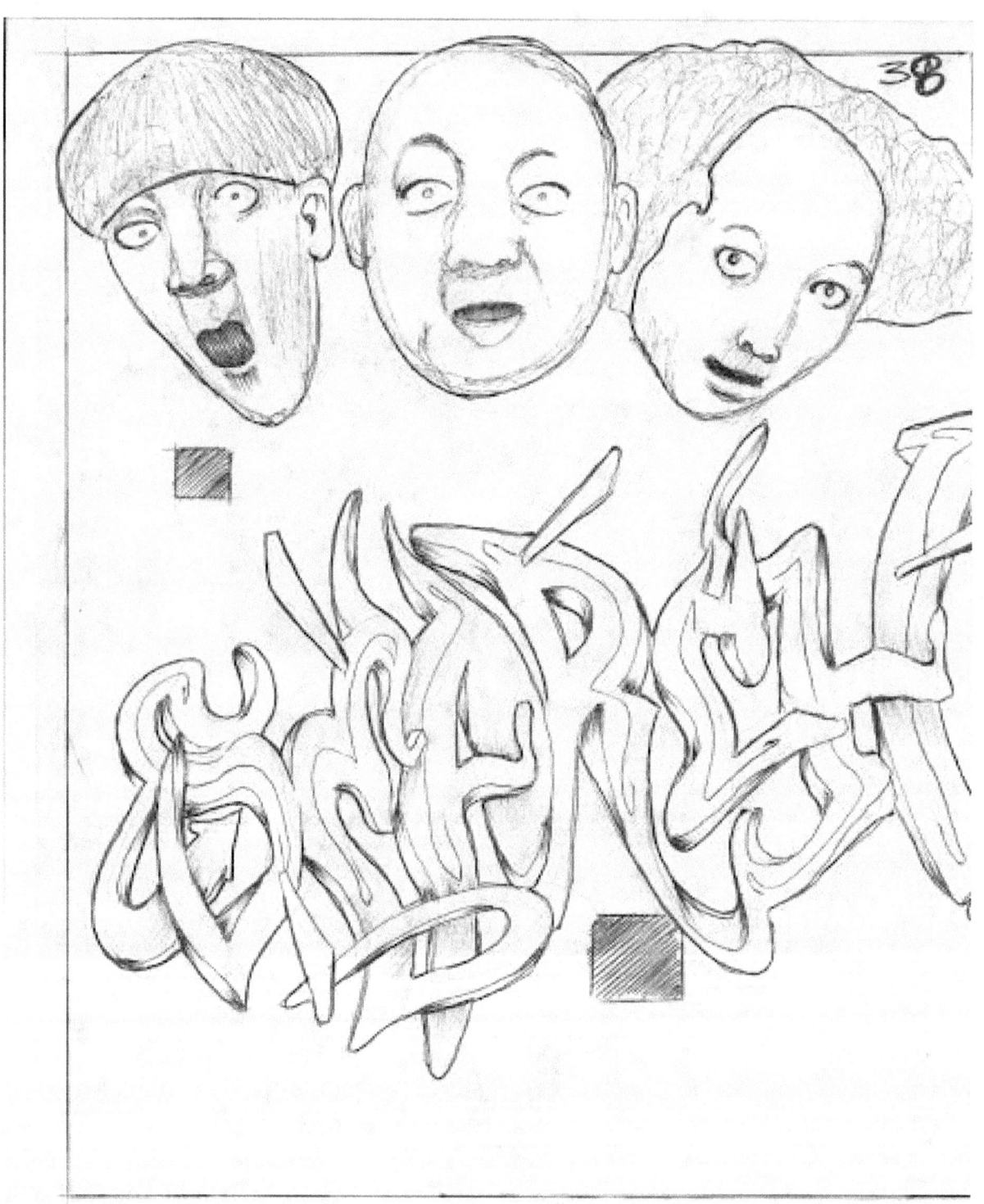

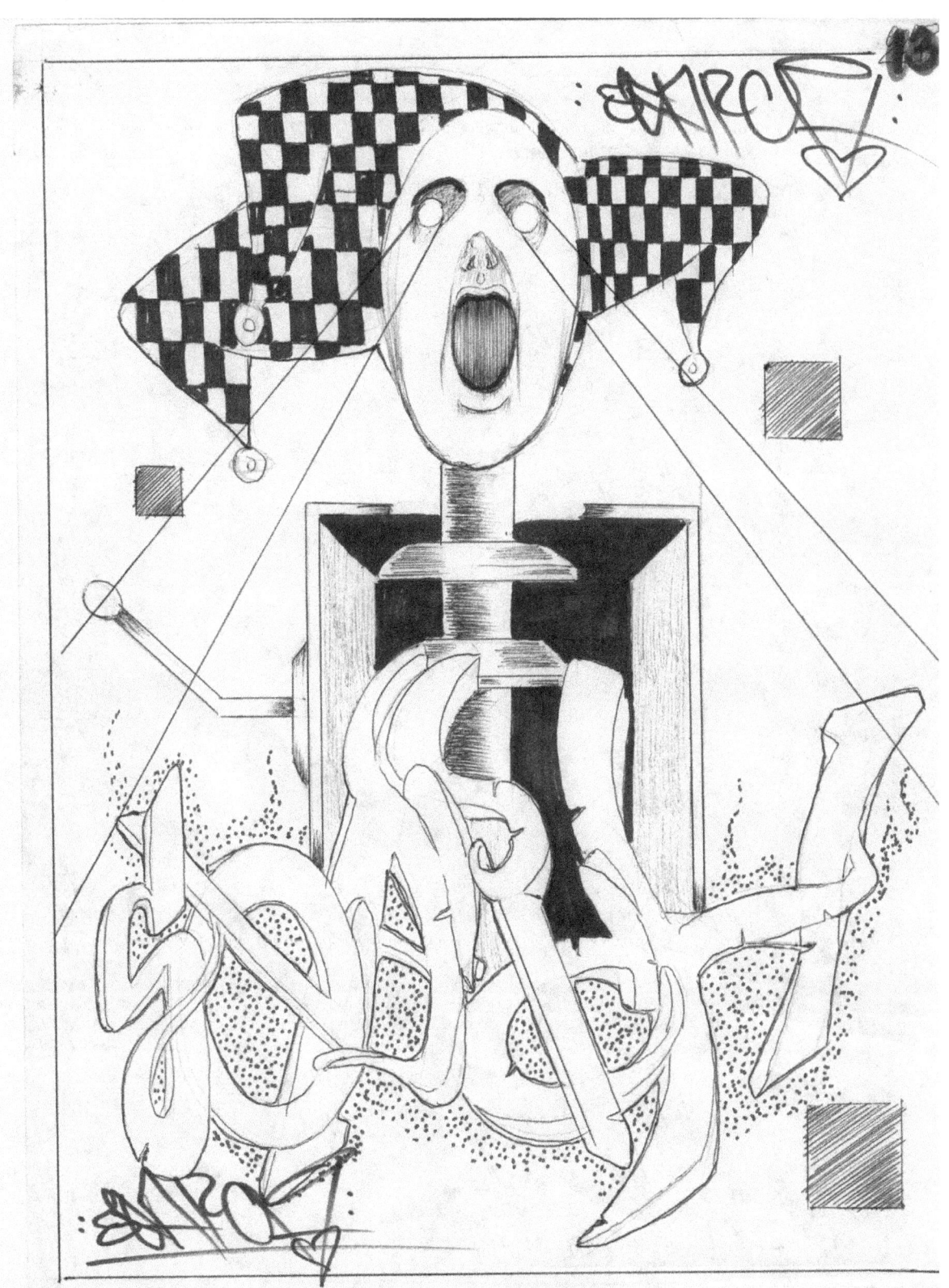

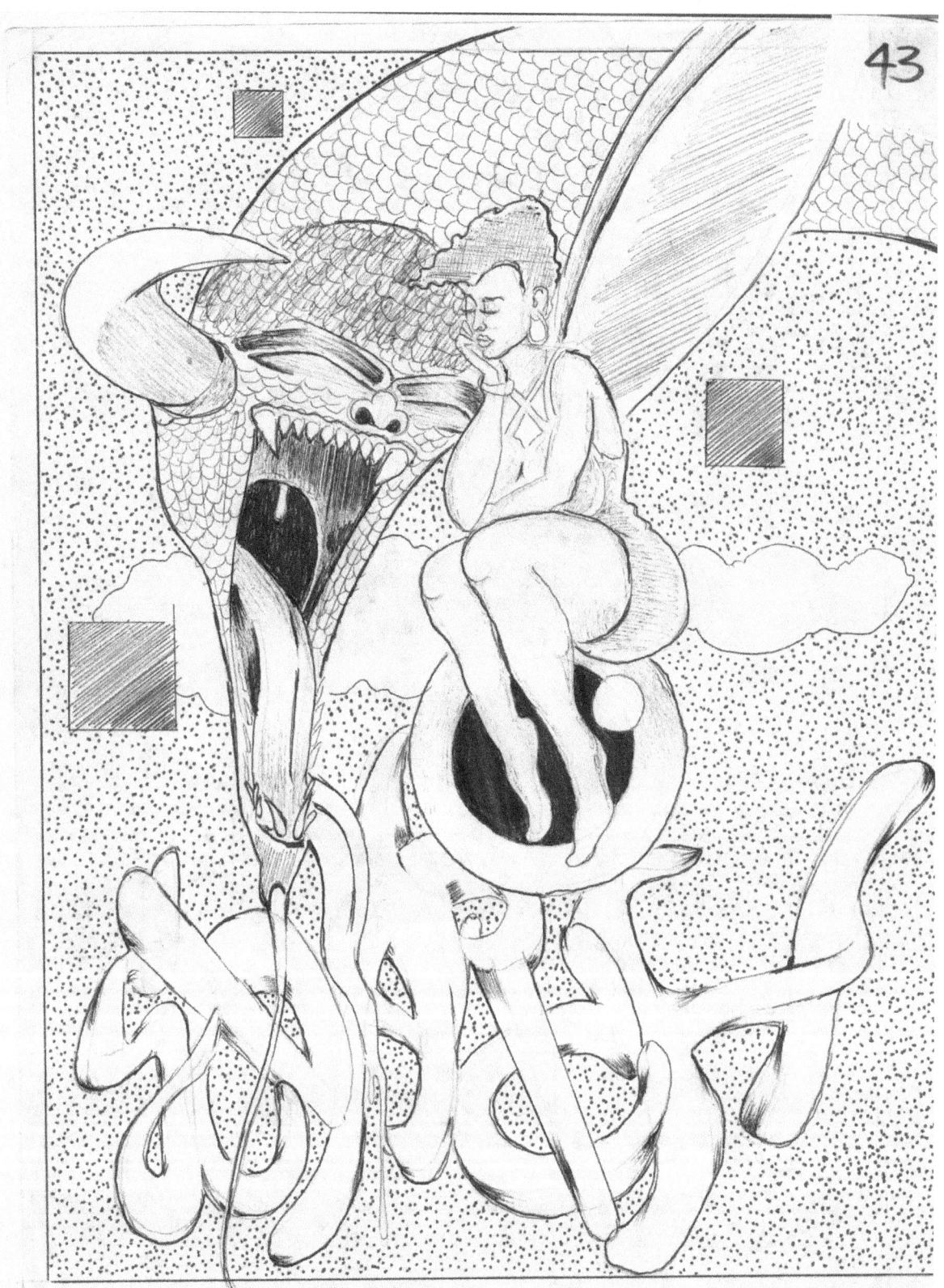

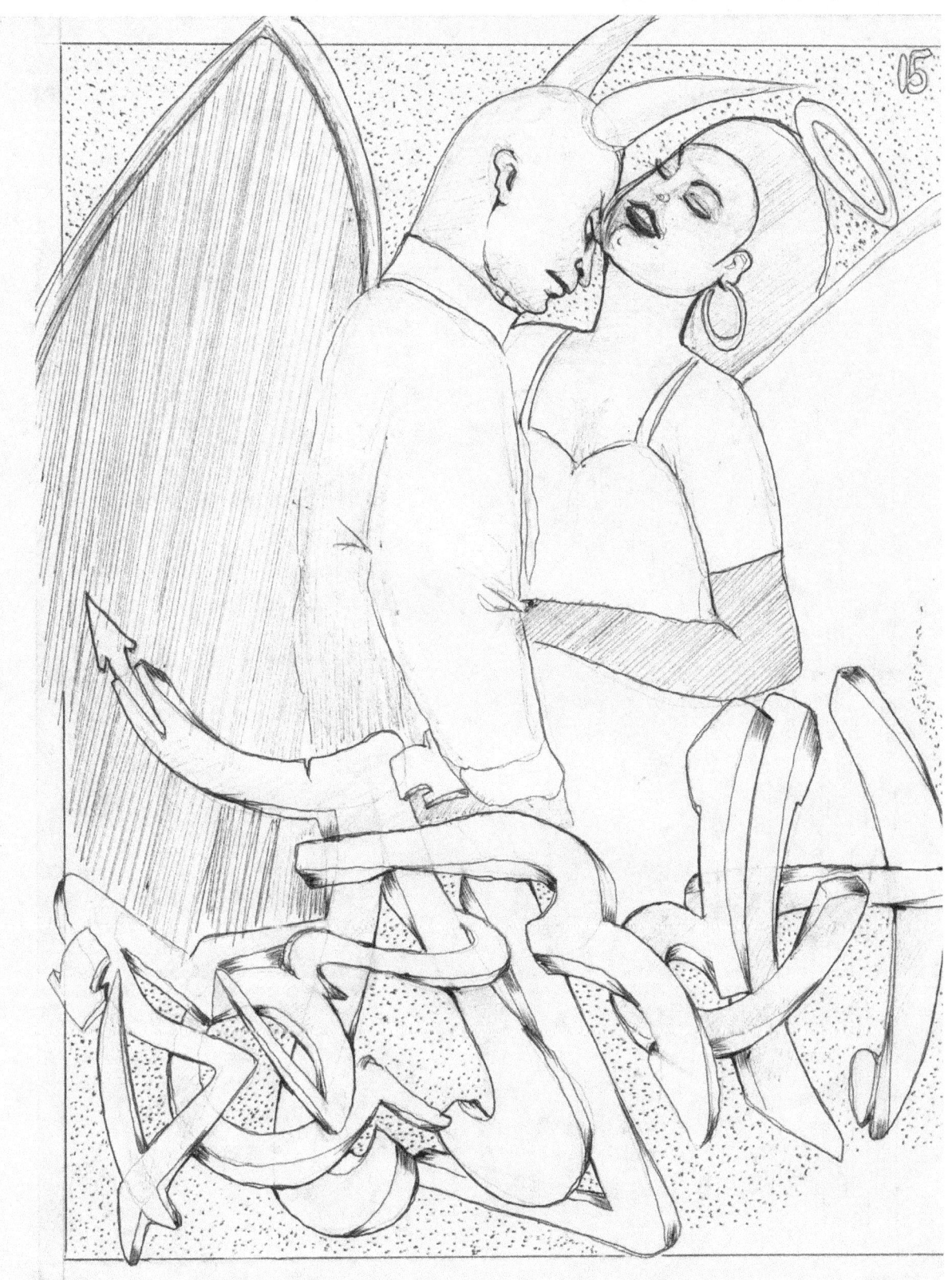

15

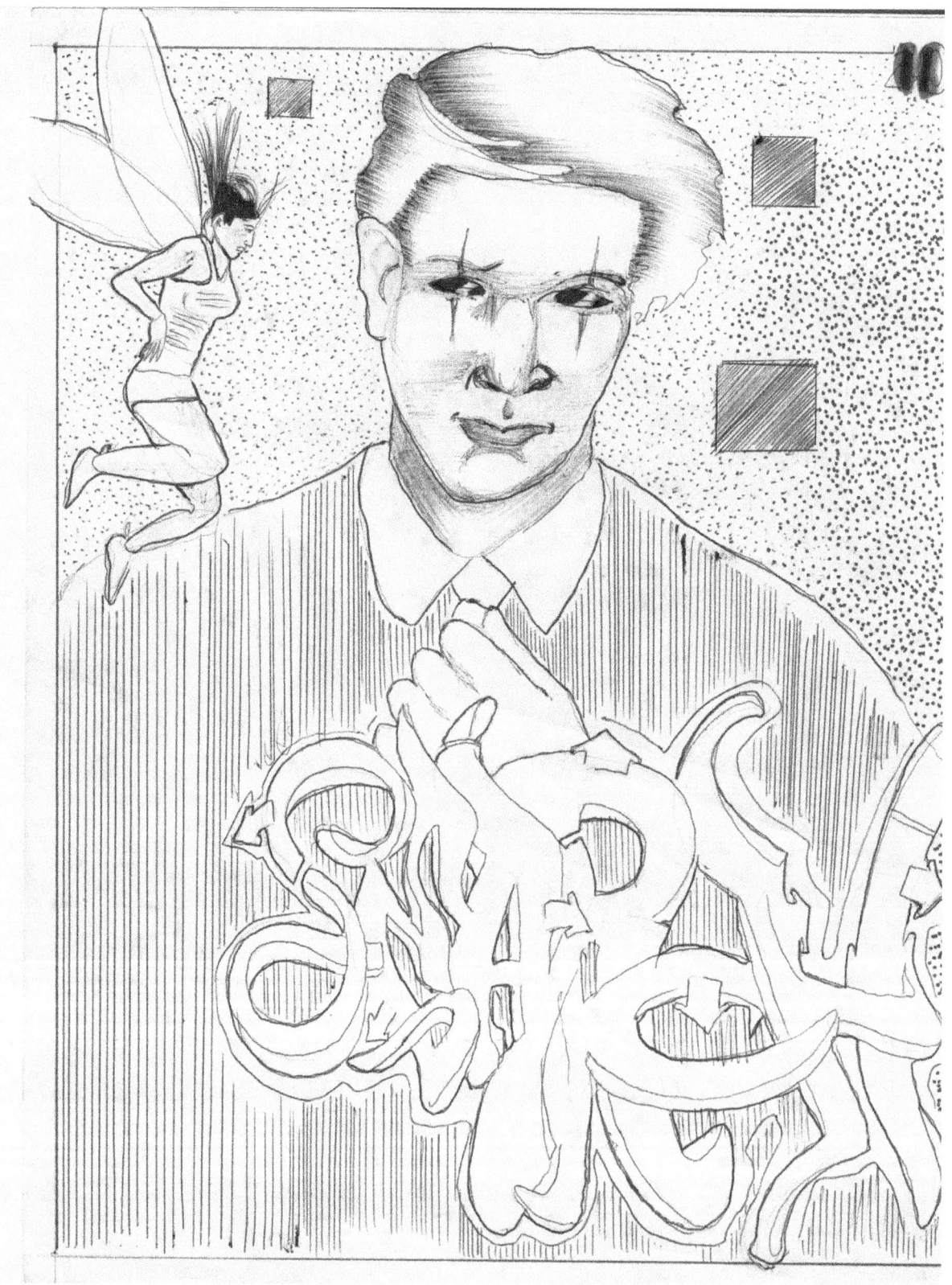

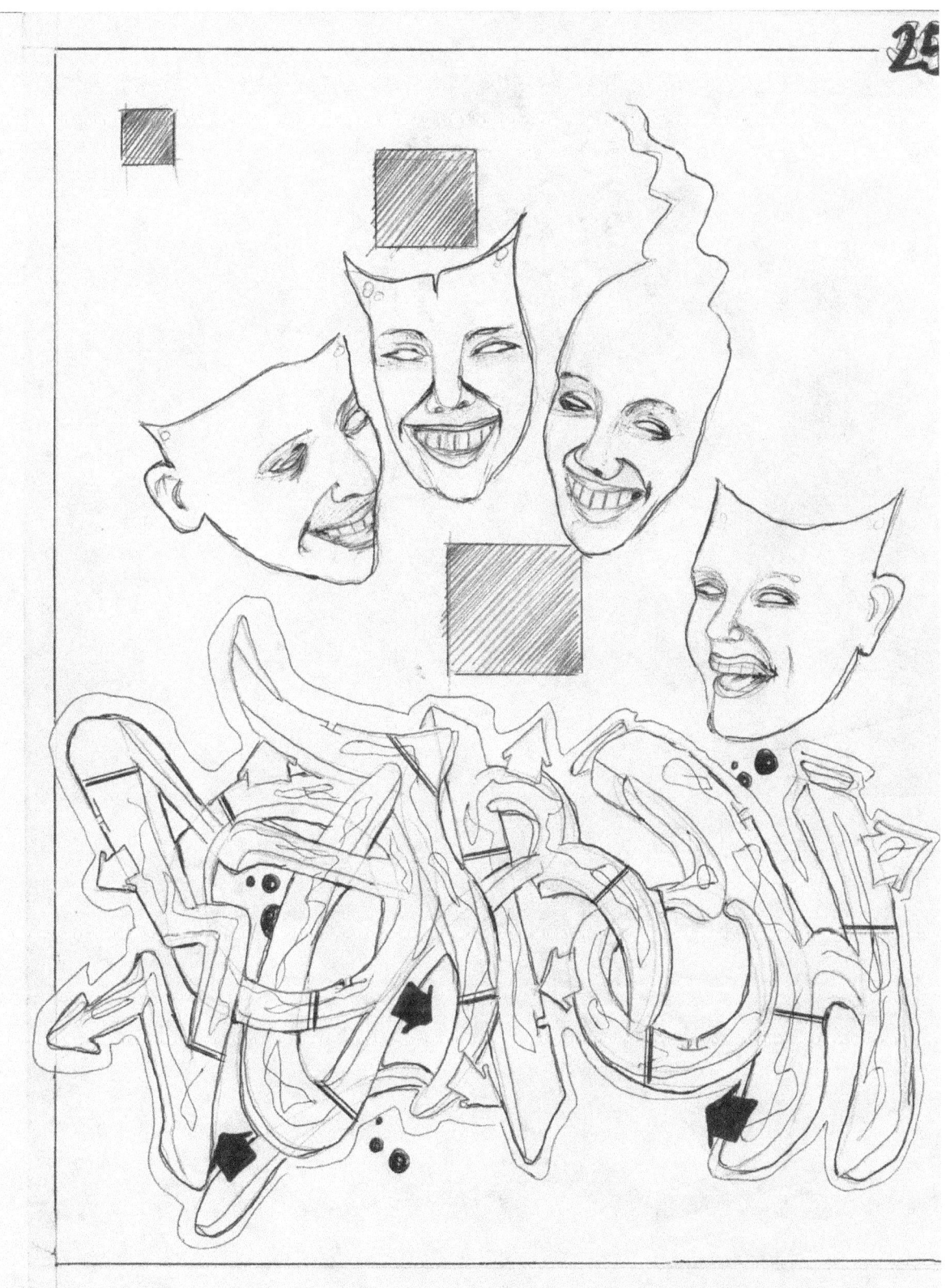

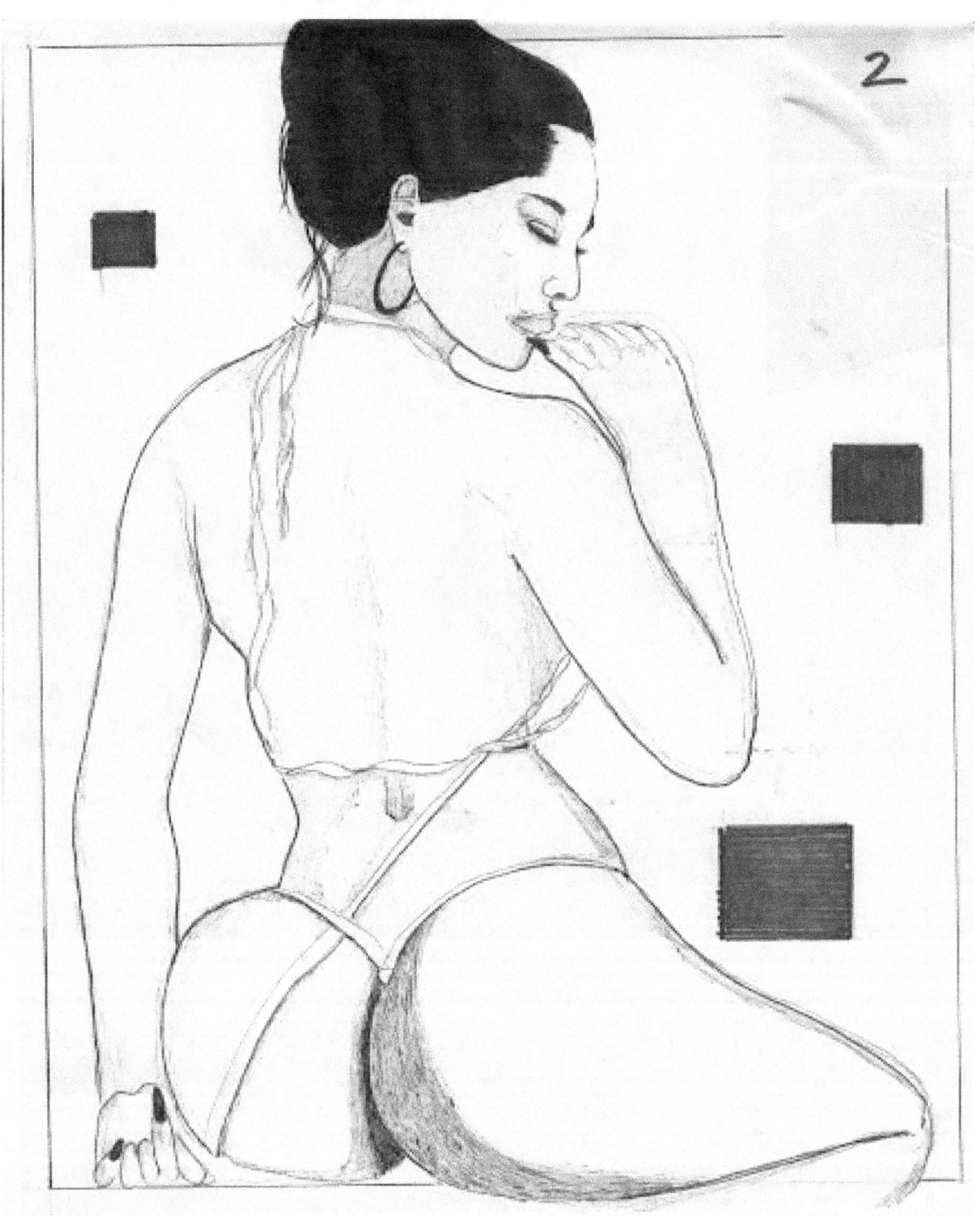

2

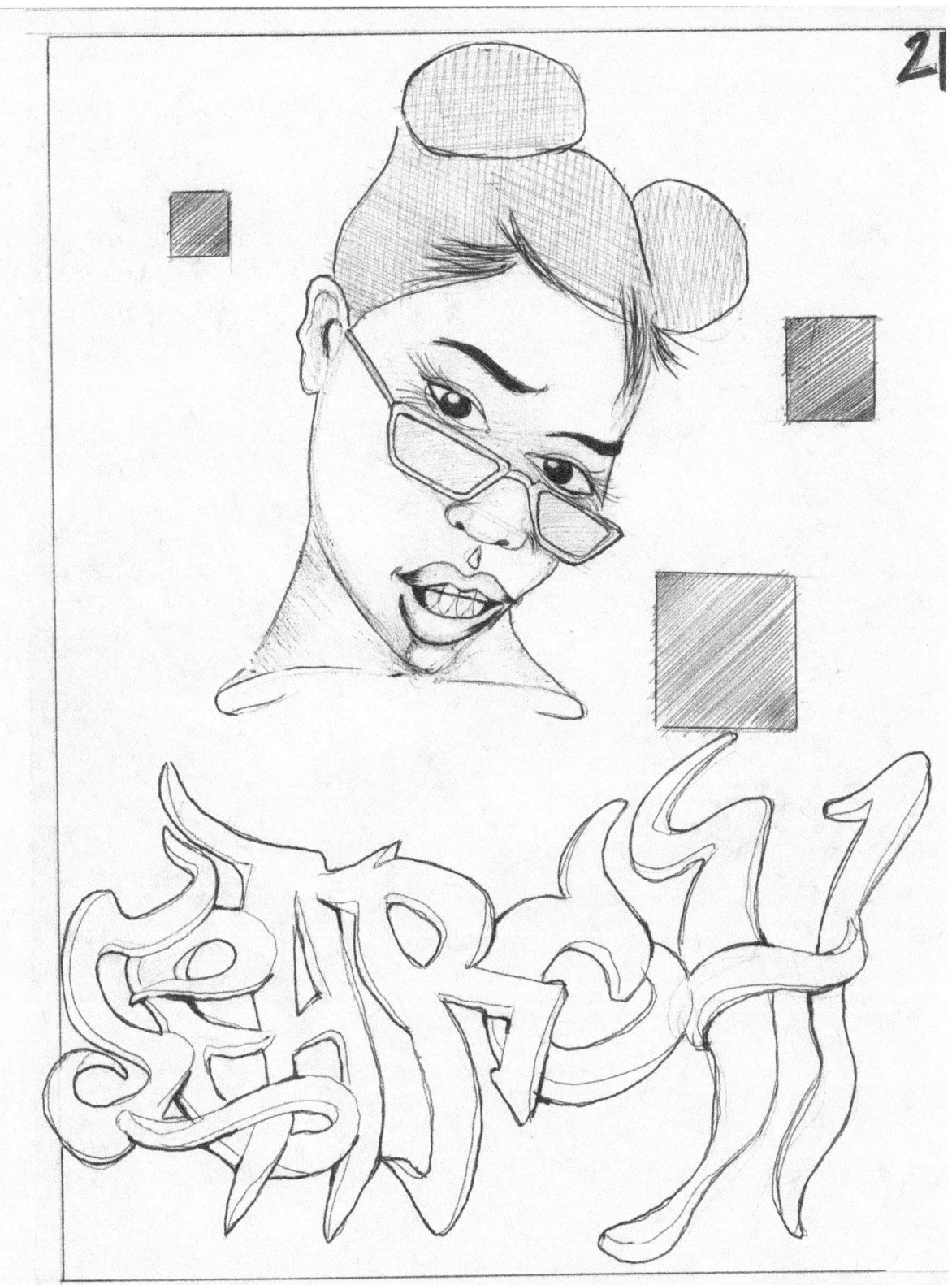

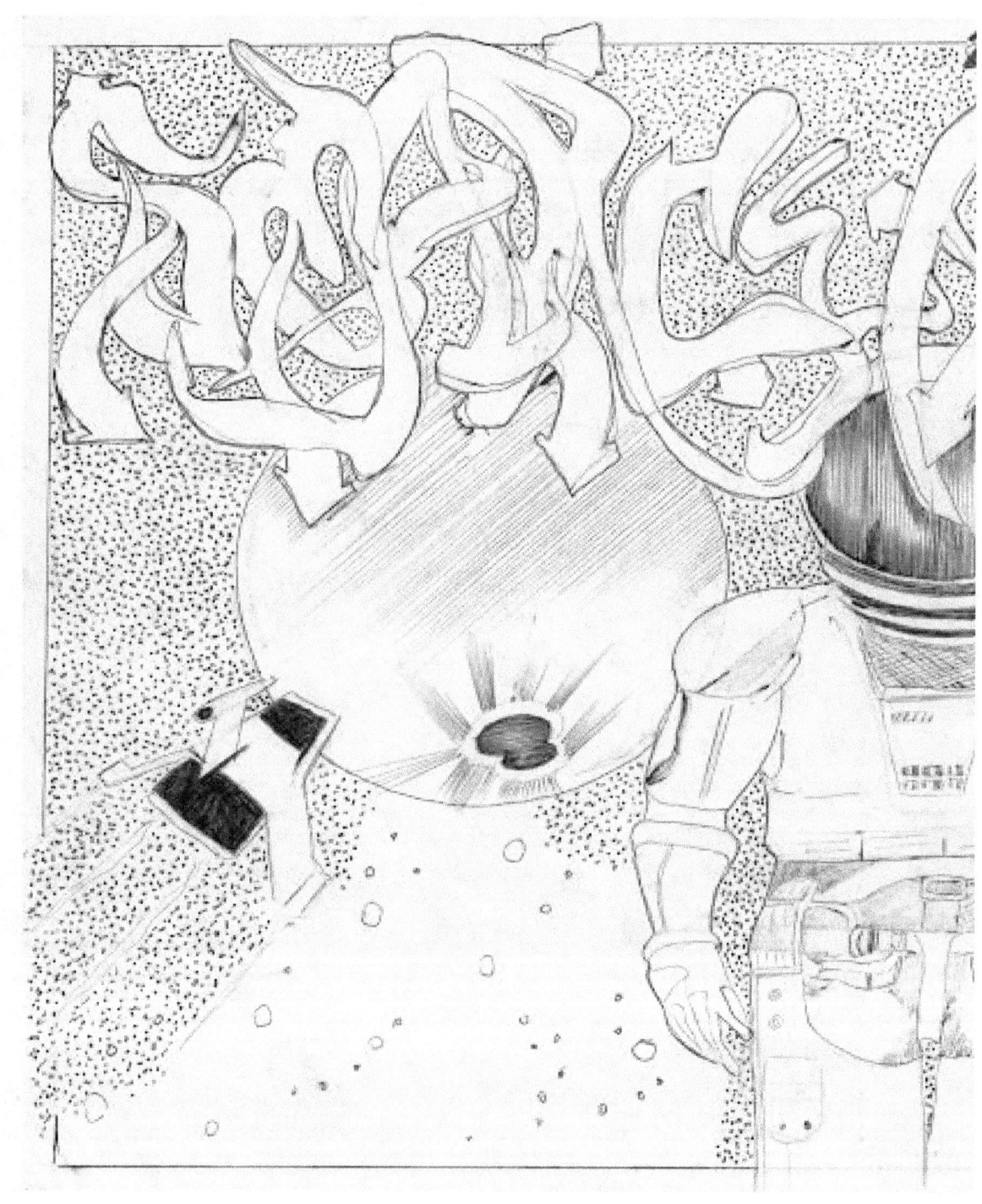

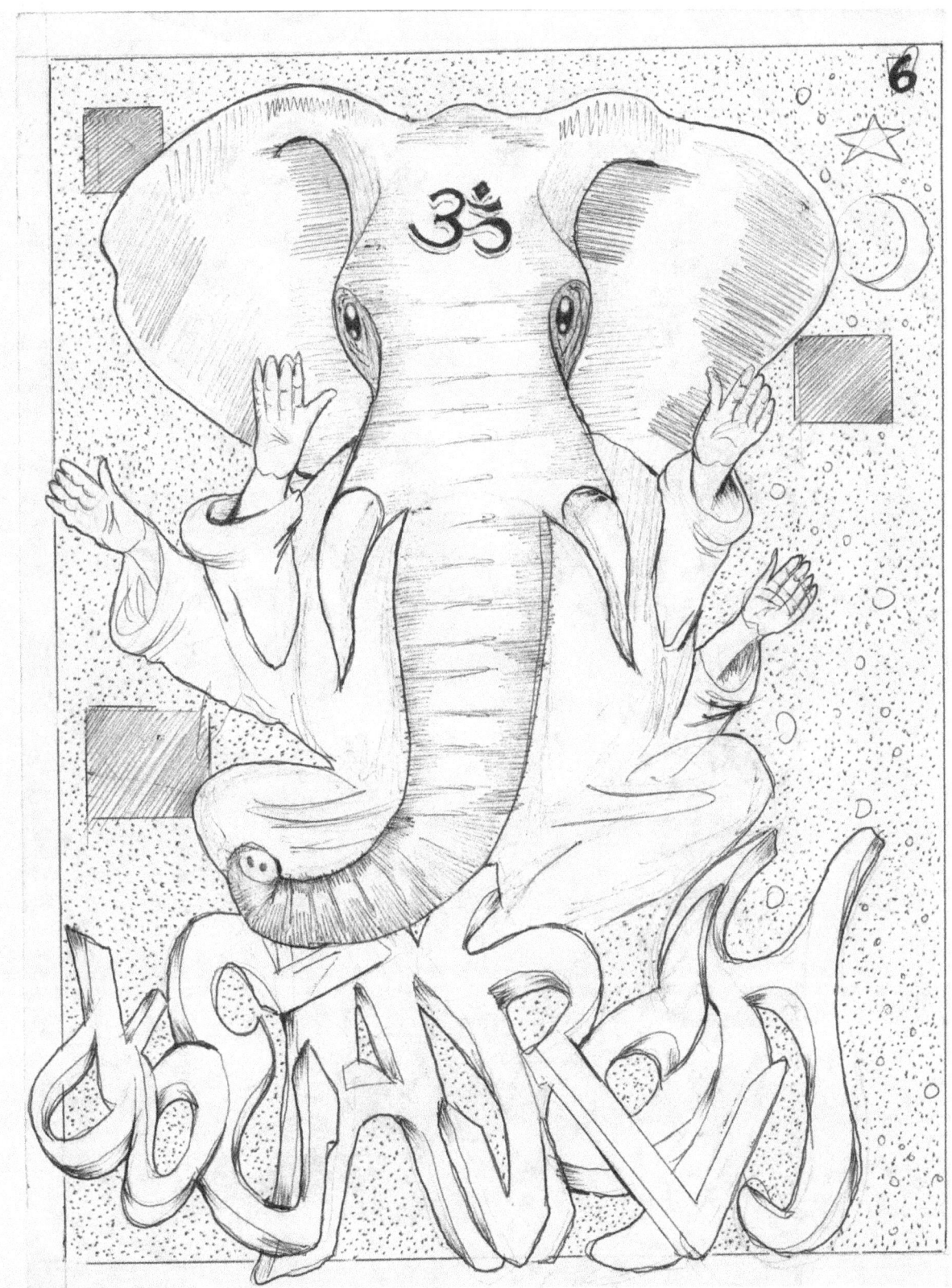

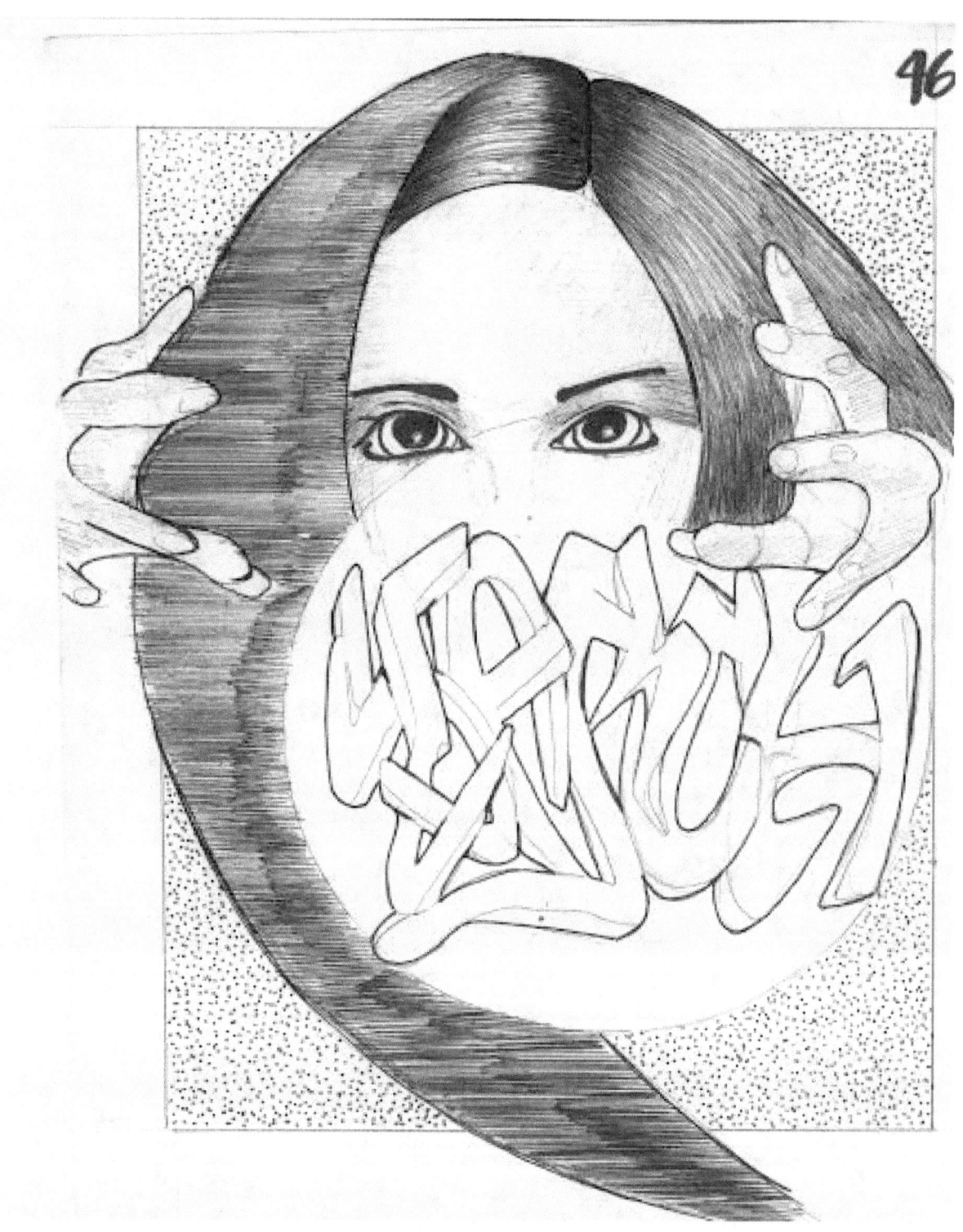

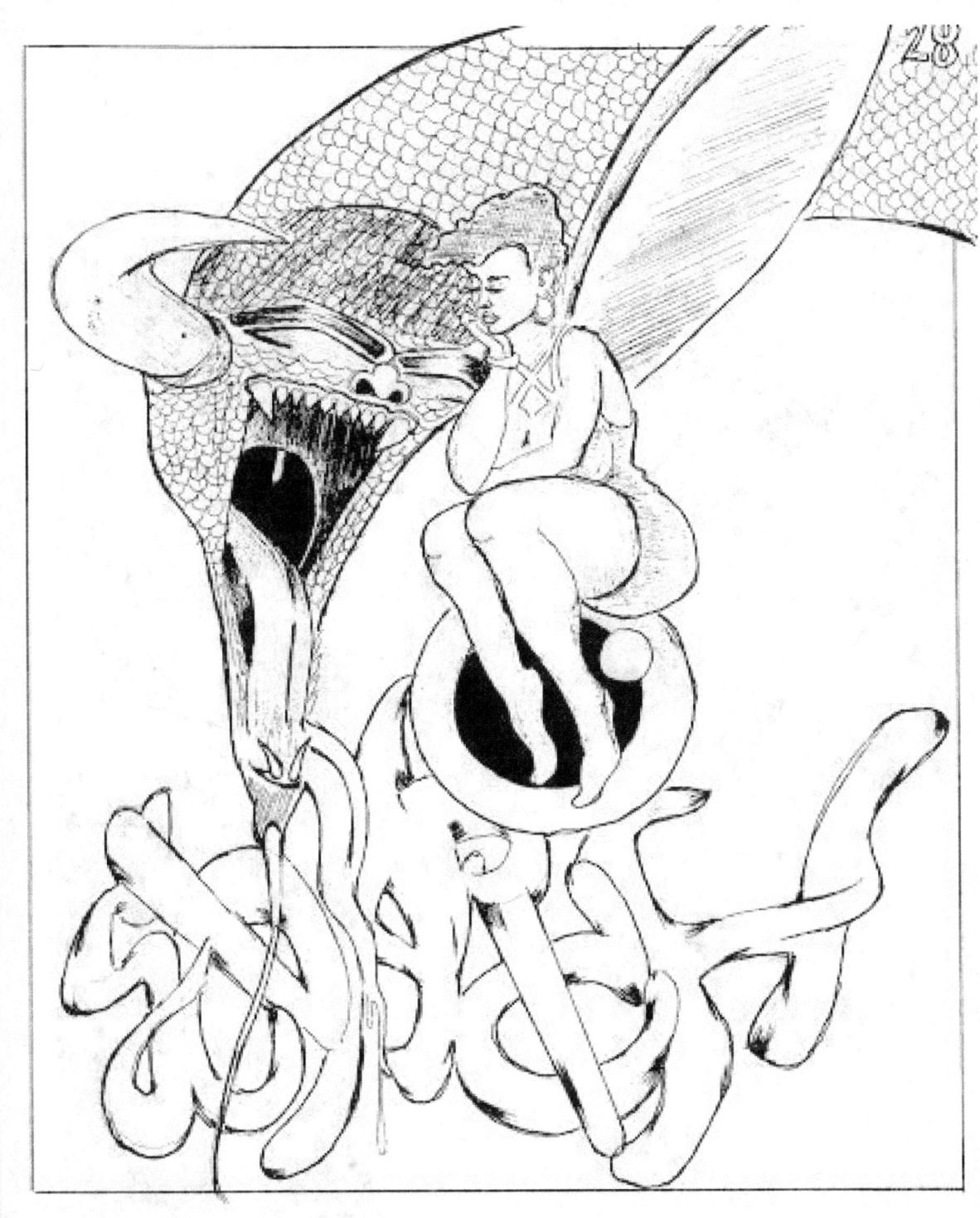

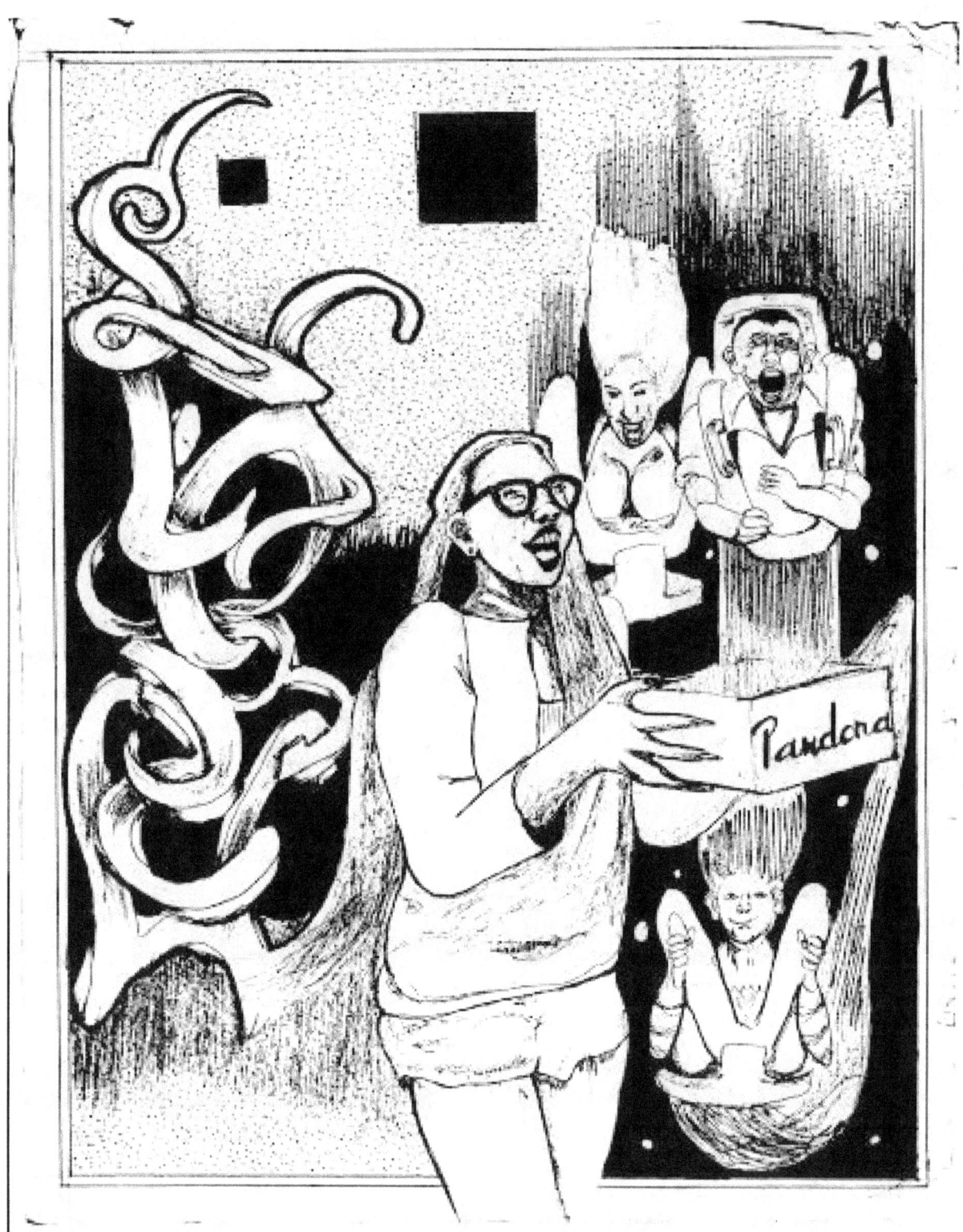

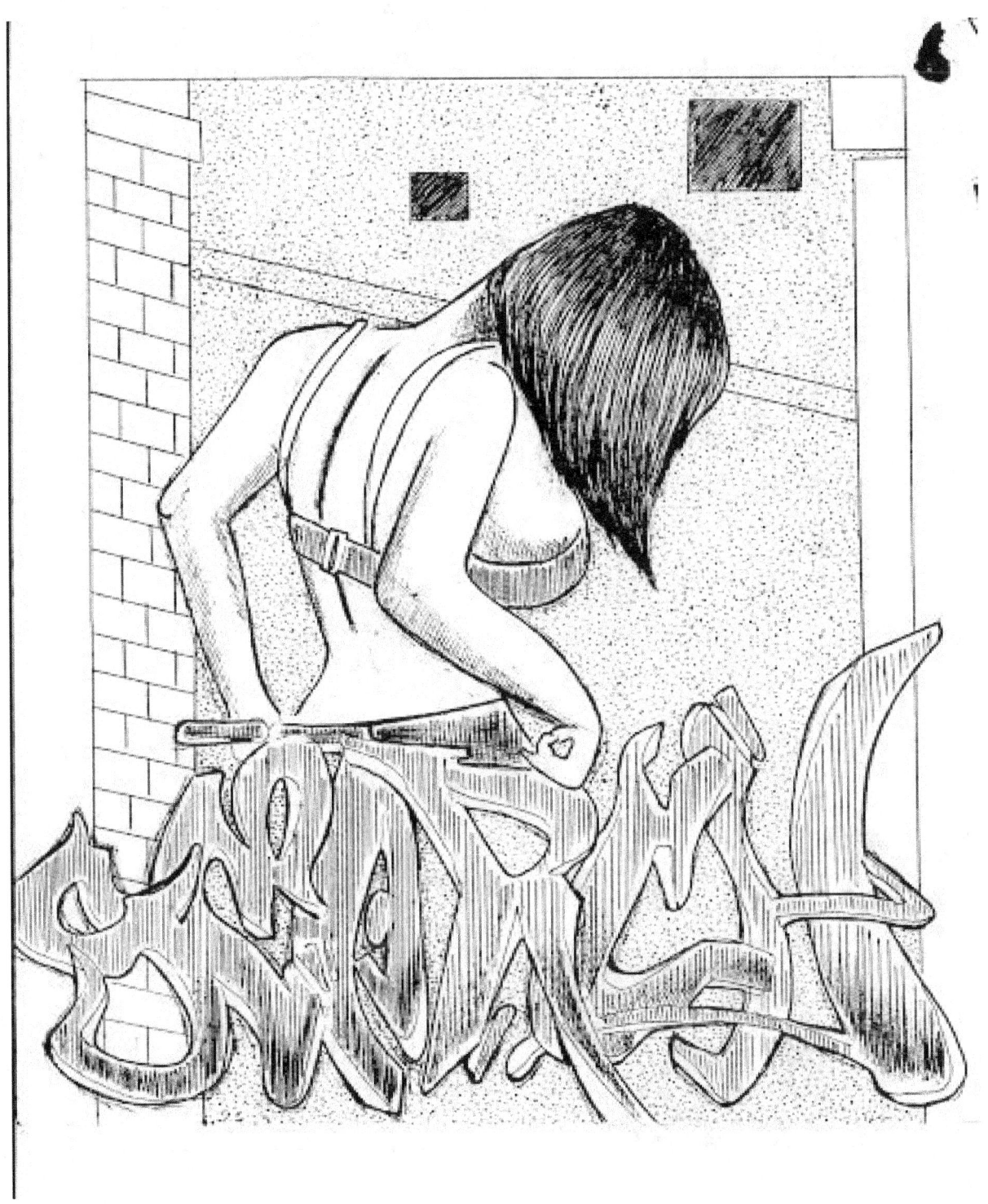

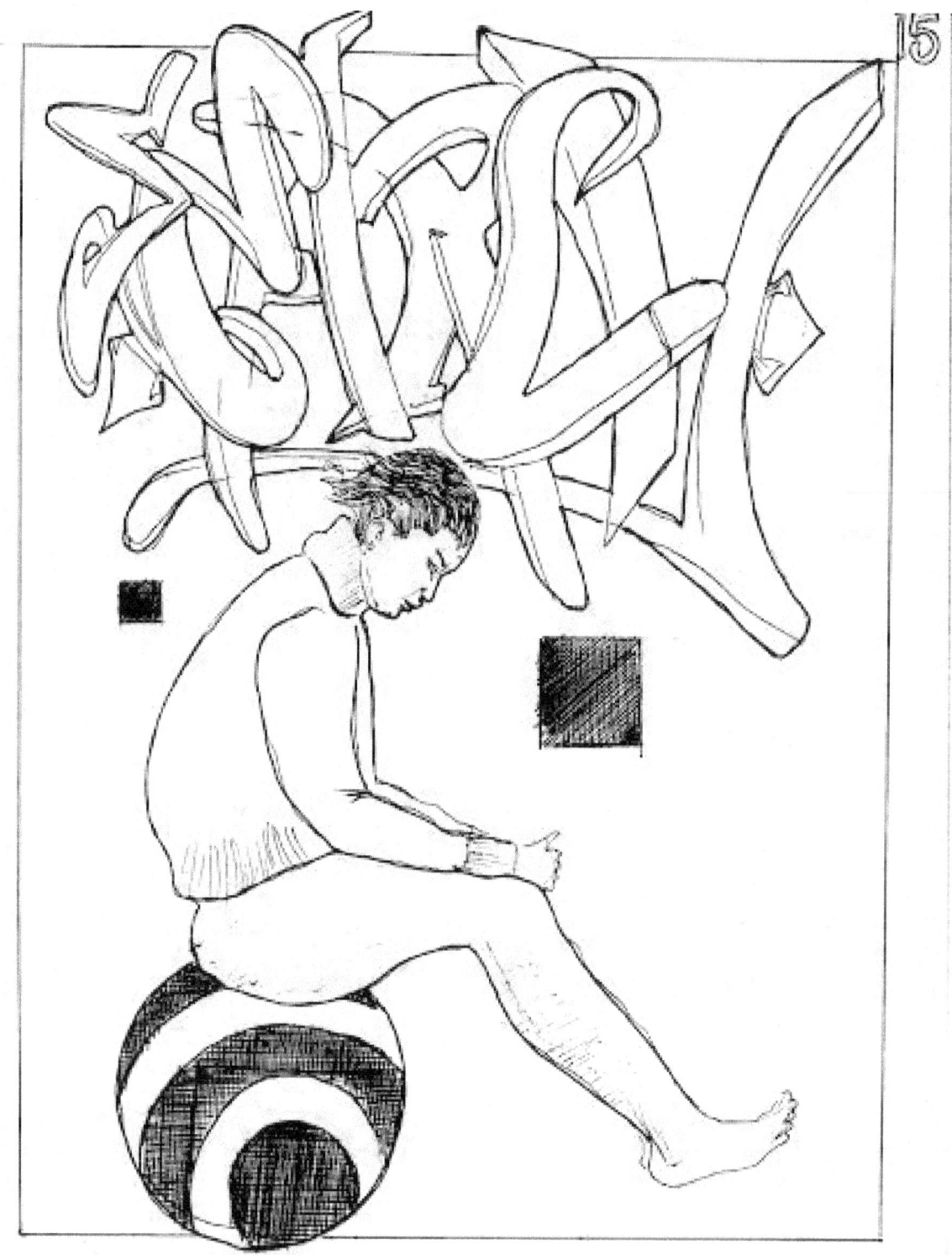

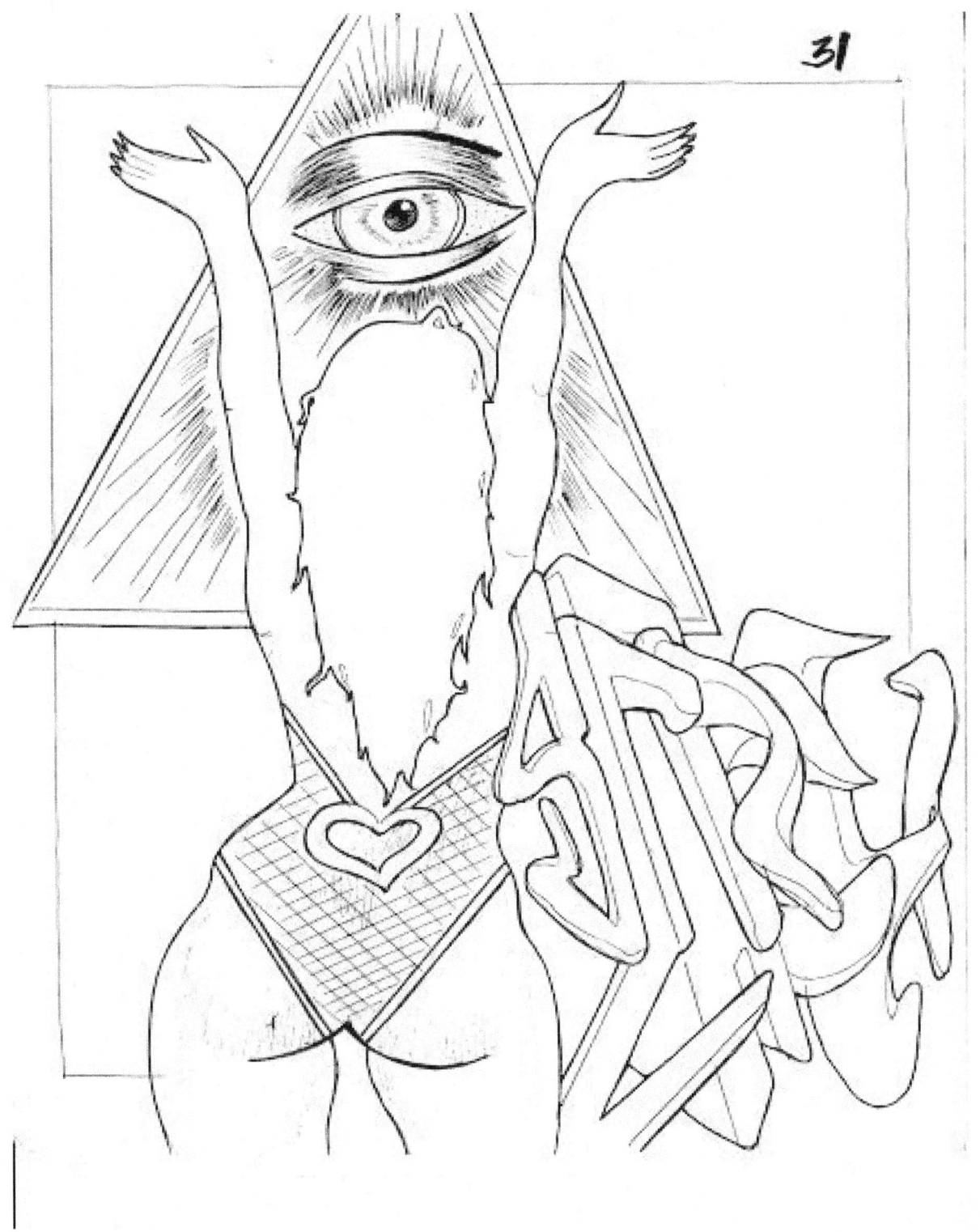

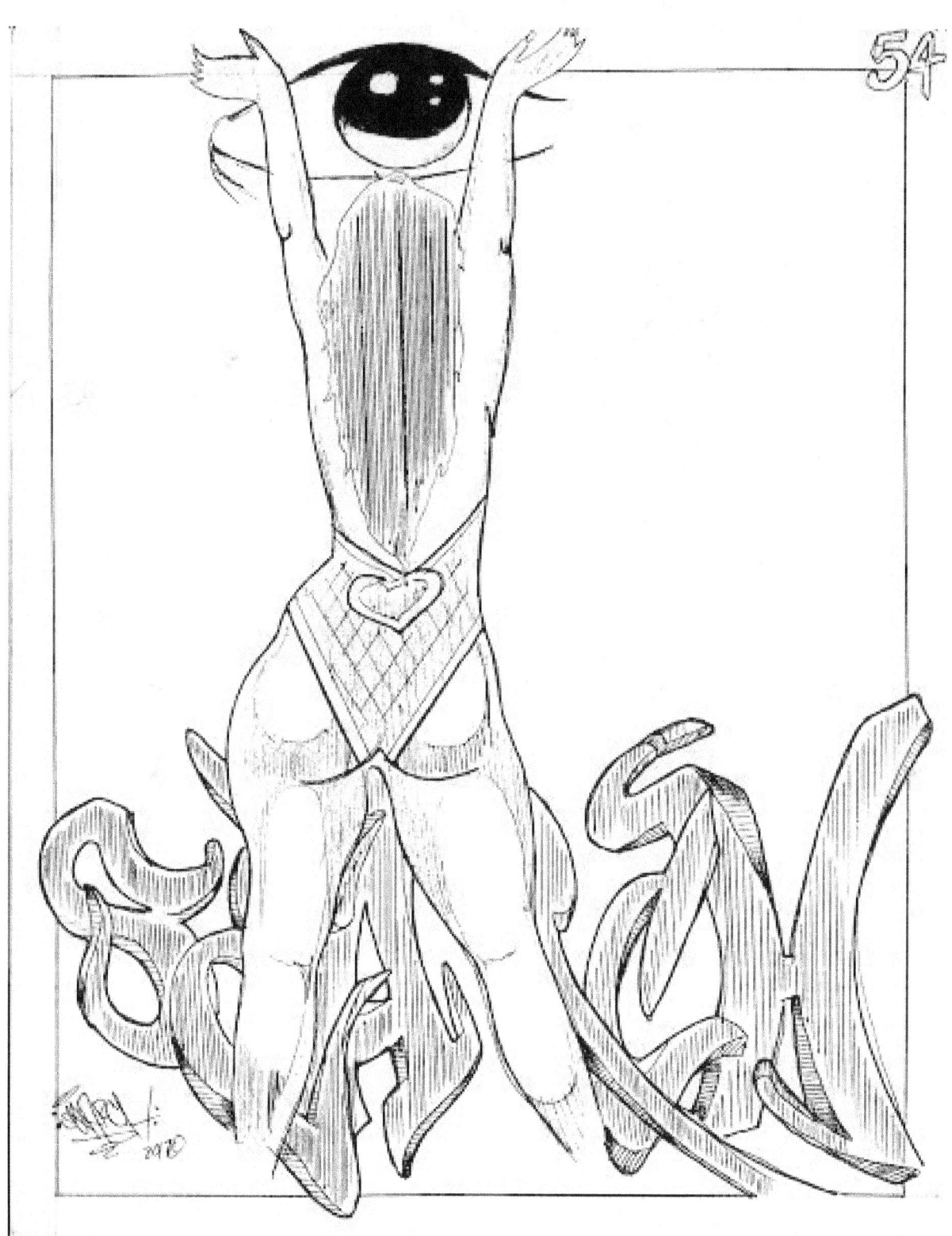

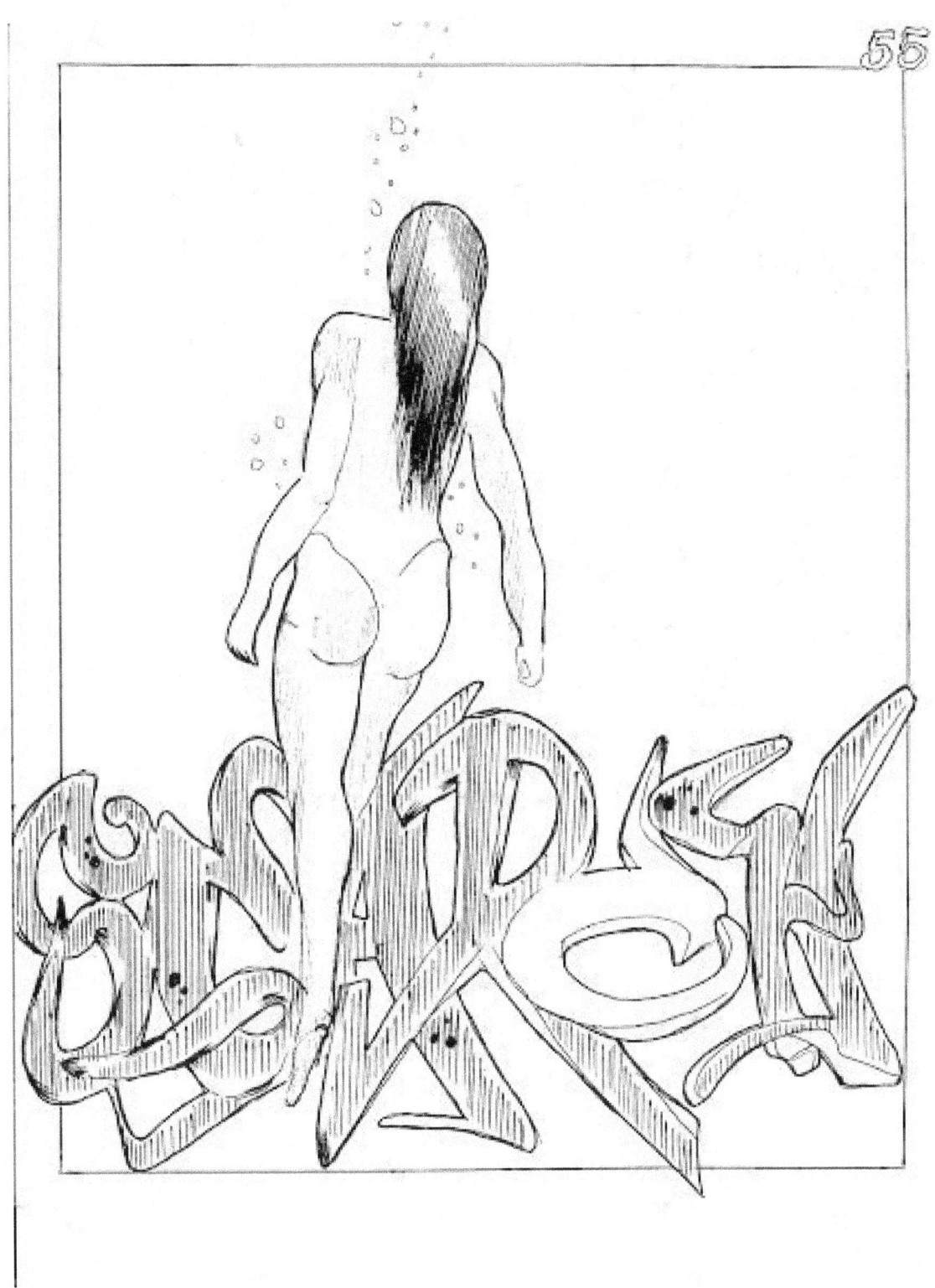

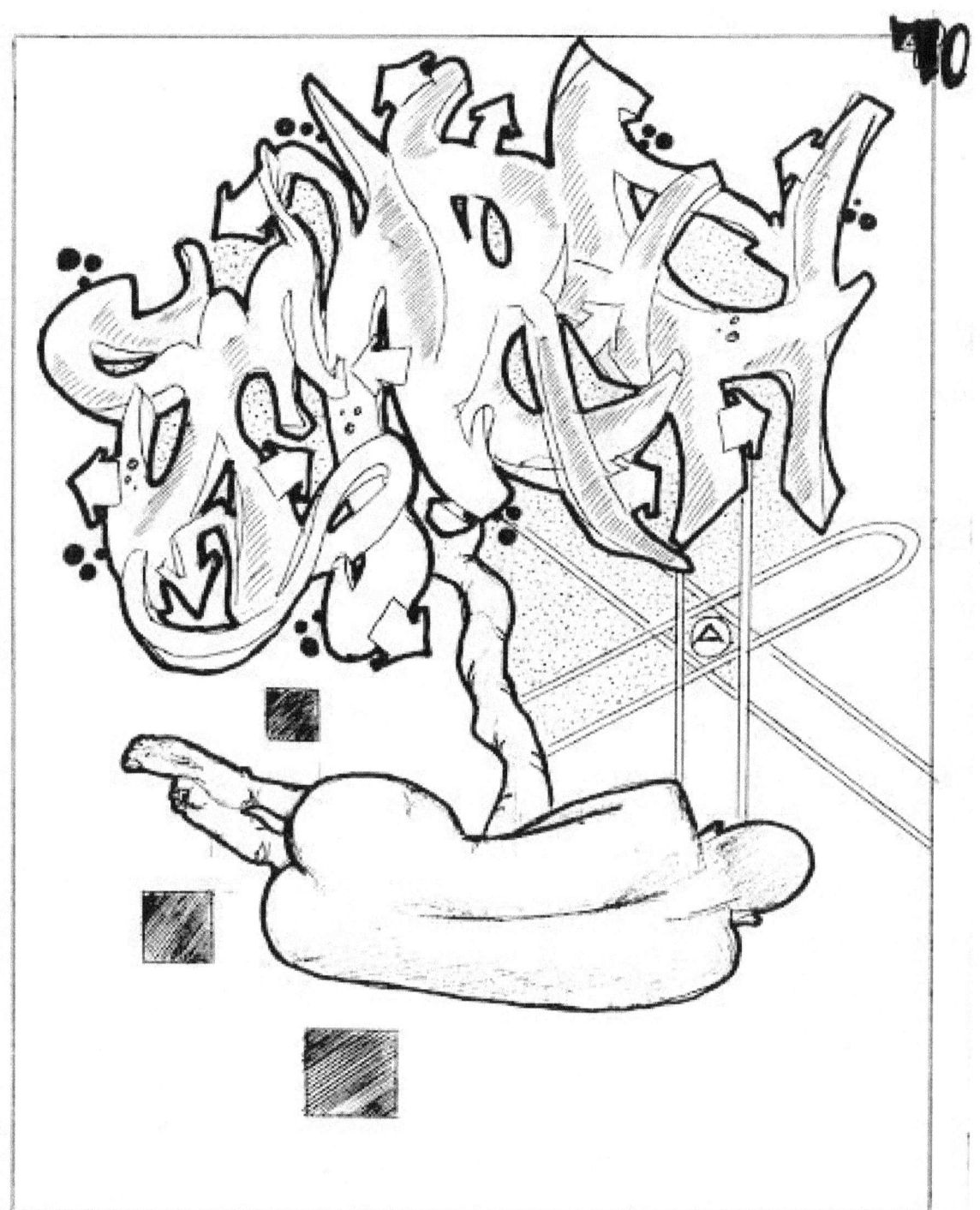

63

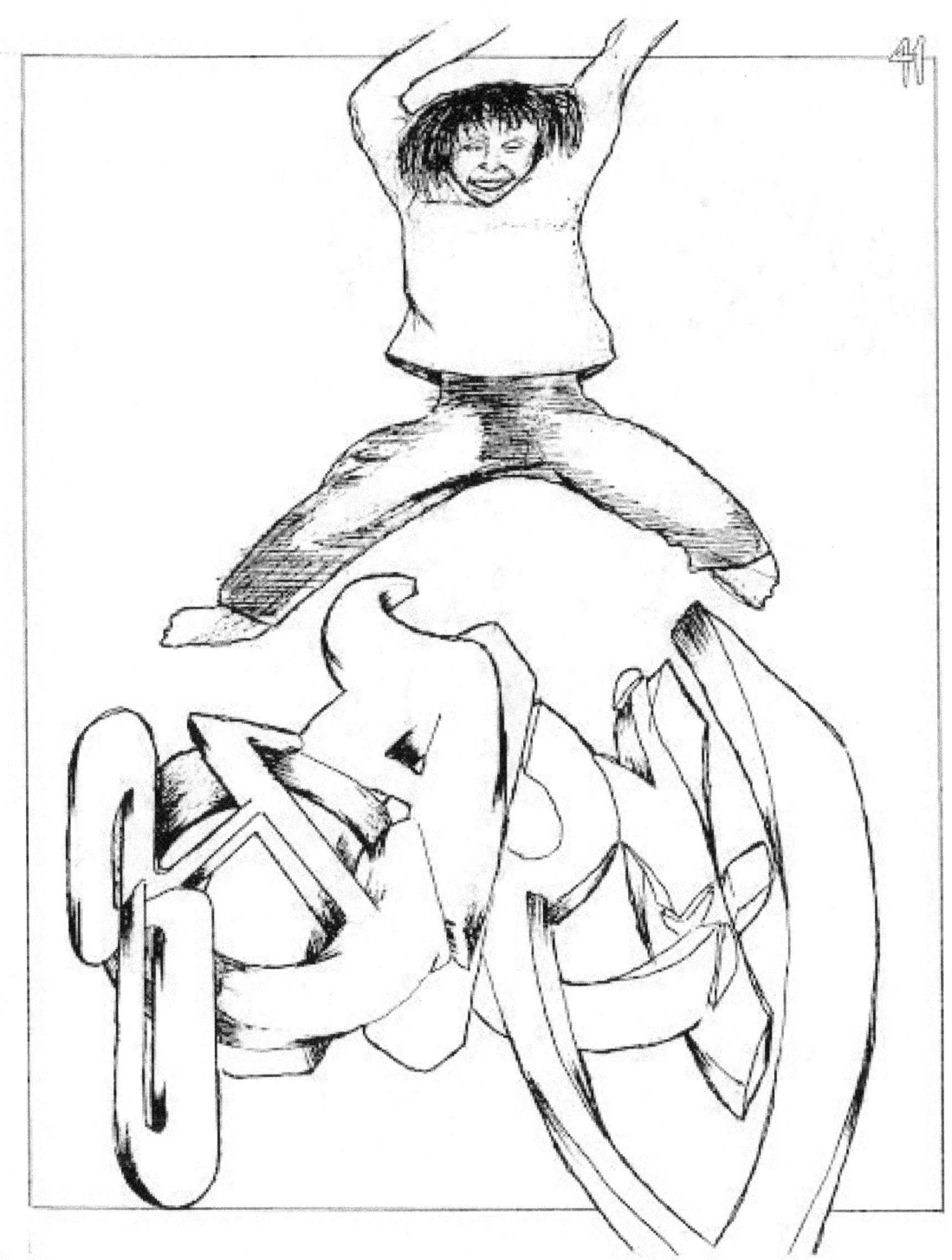

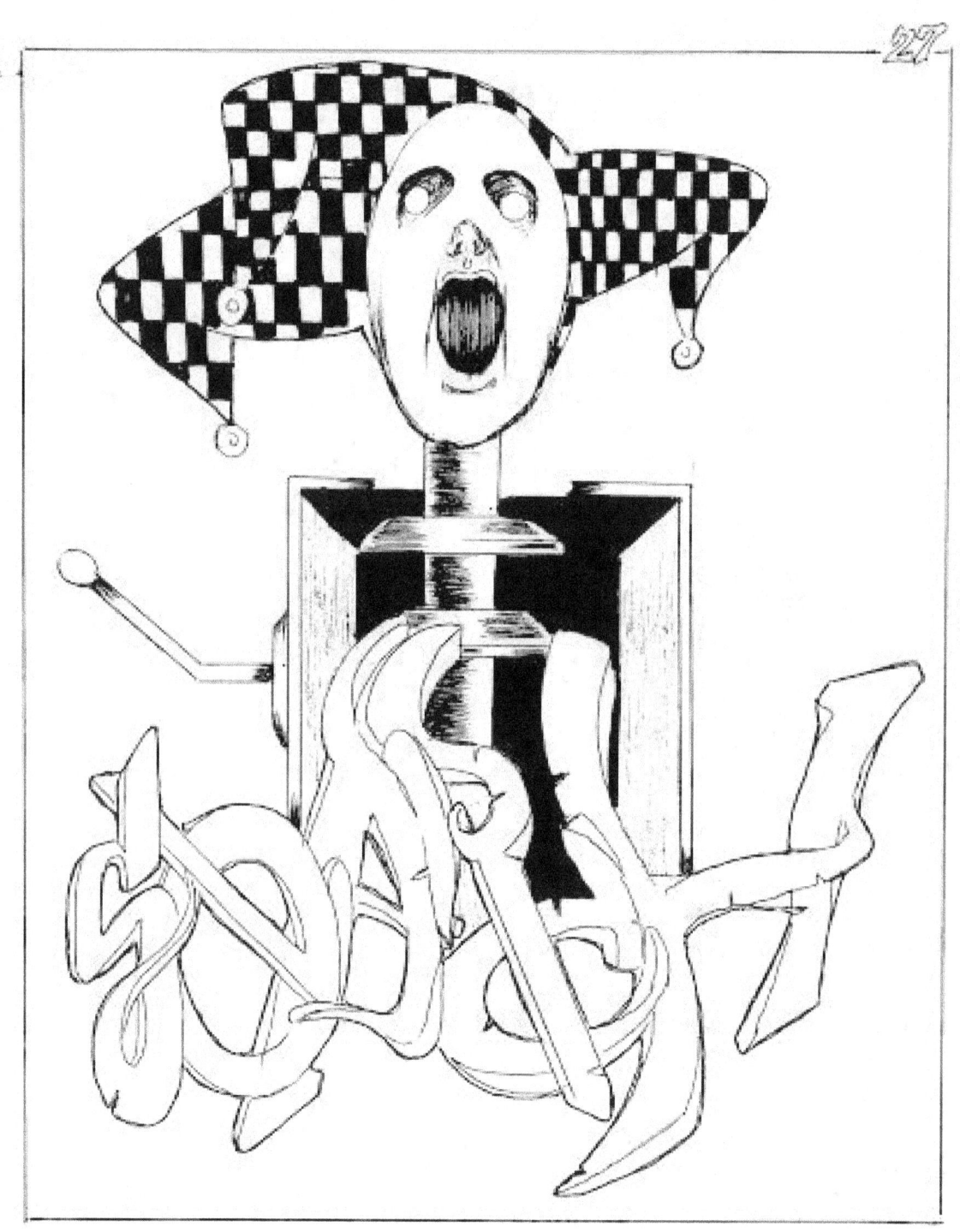

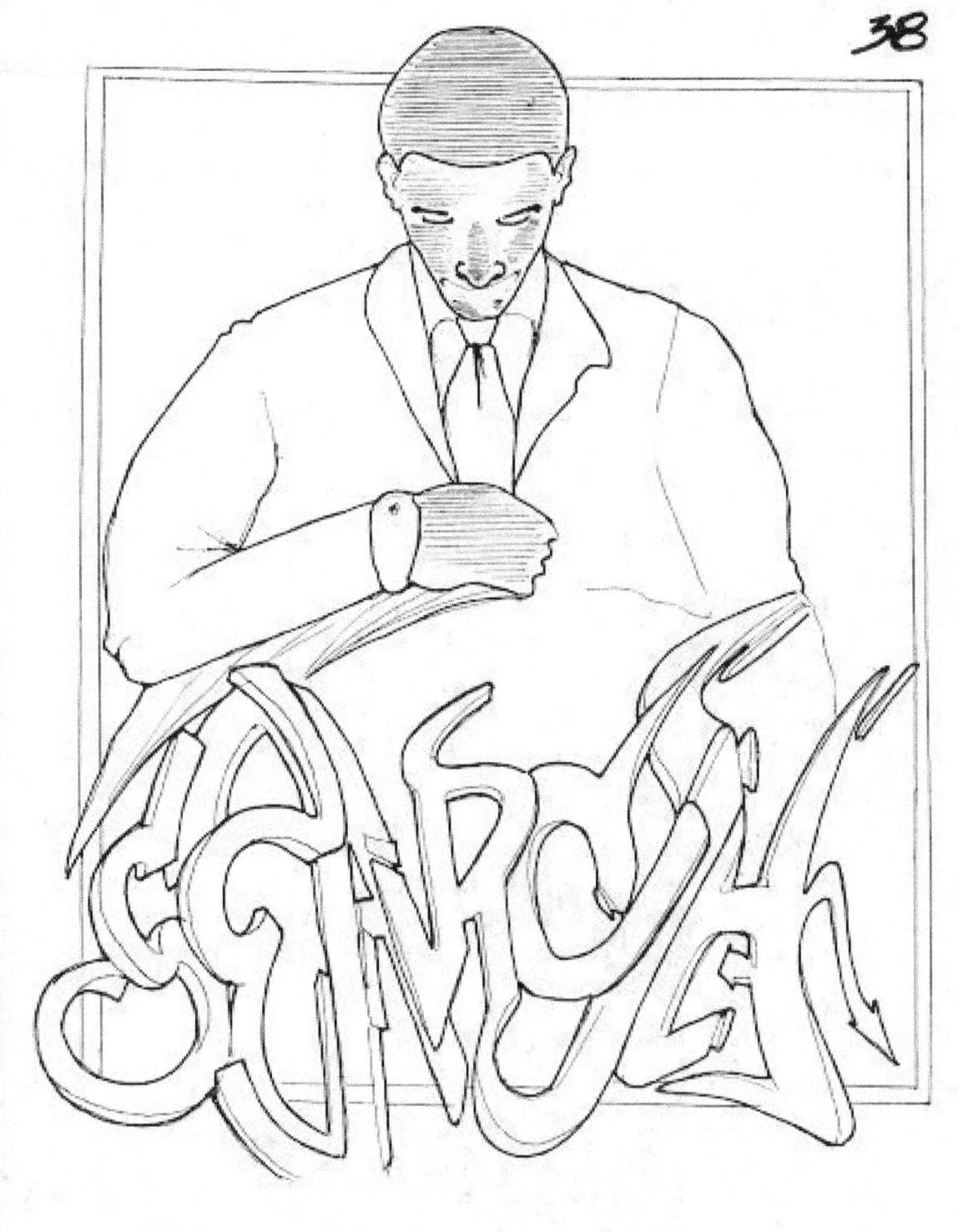

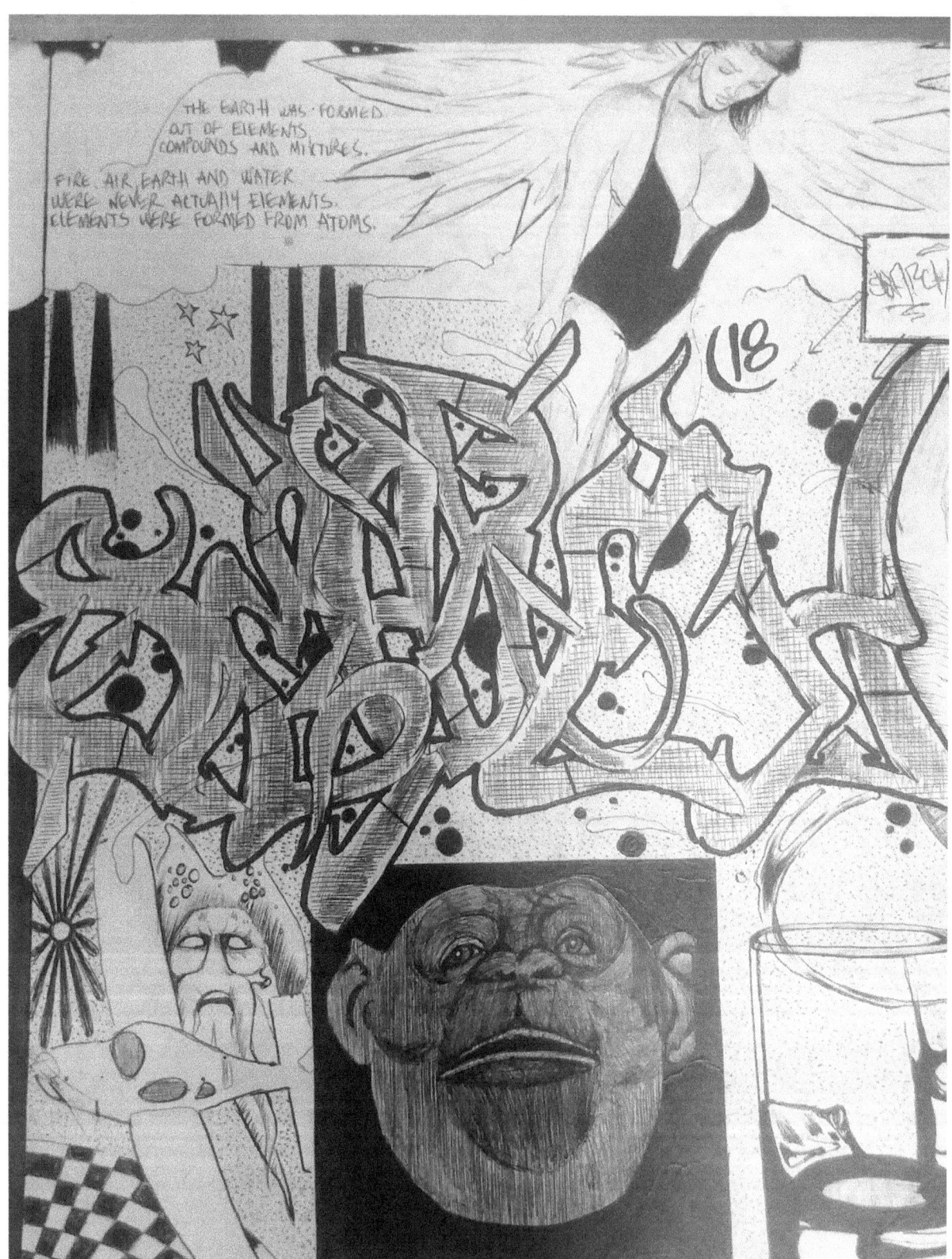

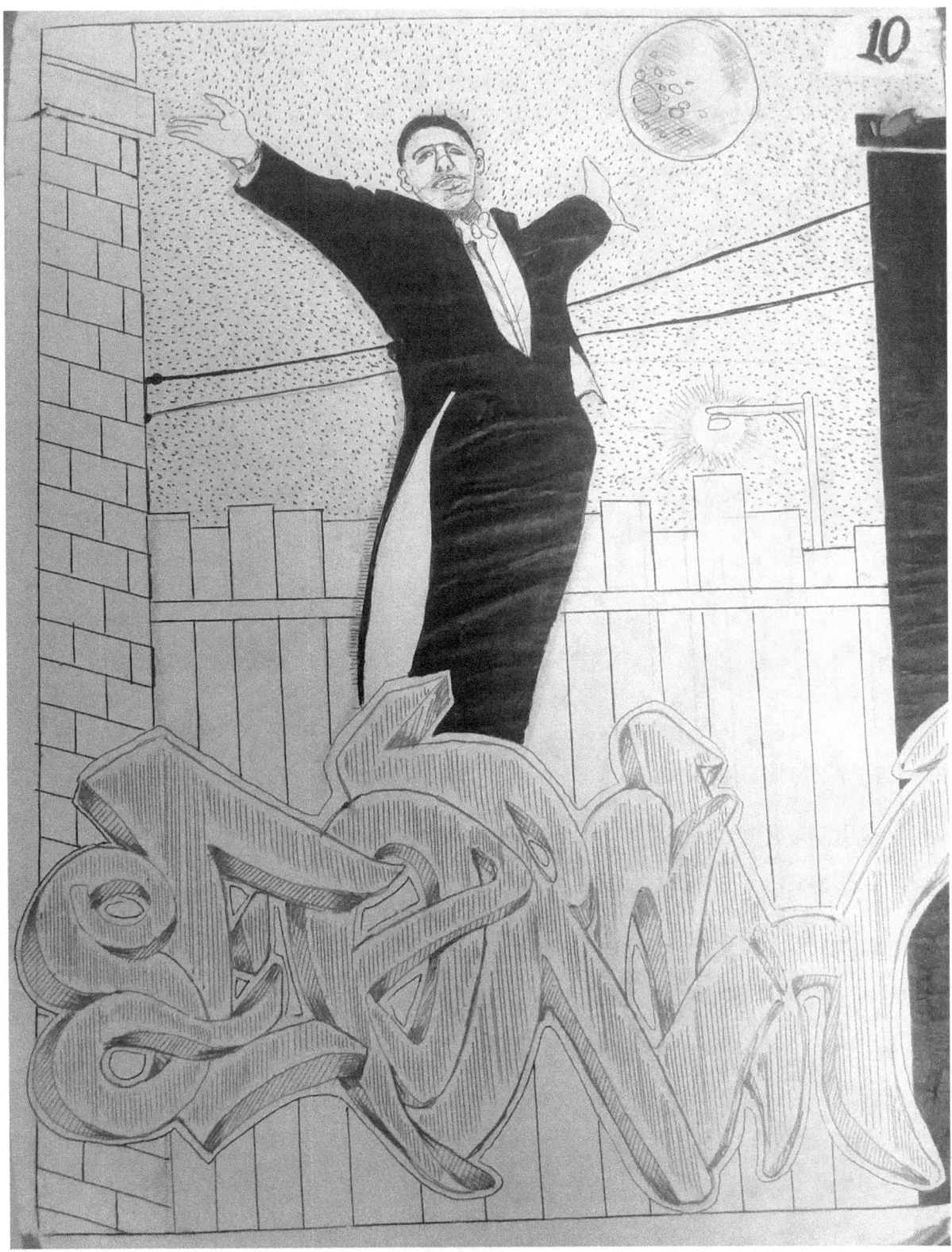

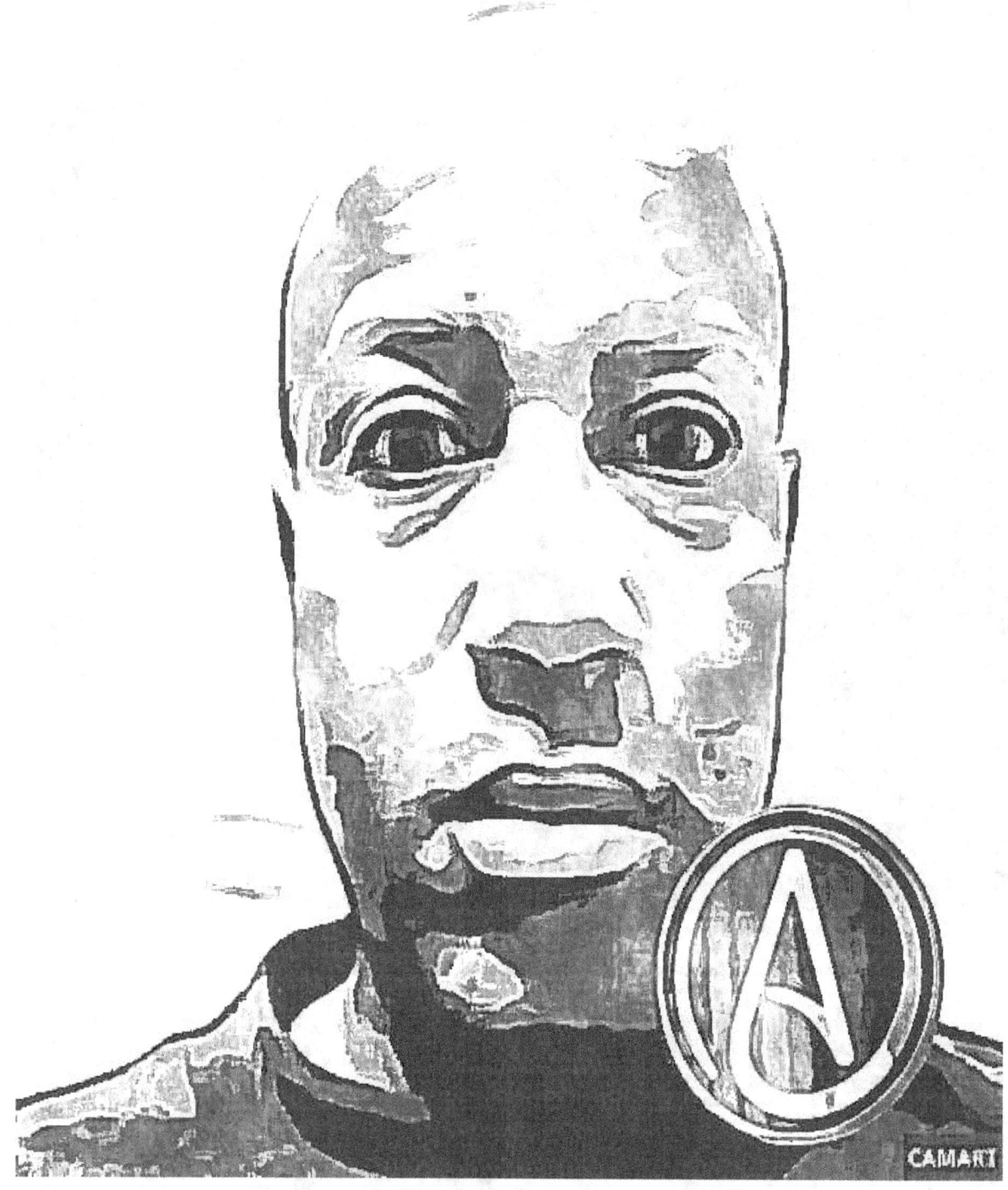

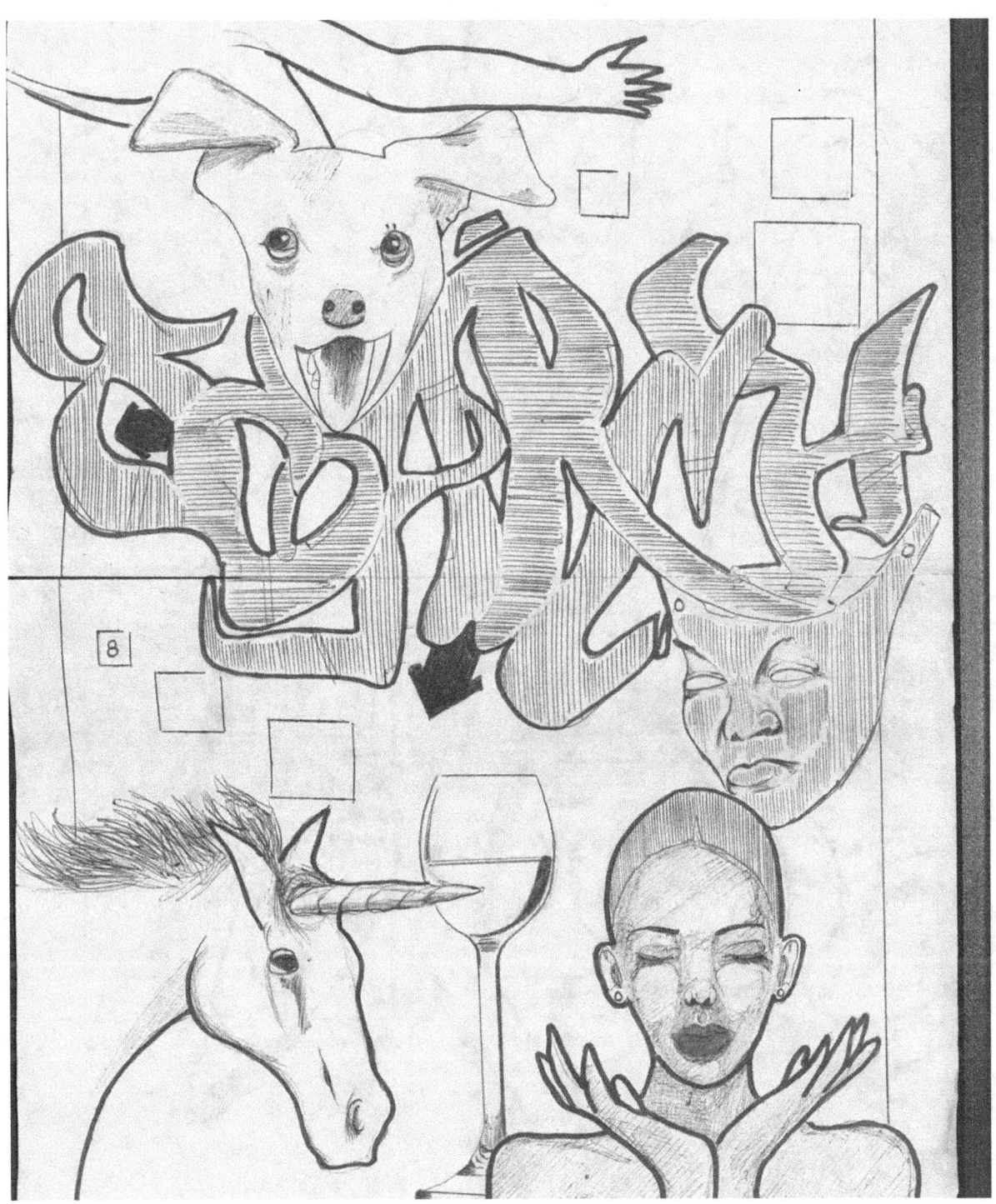

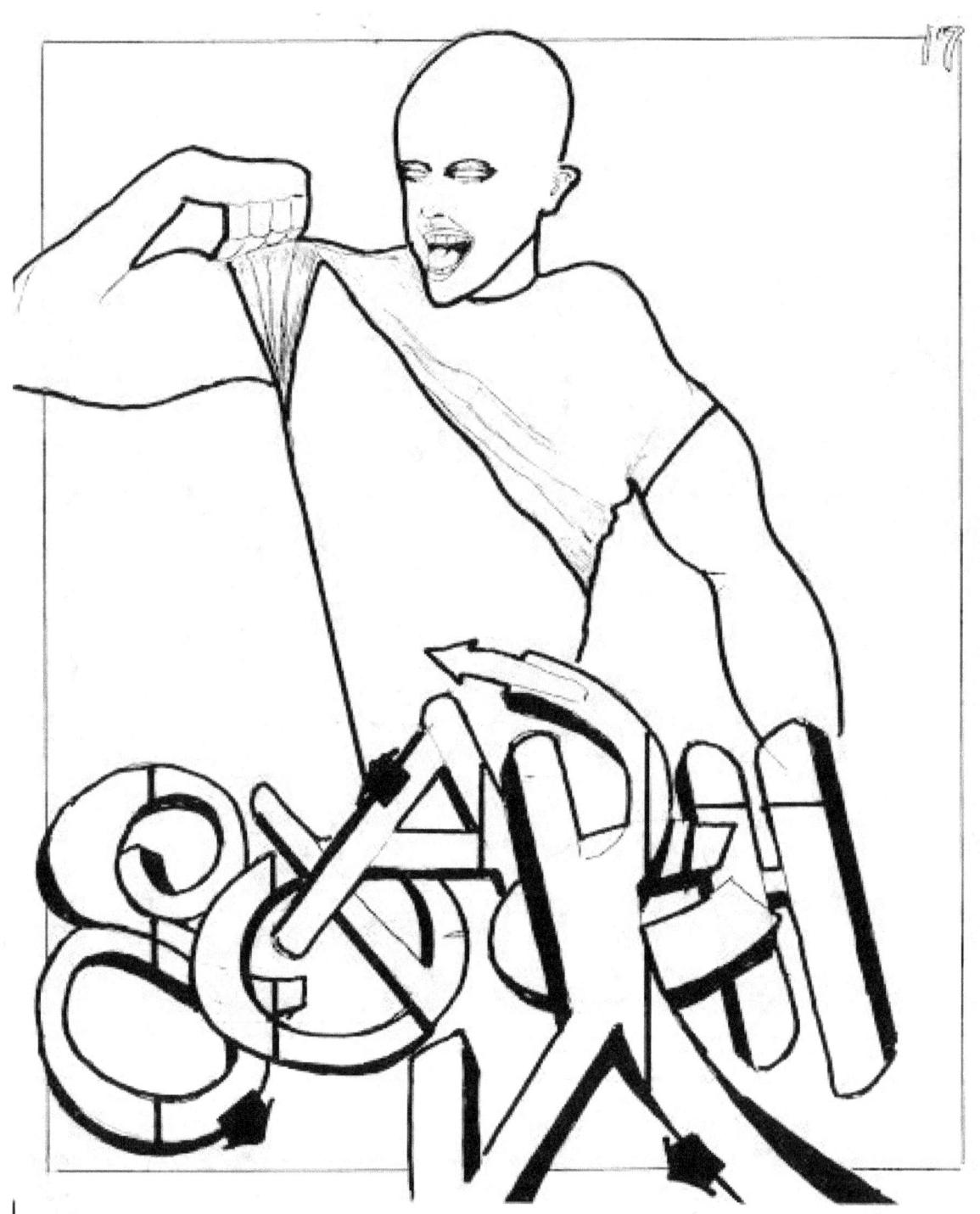

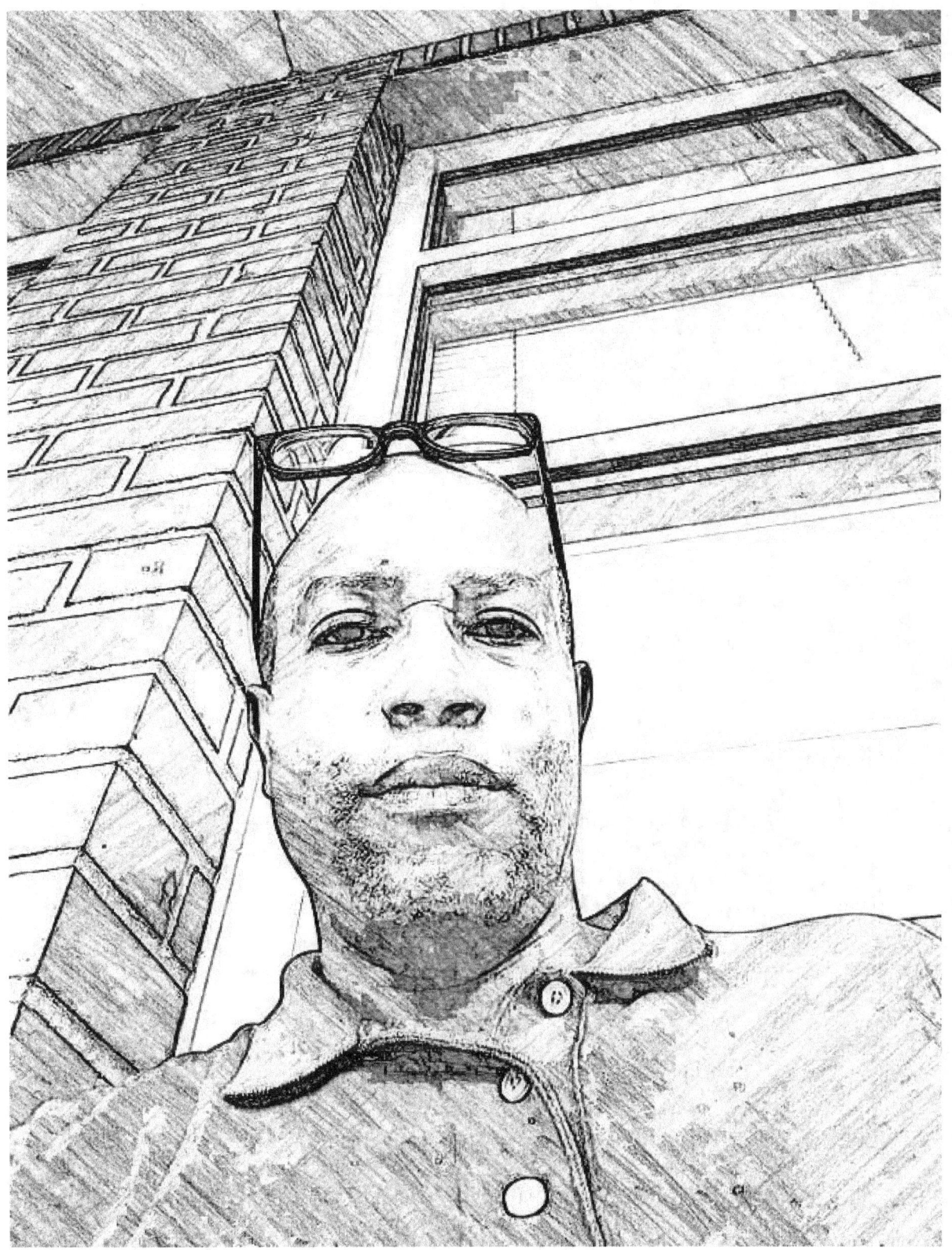

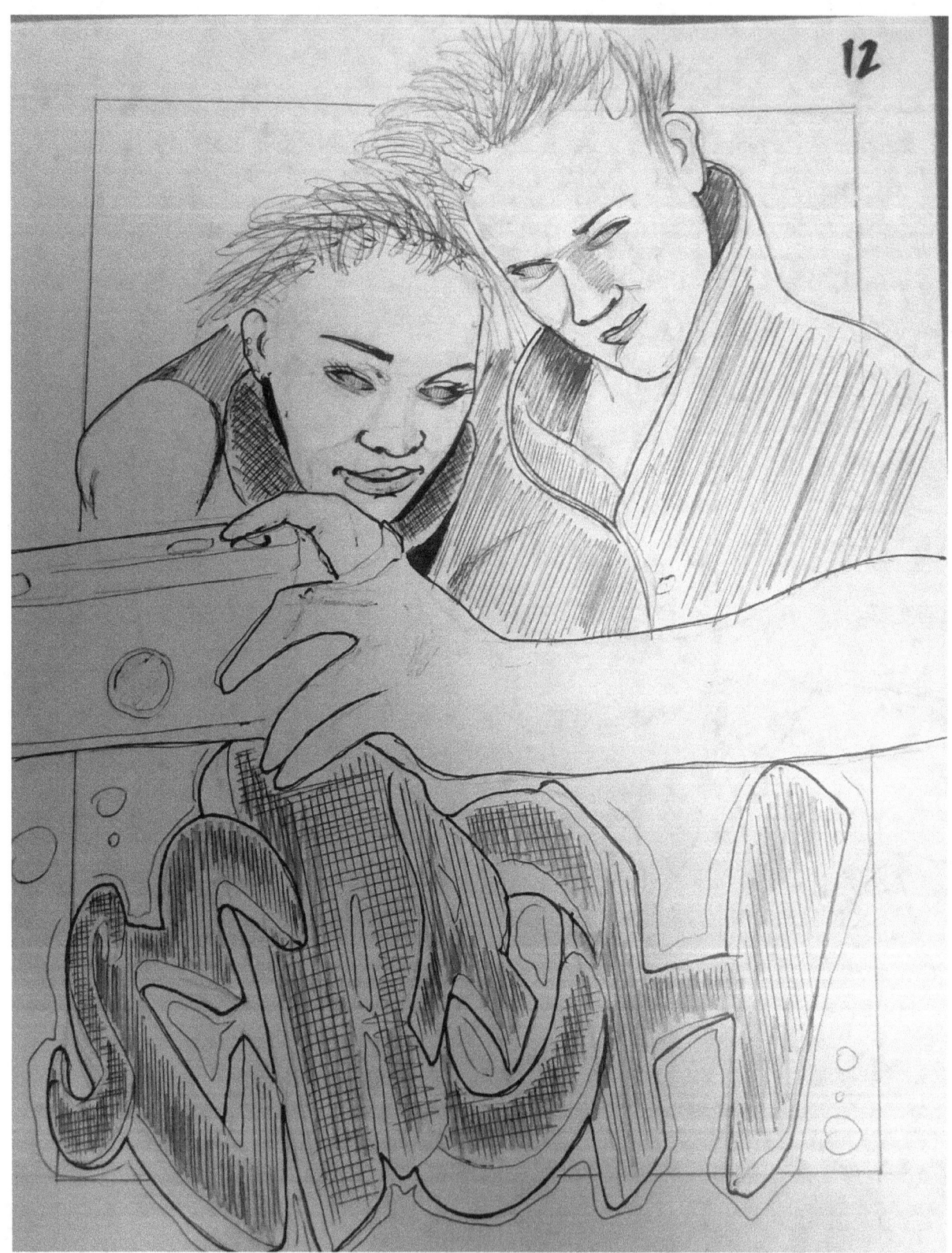

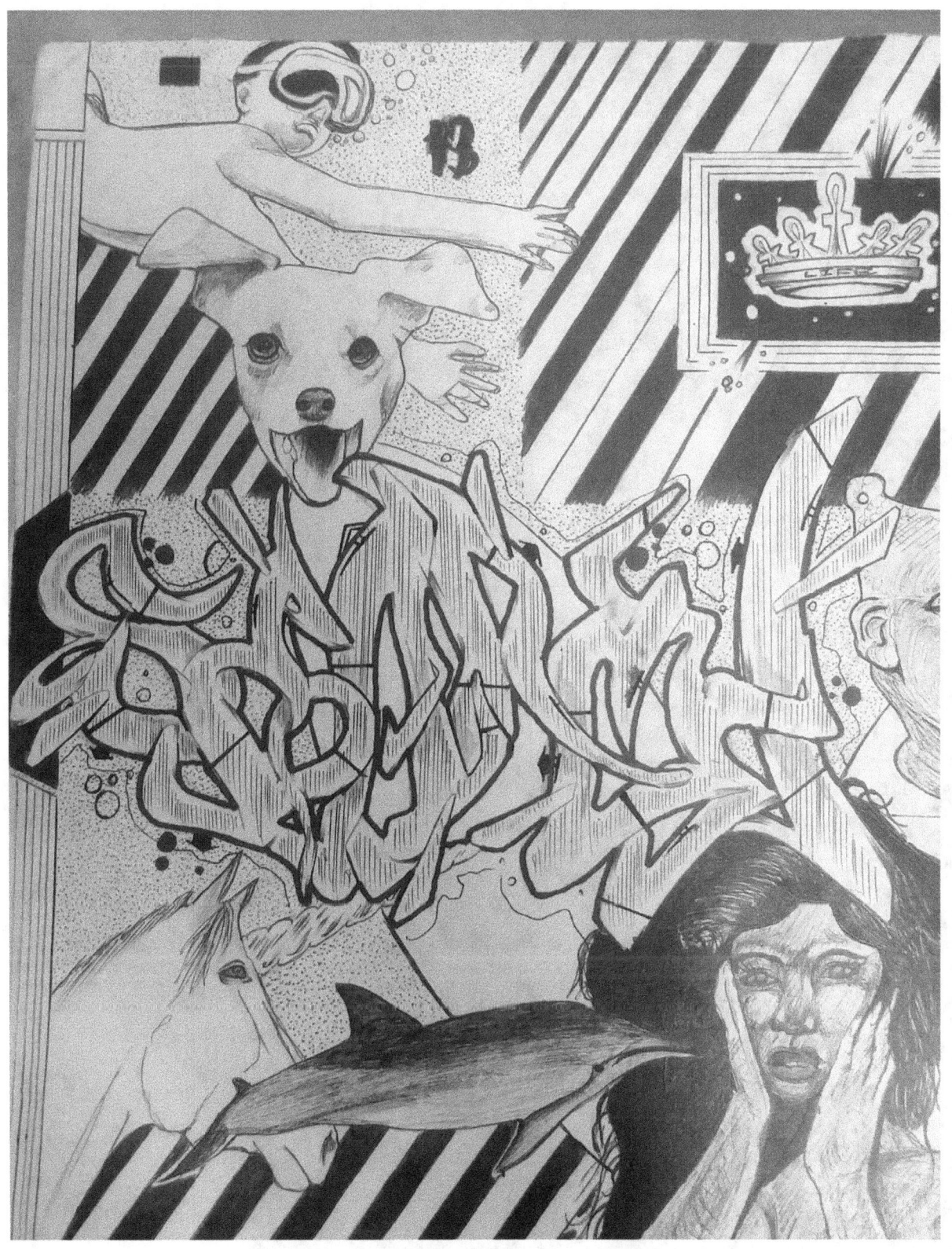

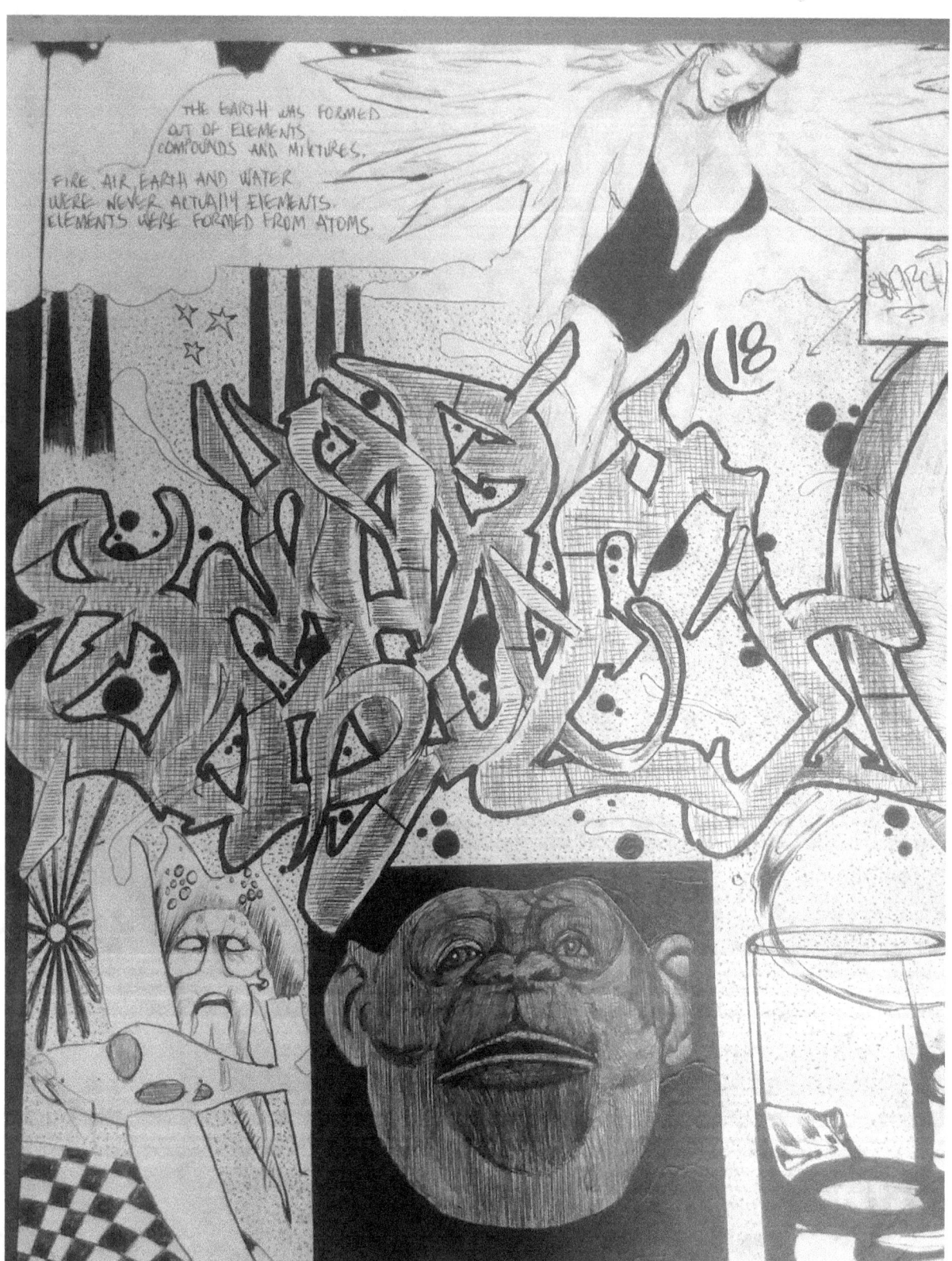

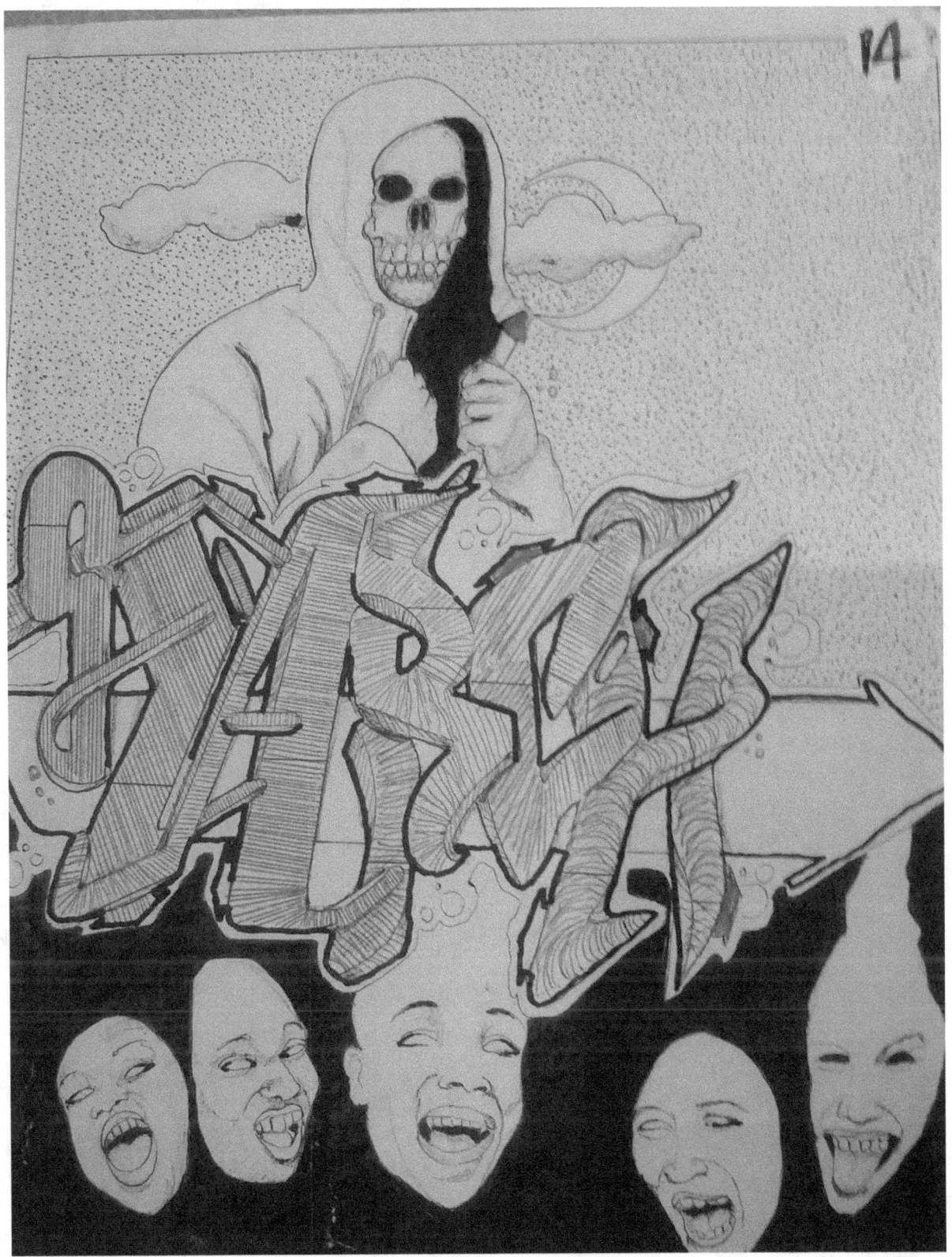

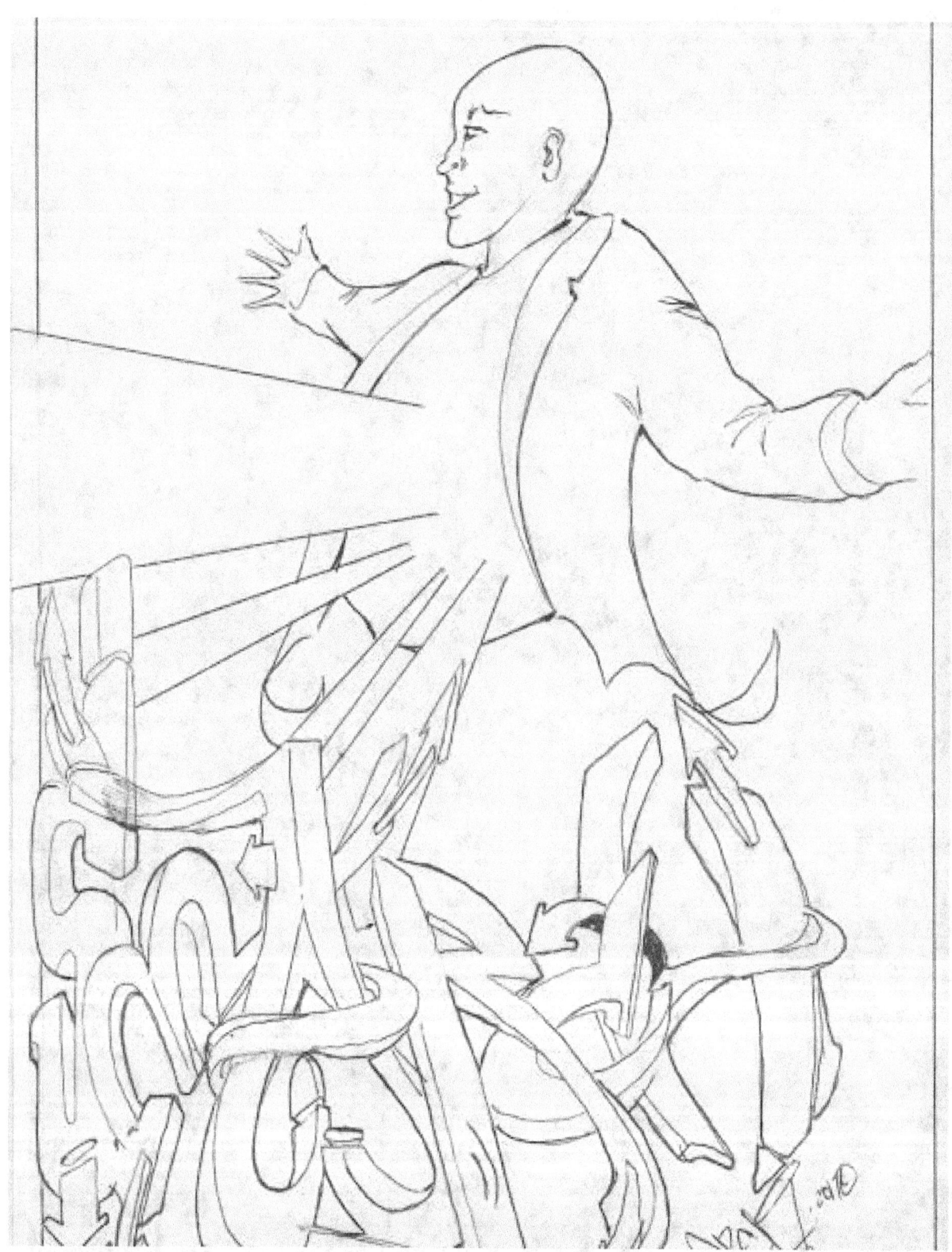

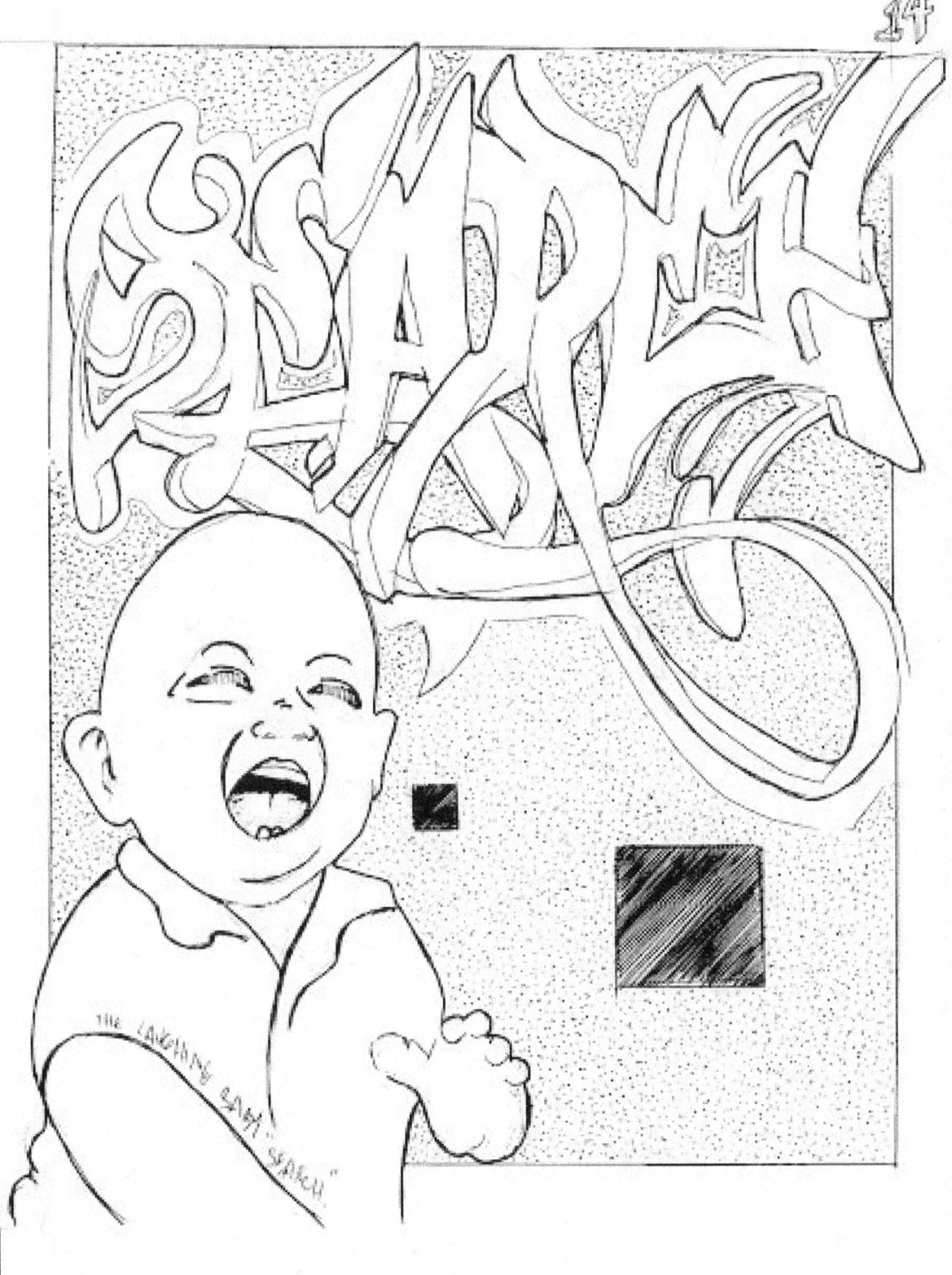

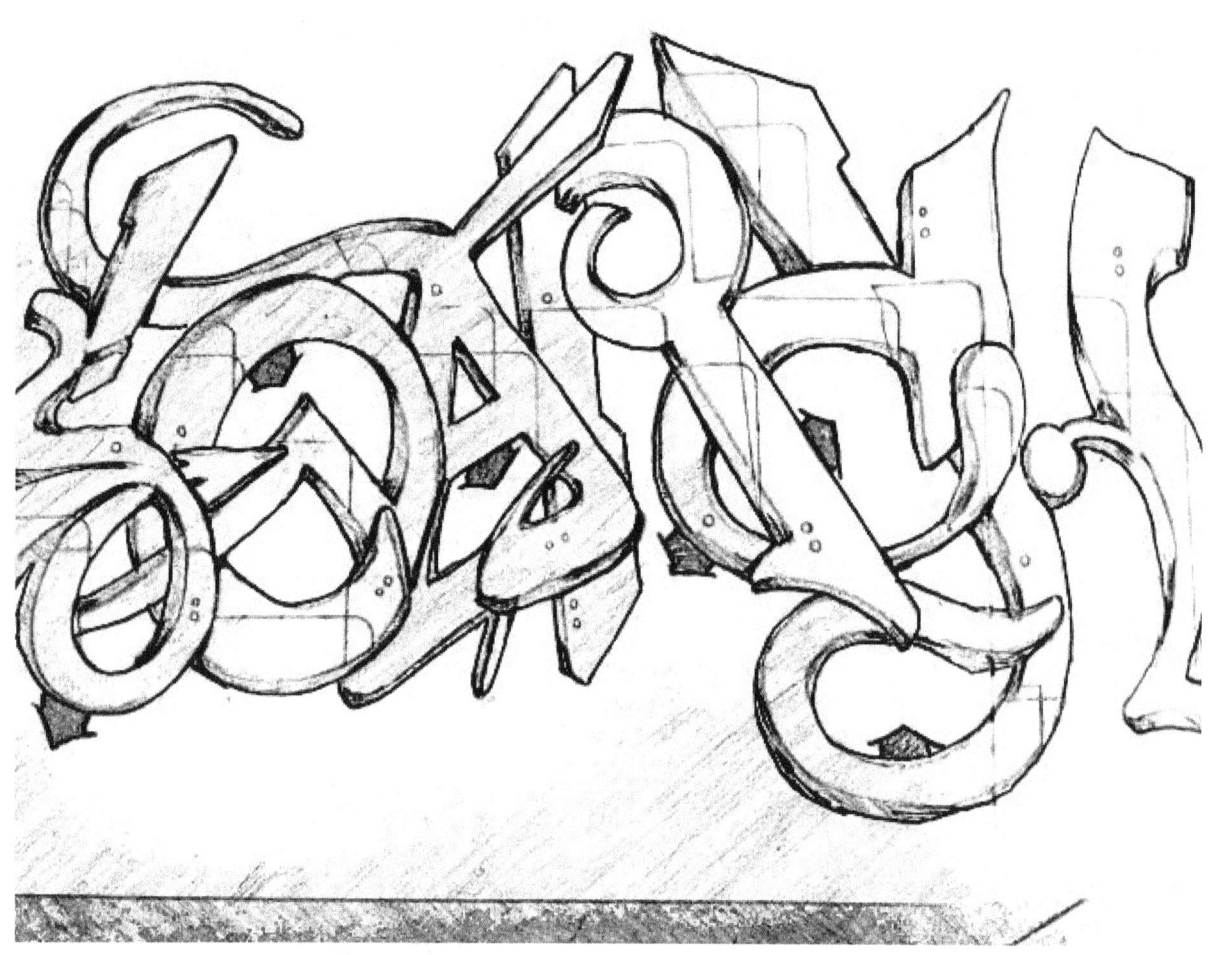

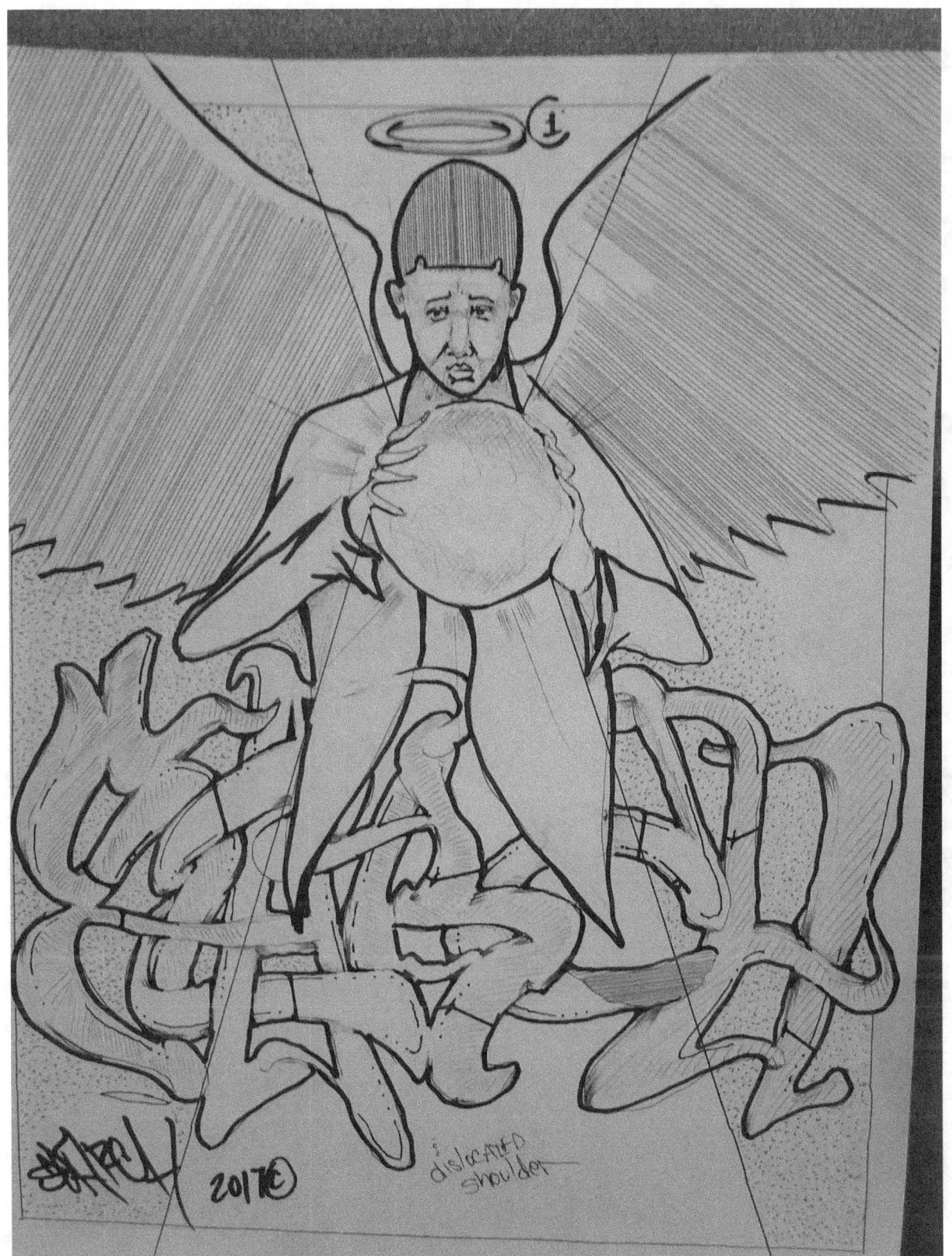

dislocated
shoulder

2017©

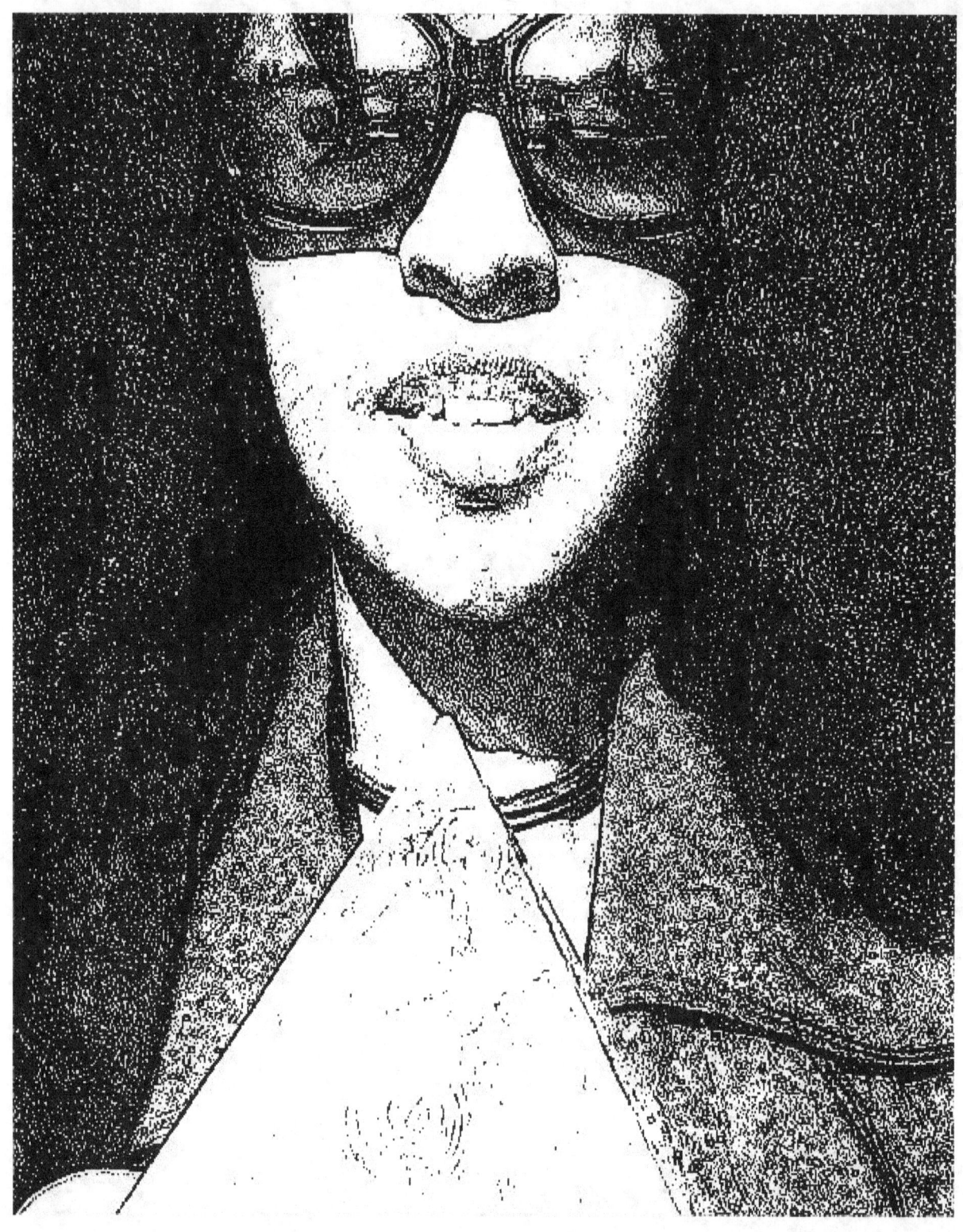

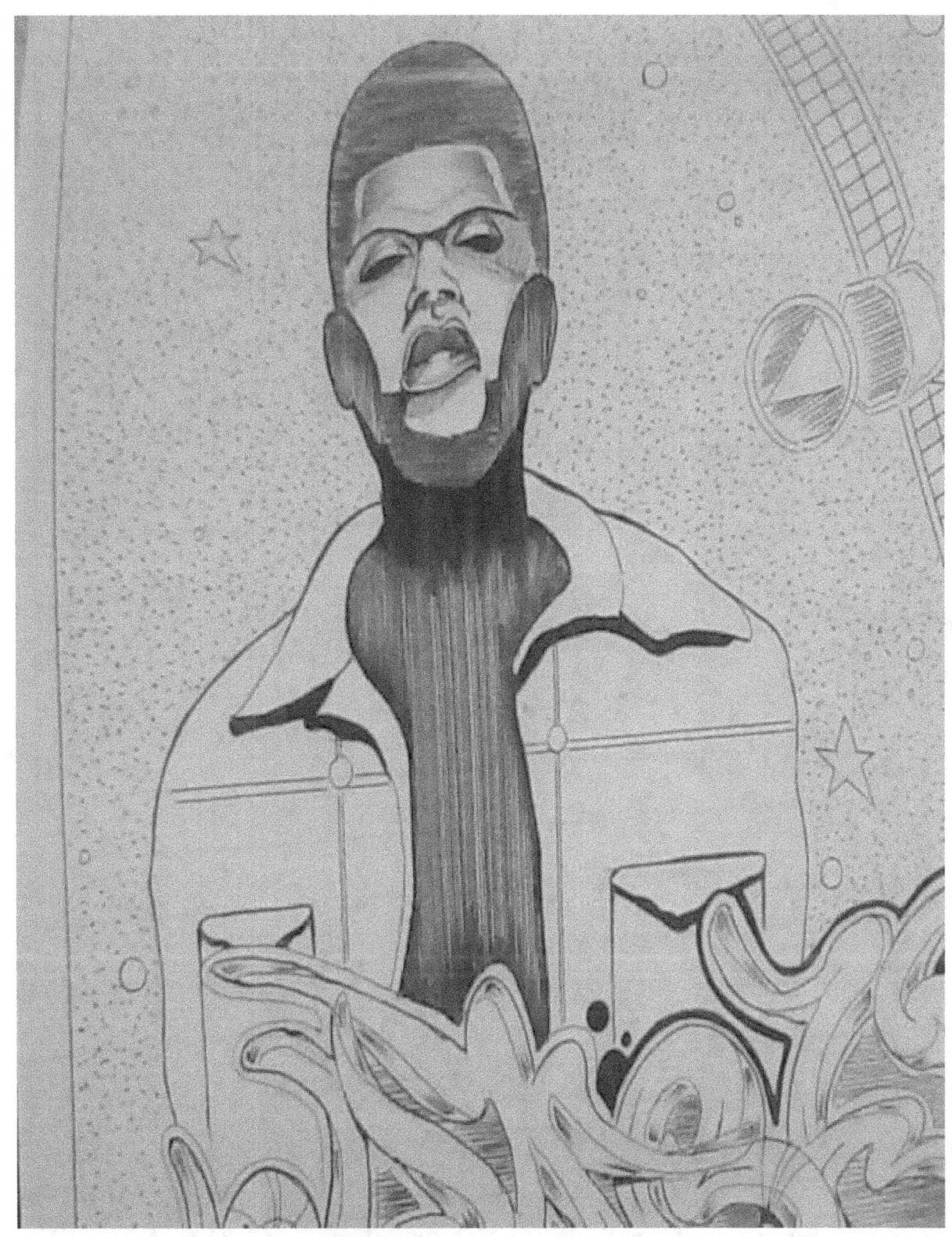

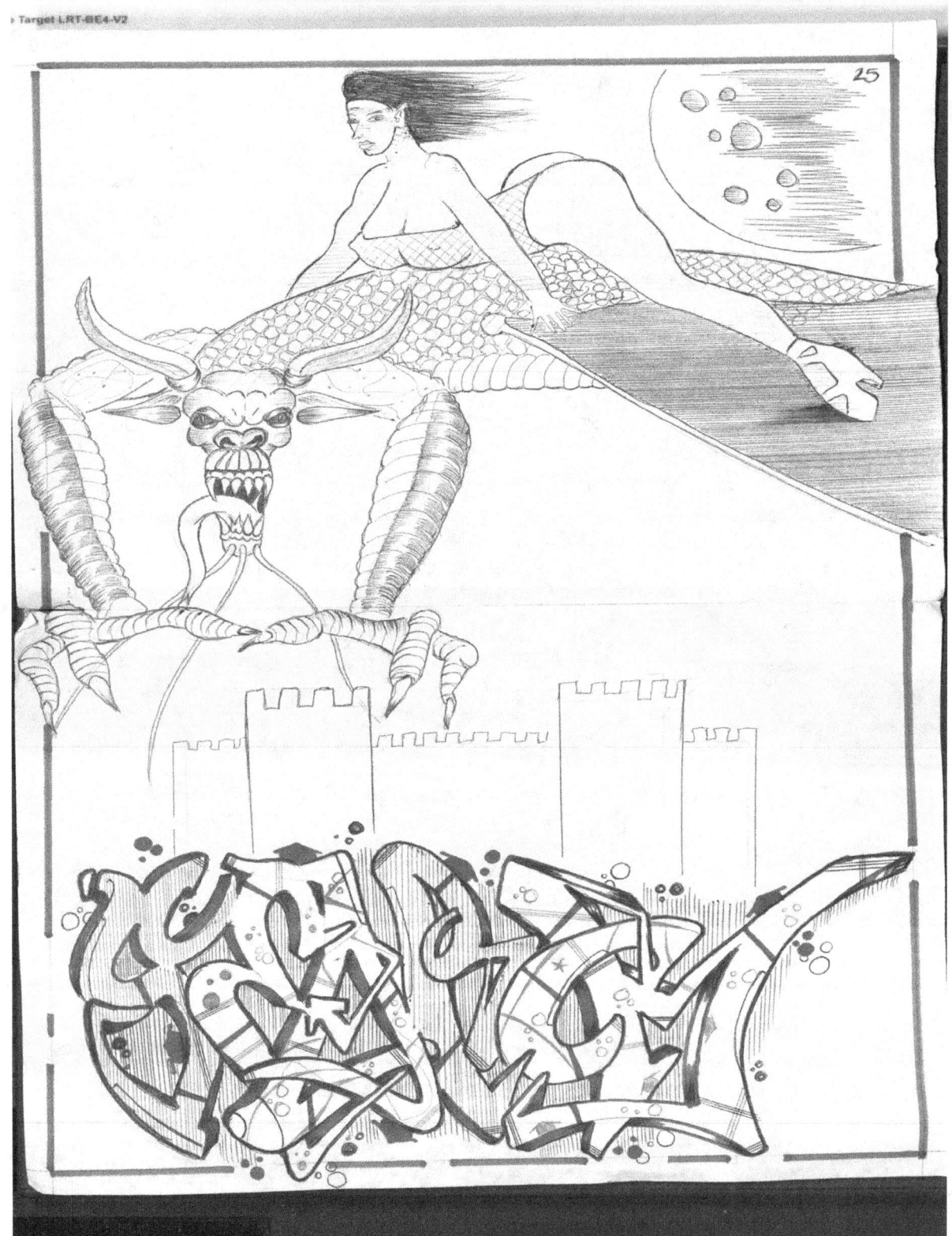

25

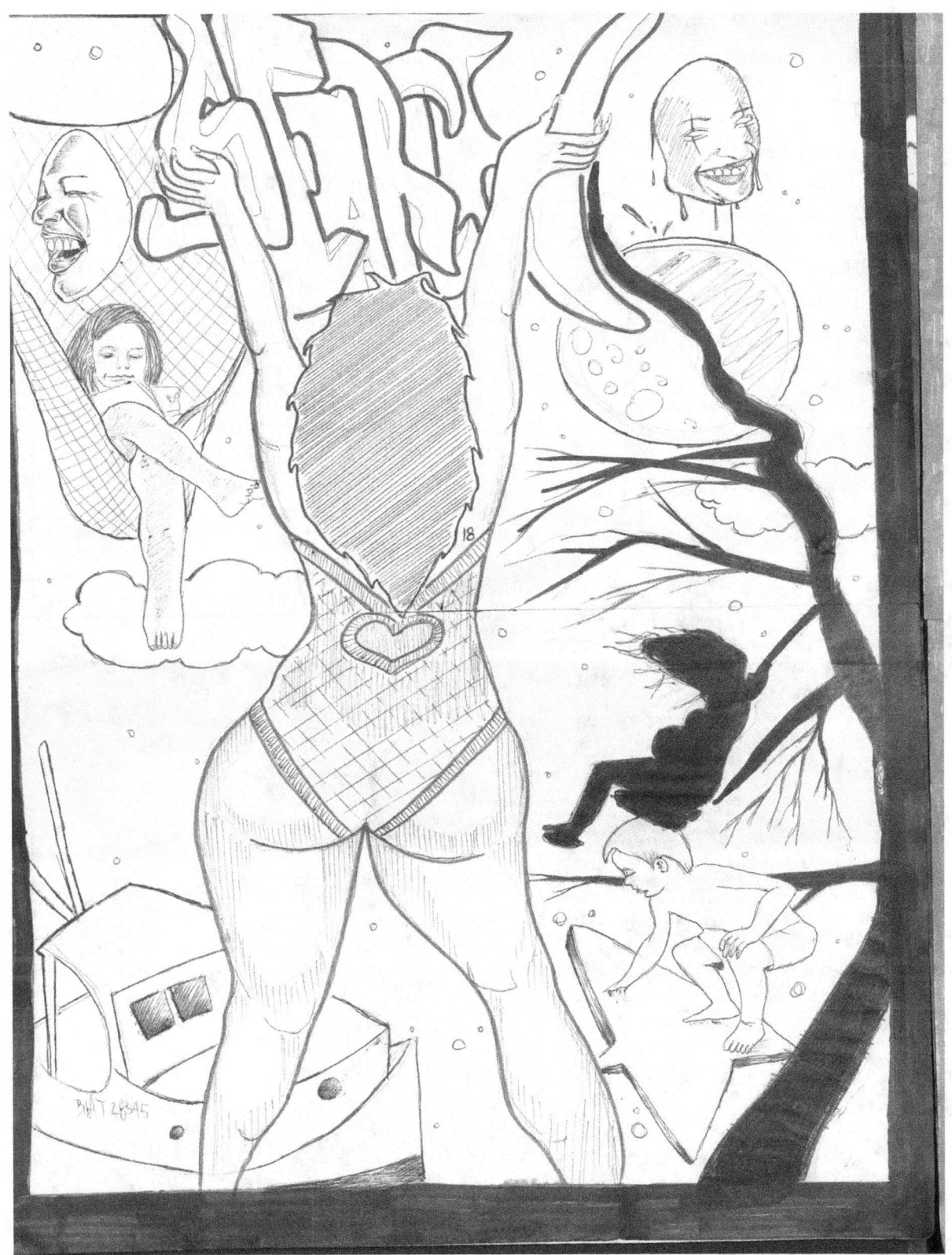

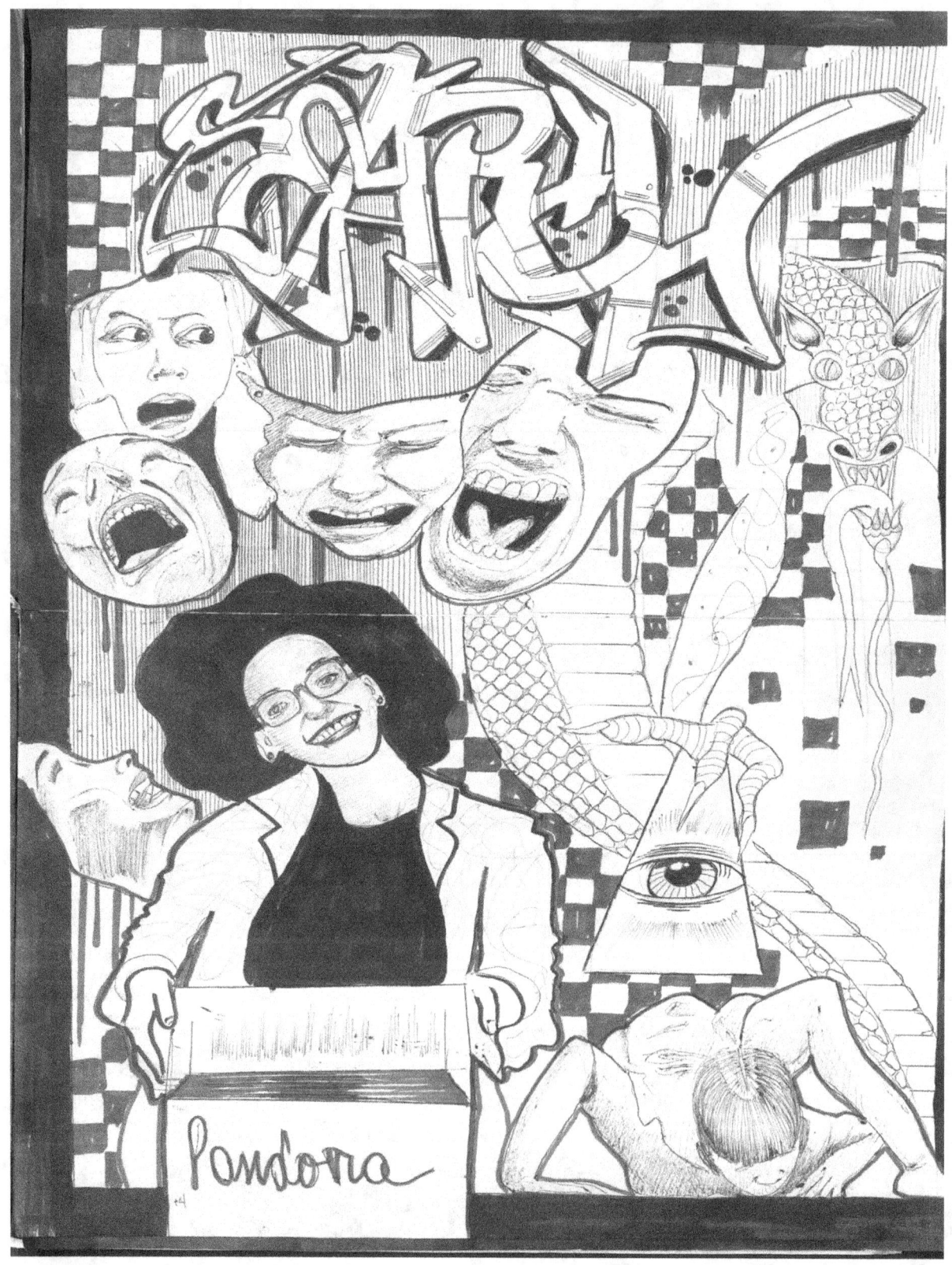

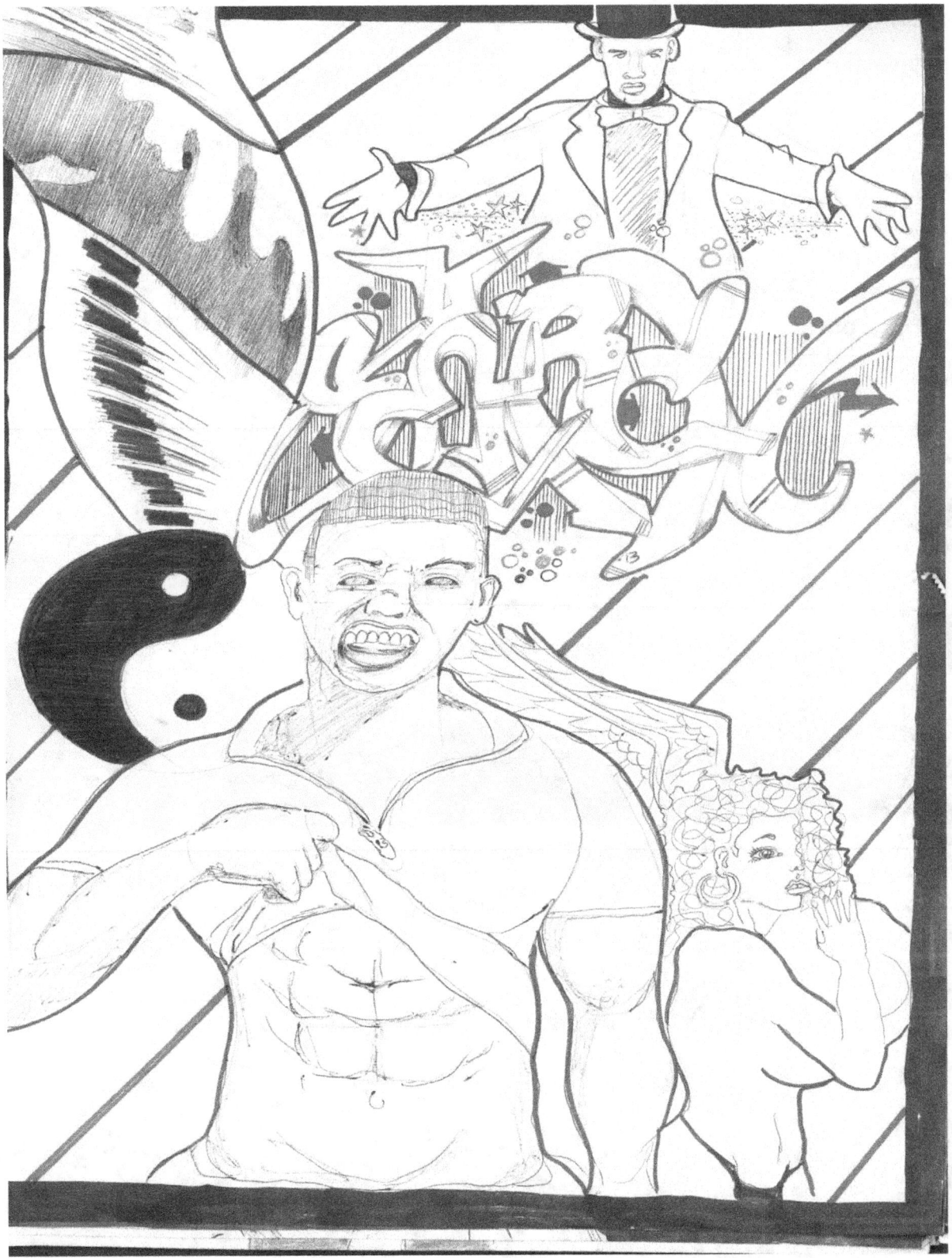

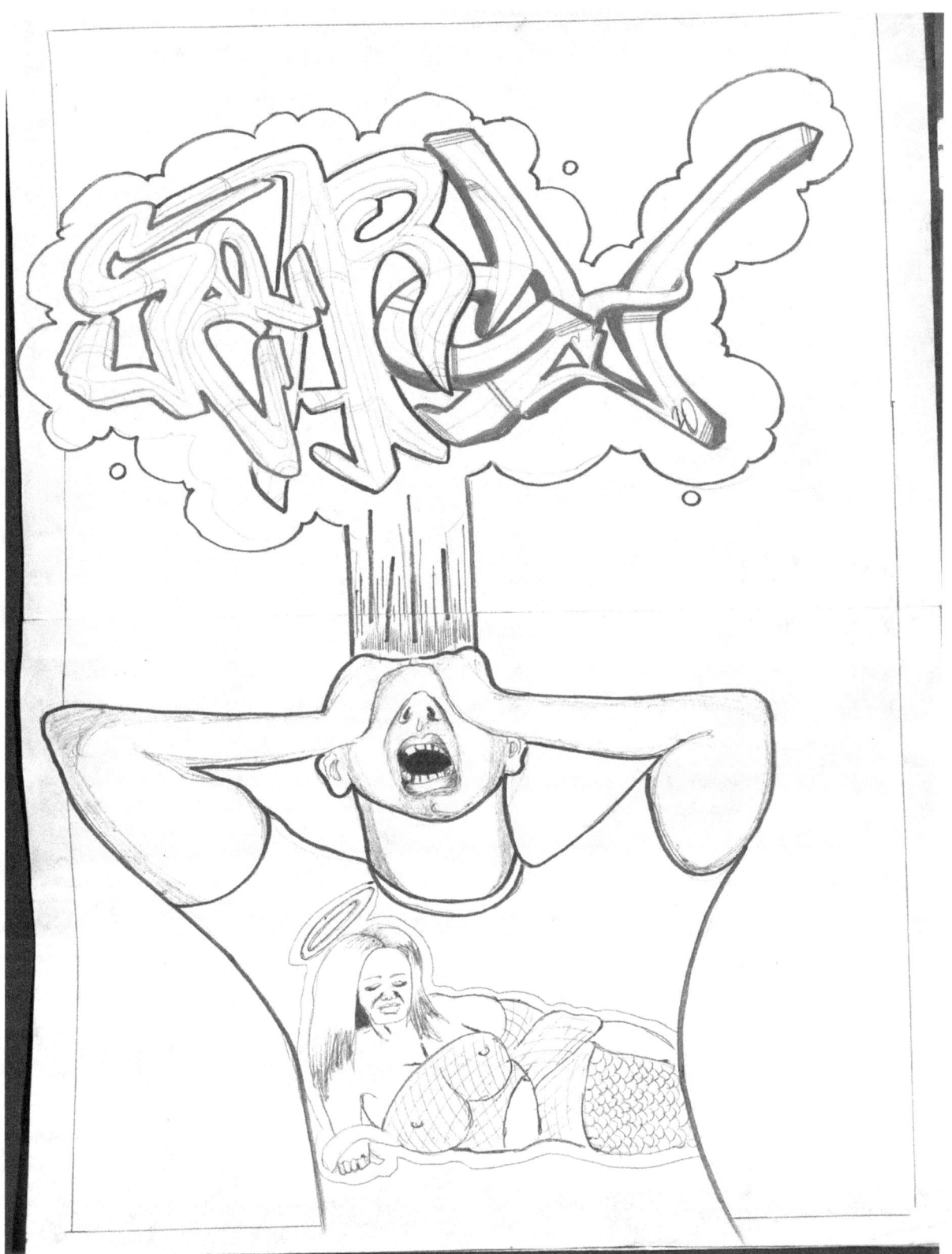

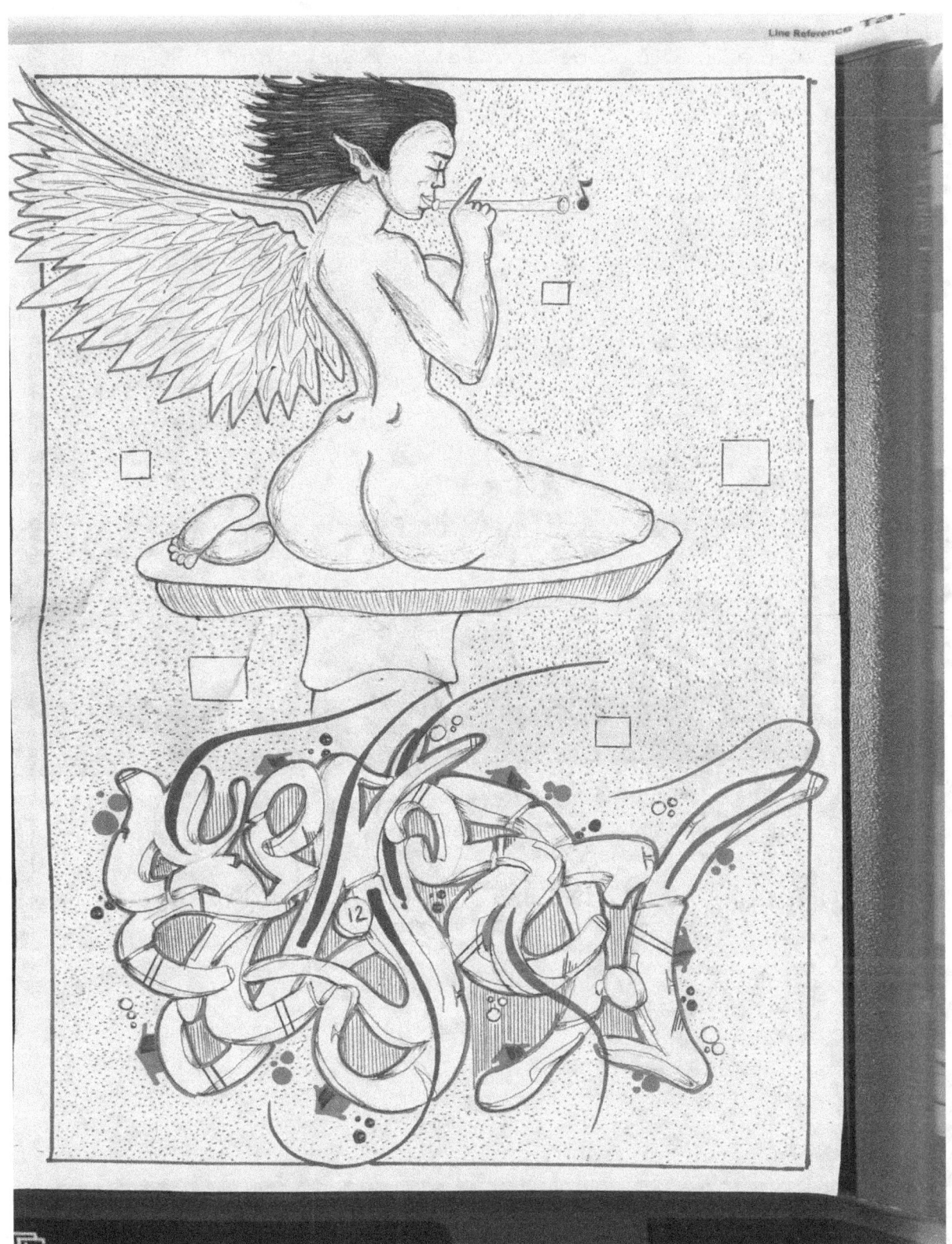

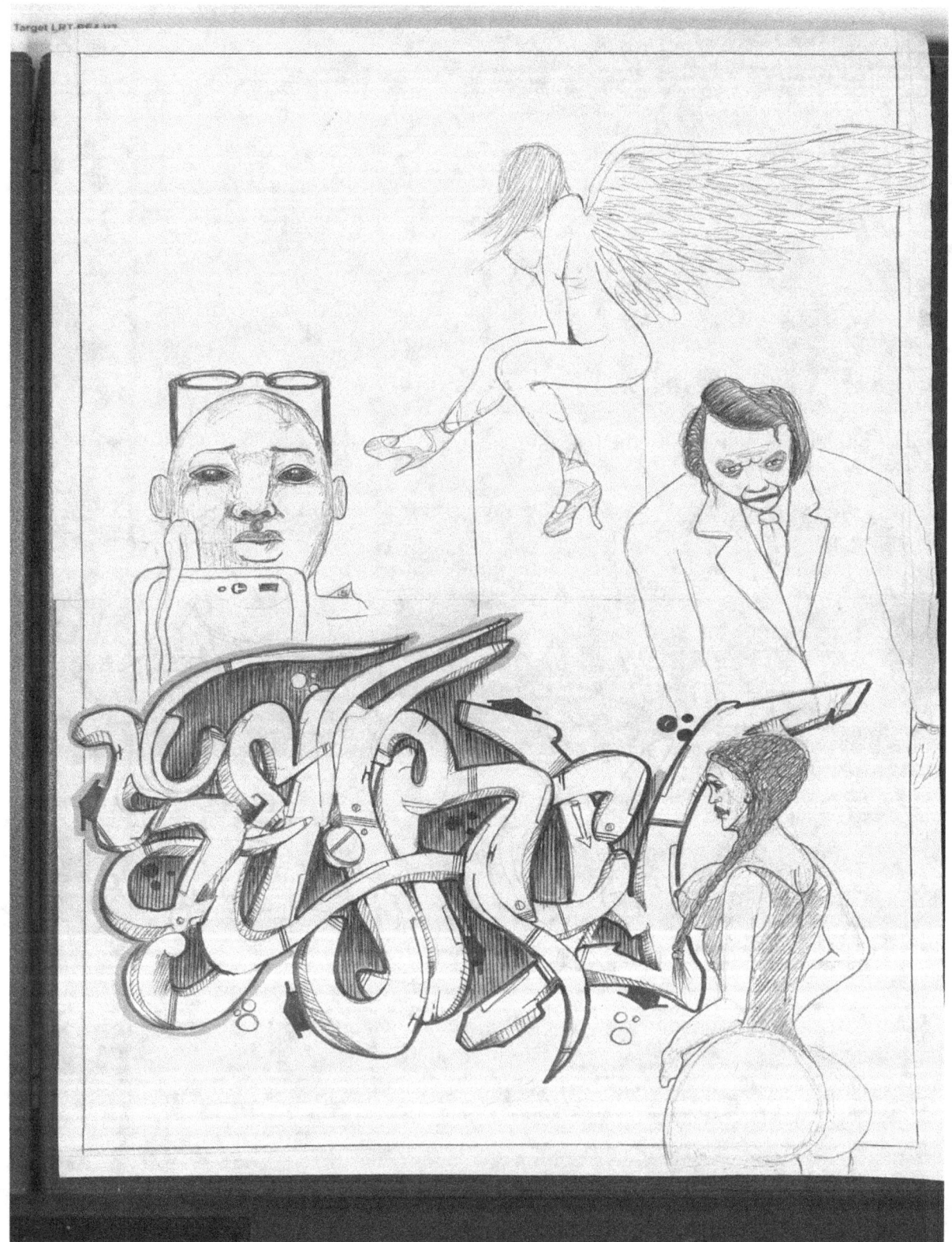

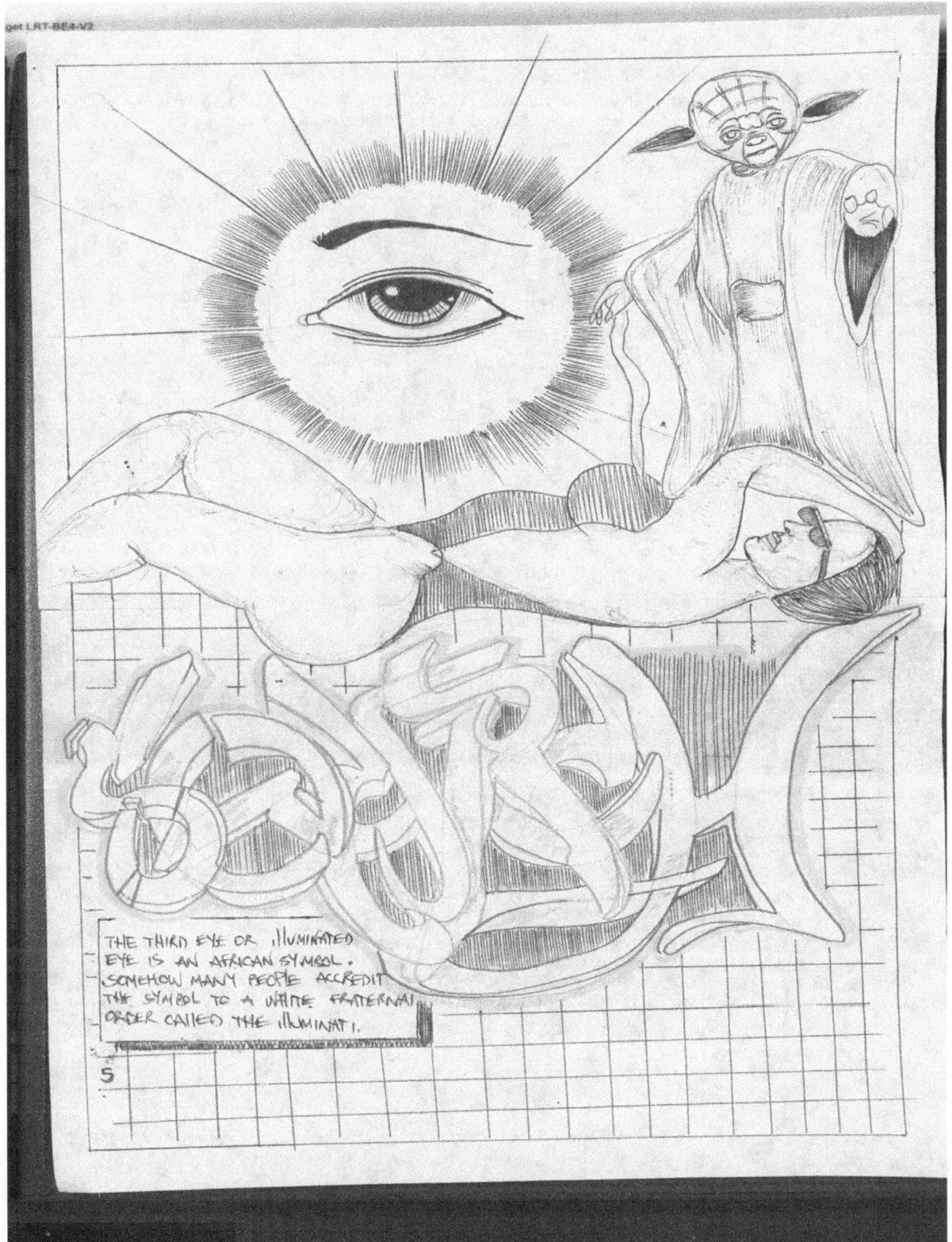

THE THIRD EYE OR ILLUMINATED
EYE IS AN AFRICAN SYMBOL.
SOMEHOW MANY PEOPLE ACCREDIT
THE SYMBOL TO A WHITE FRATERNAL
ORDER CALLED THE ILLUMINATI.

S

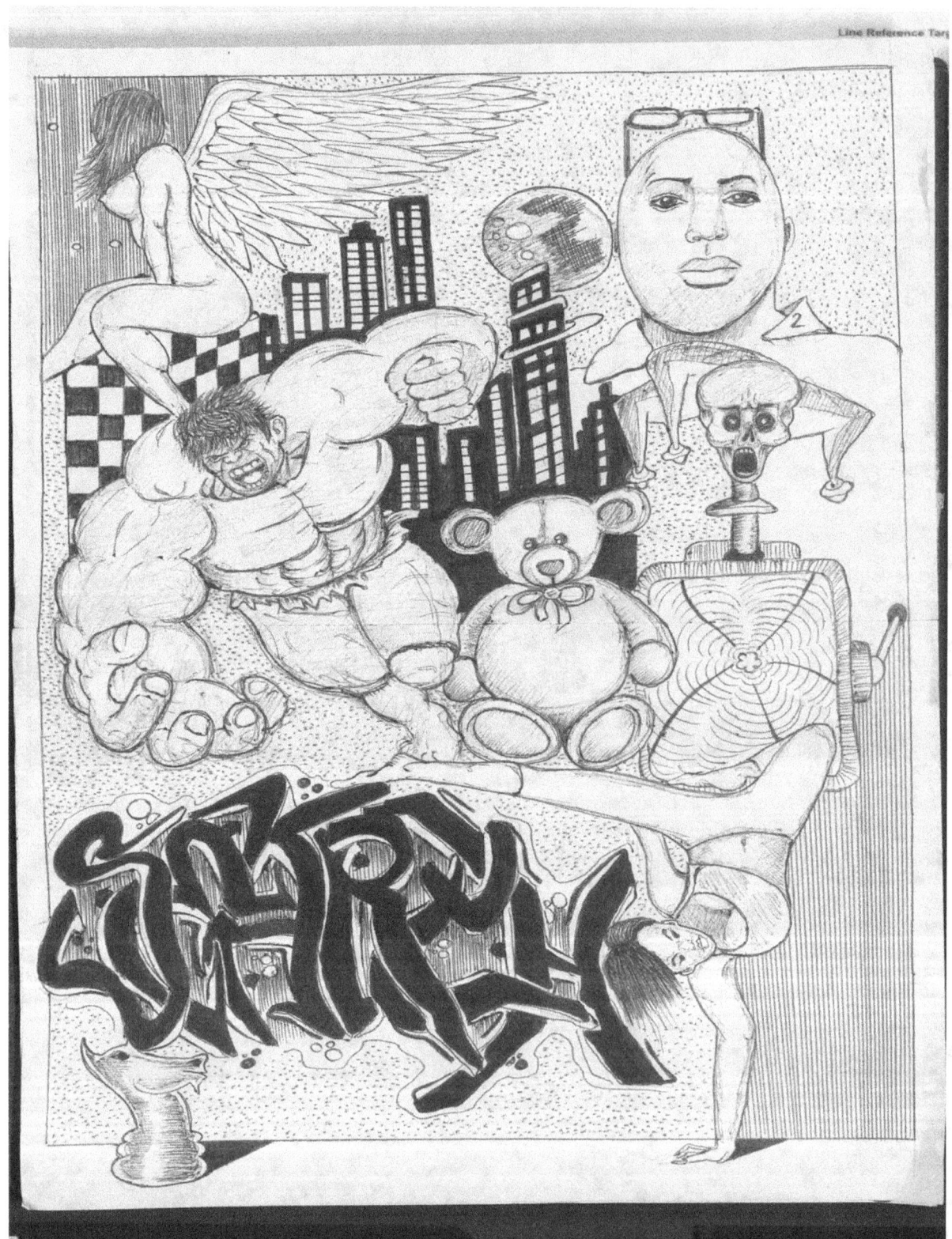

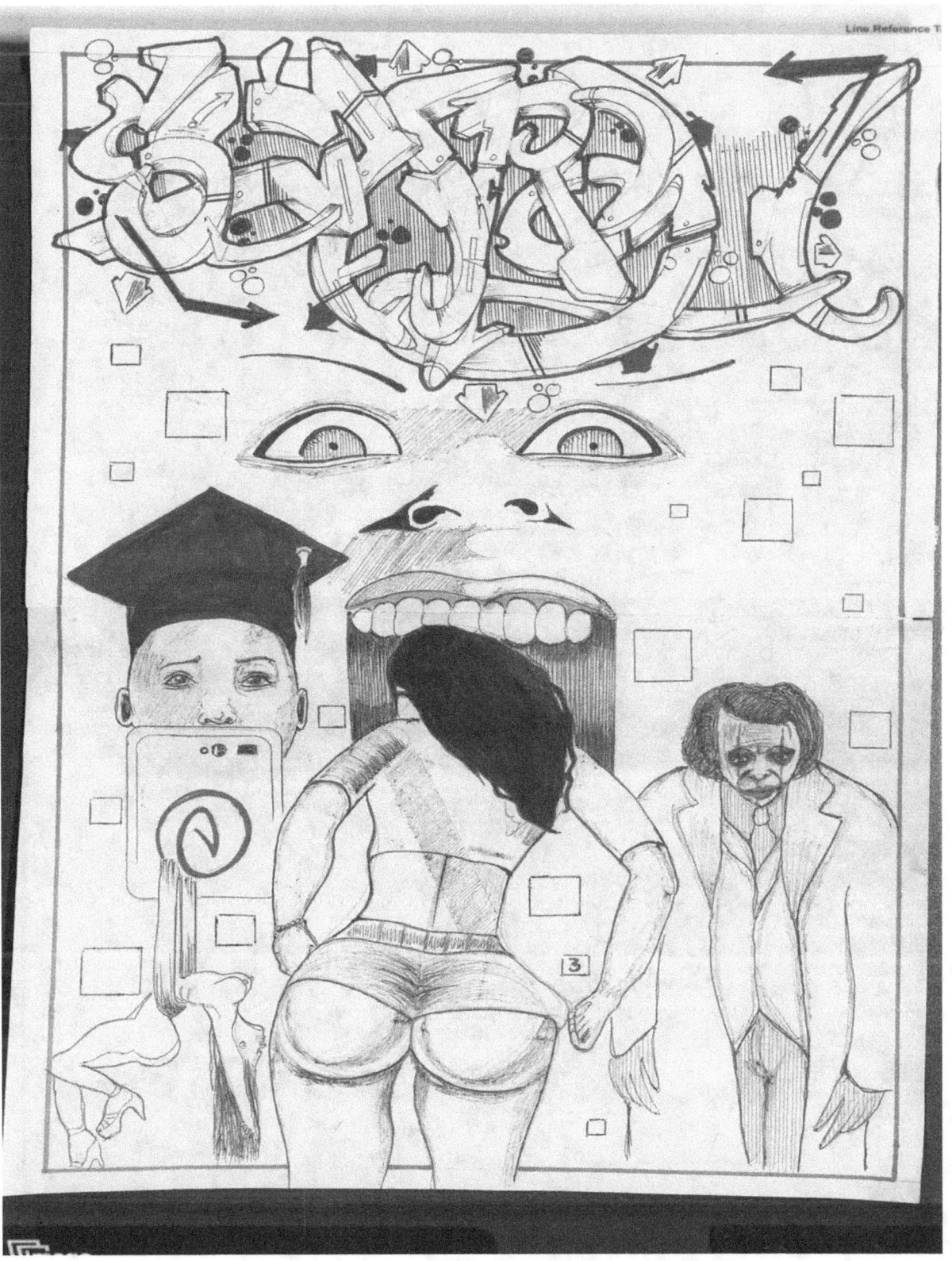

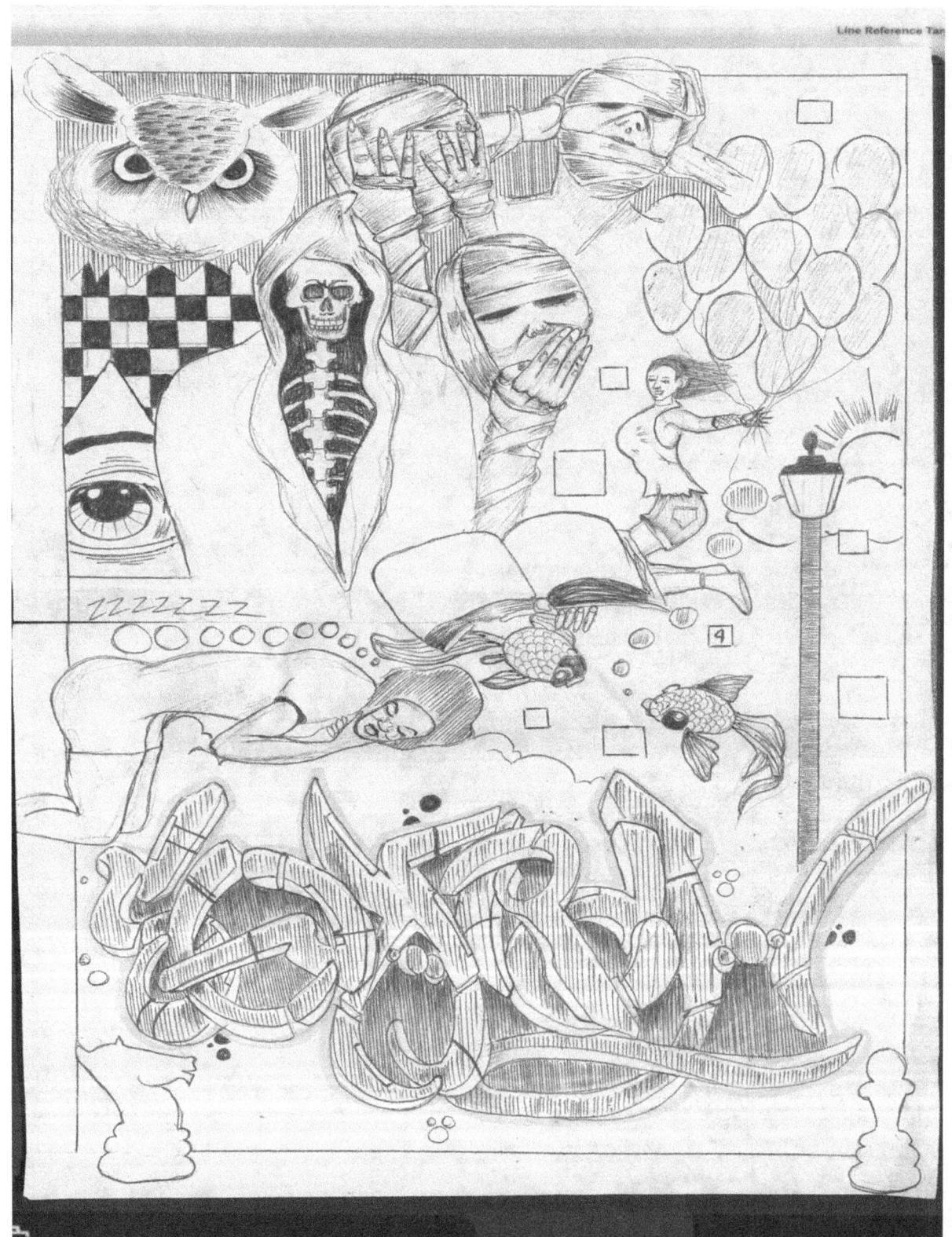

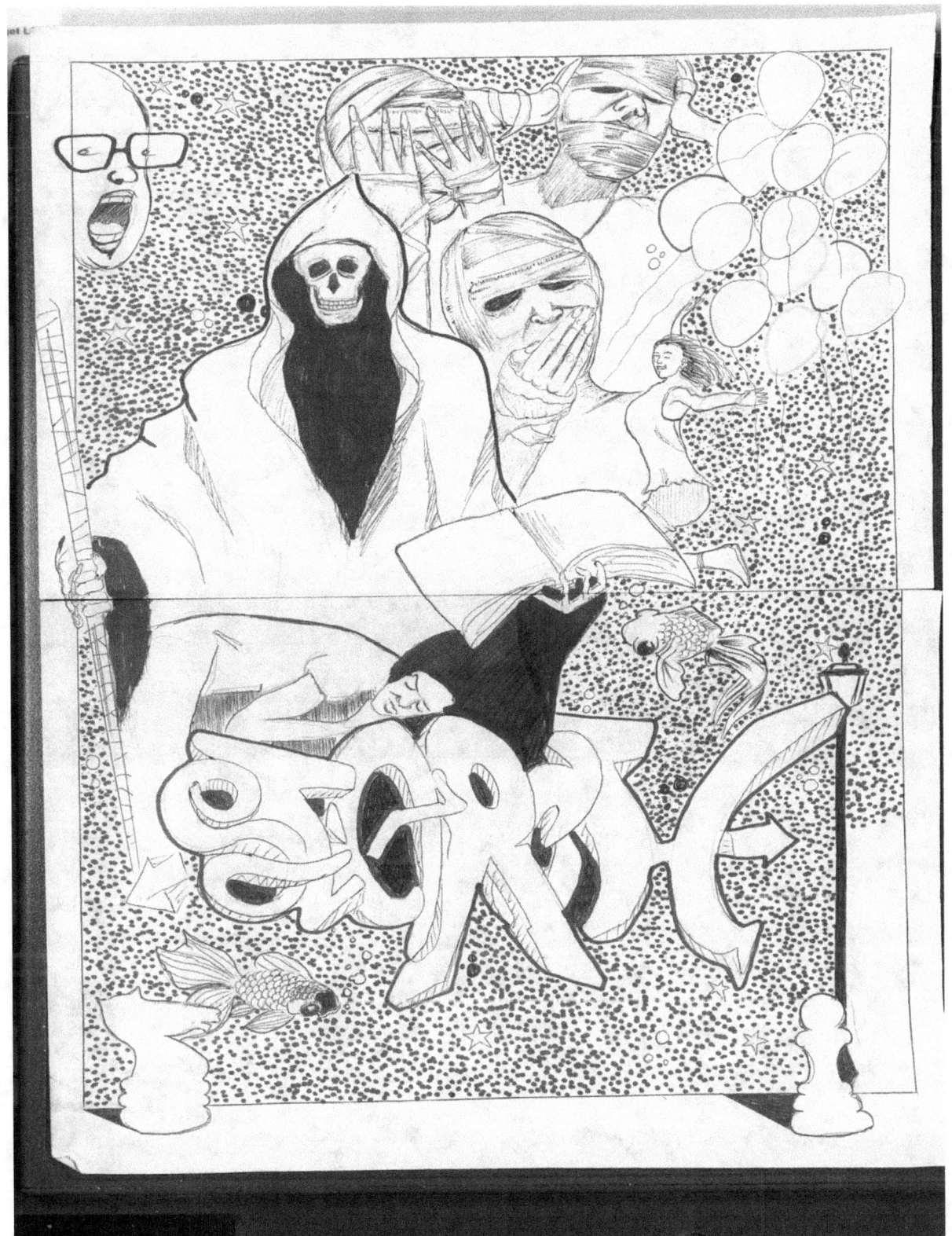

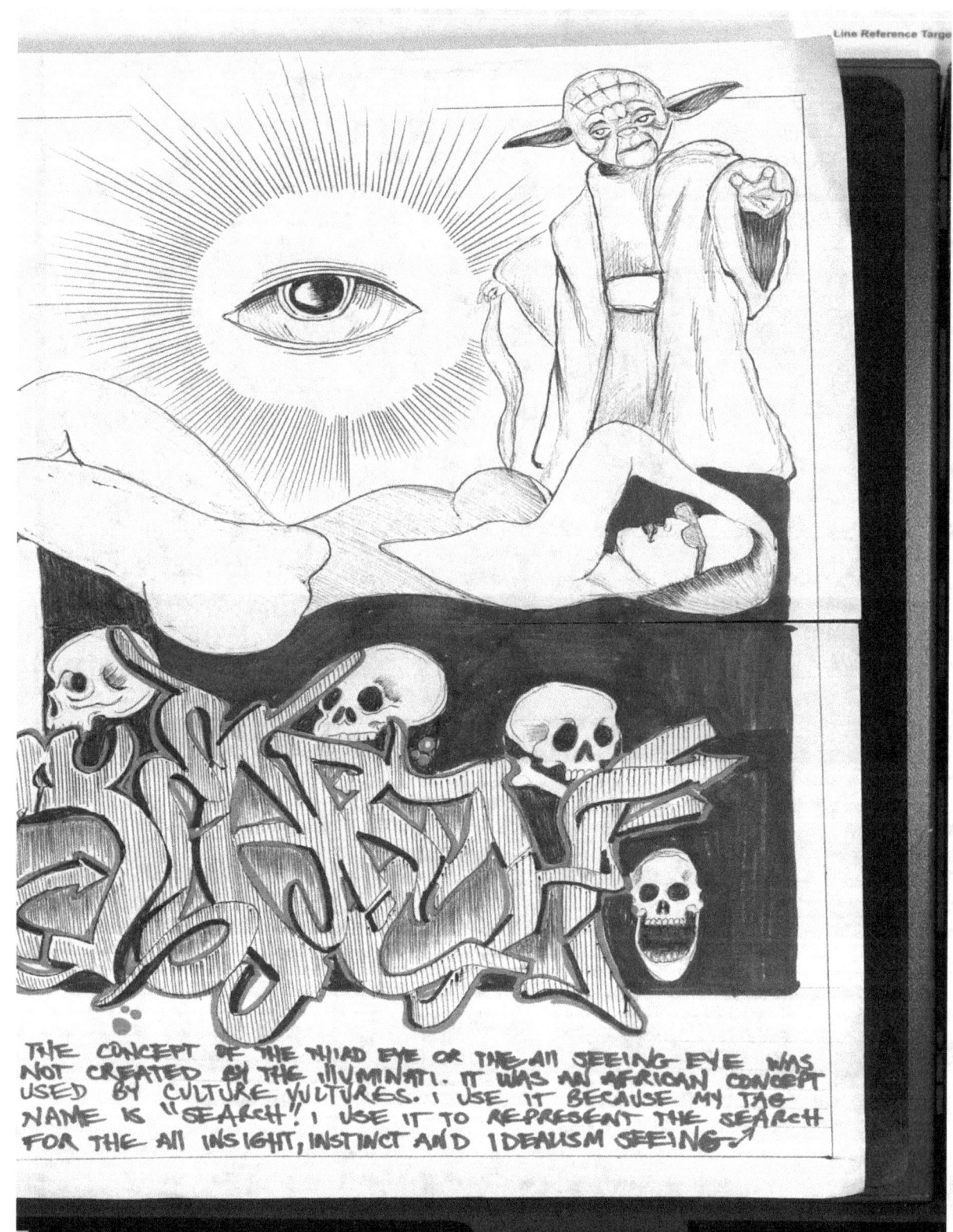

THE CONCEPT OF THE THIRD EYE OR THE ALL SEEING EYE WAS NOT CREATED BY THE ILLUMINATI. IT WAS AN AFRICAN CONCEPT USED BY CULTURE VULTURES. I USE IT BECAUSE MY TAG NAME IS "SEARCH". I USE IT TO REPRESENT THE SEARCH FOR THE ALL INSIGHT, INSTINCT AND IDEALISM SEEING.

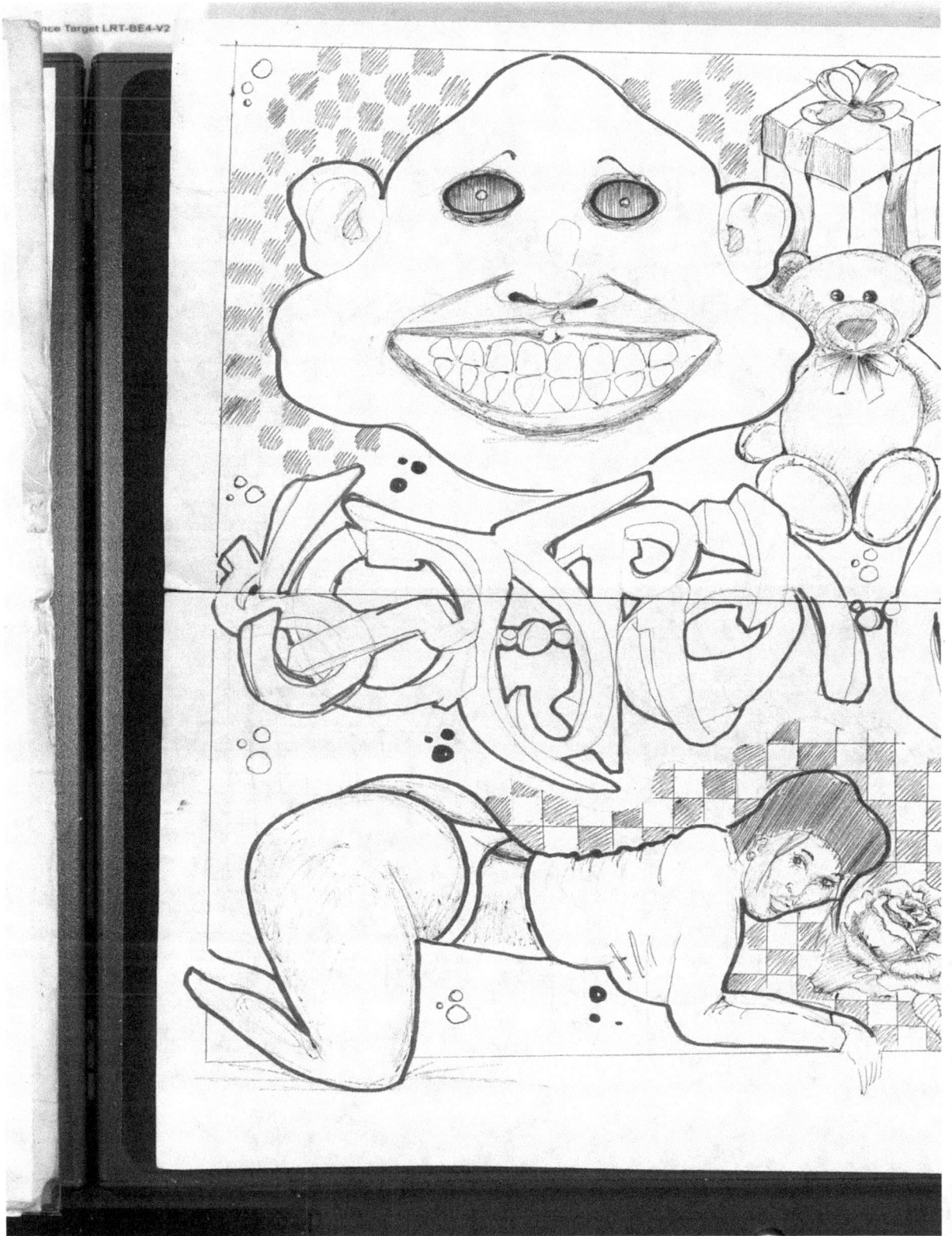

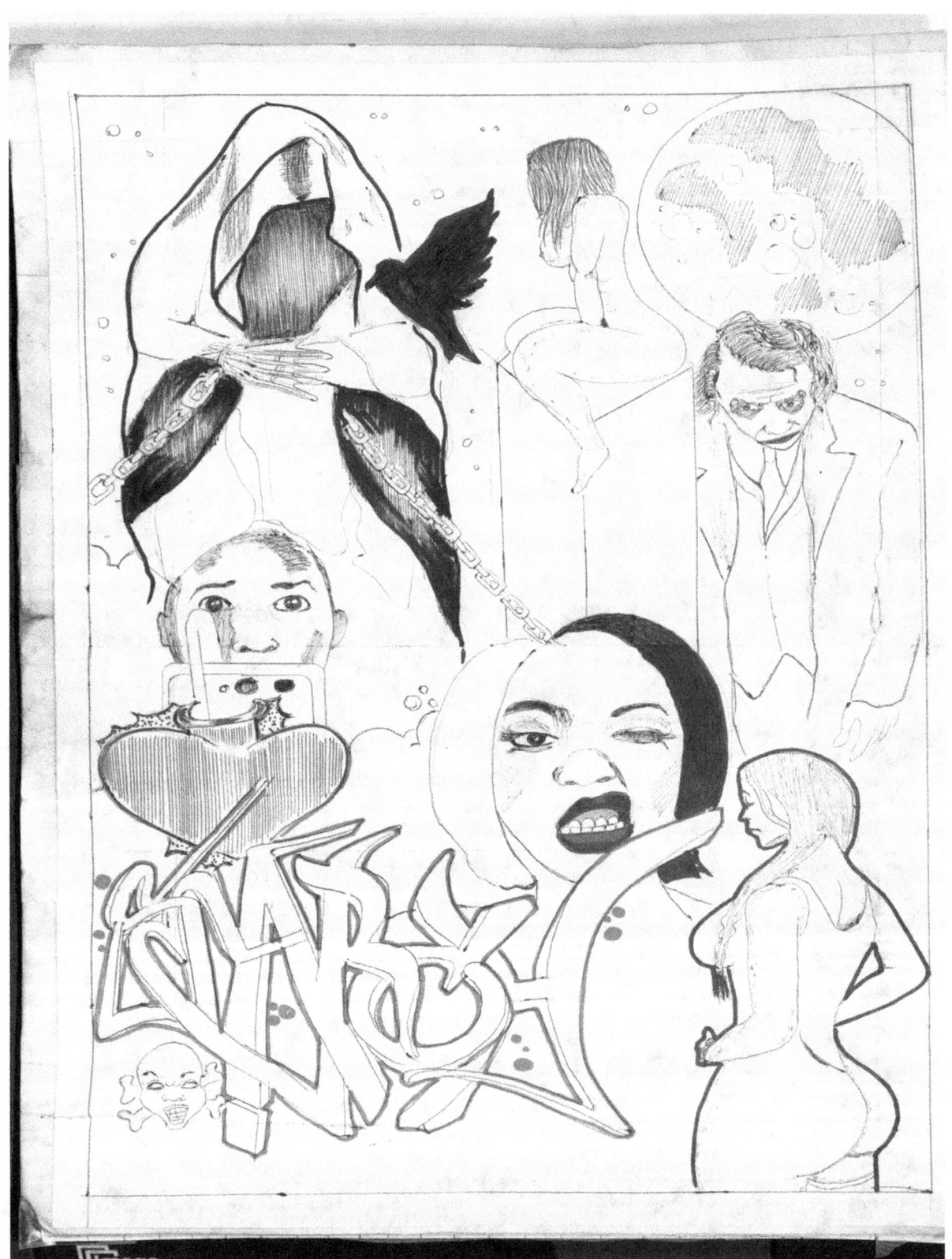

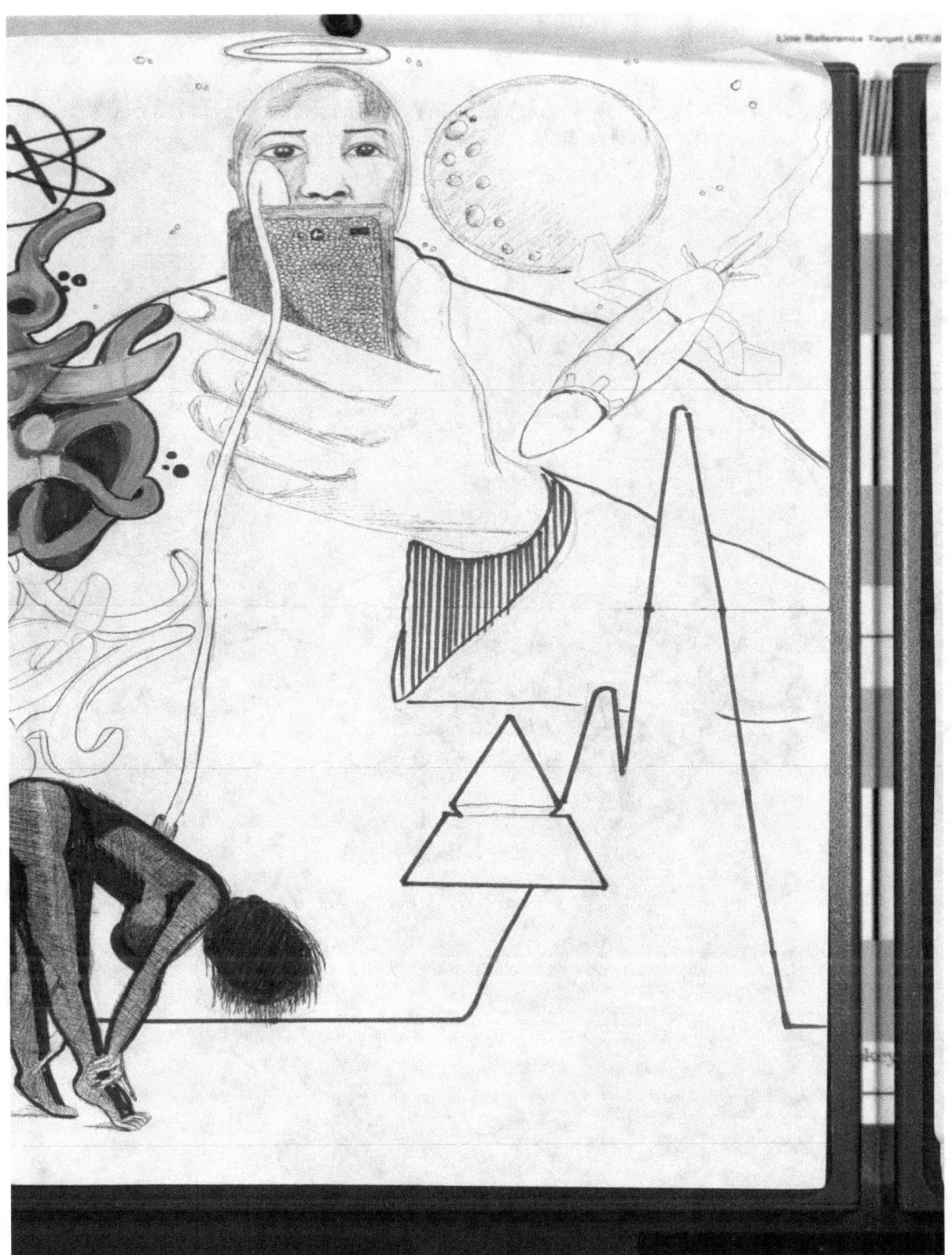

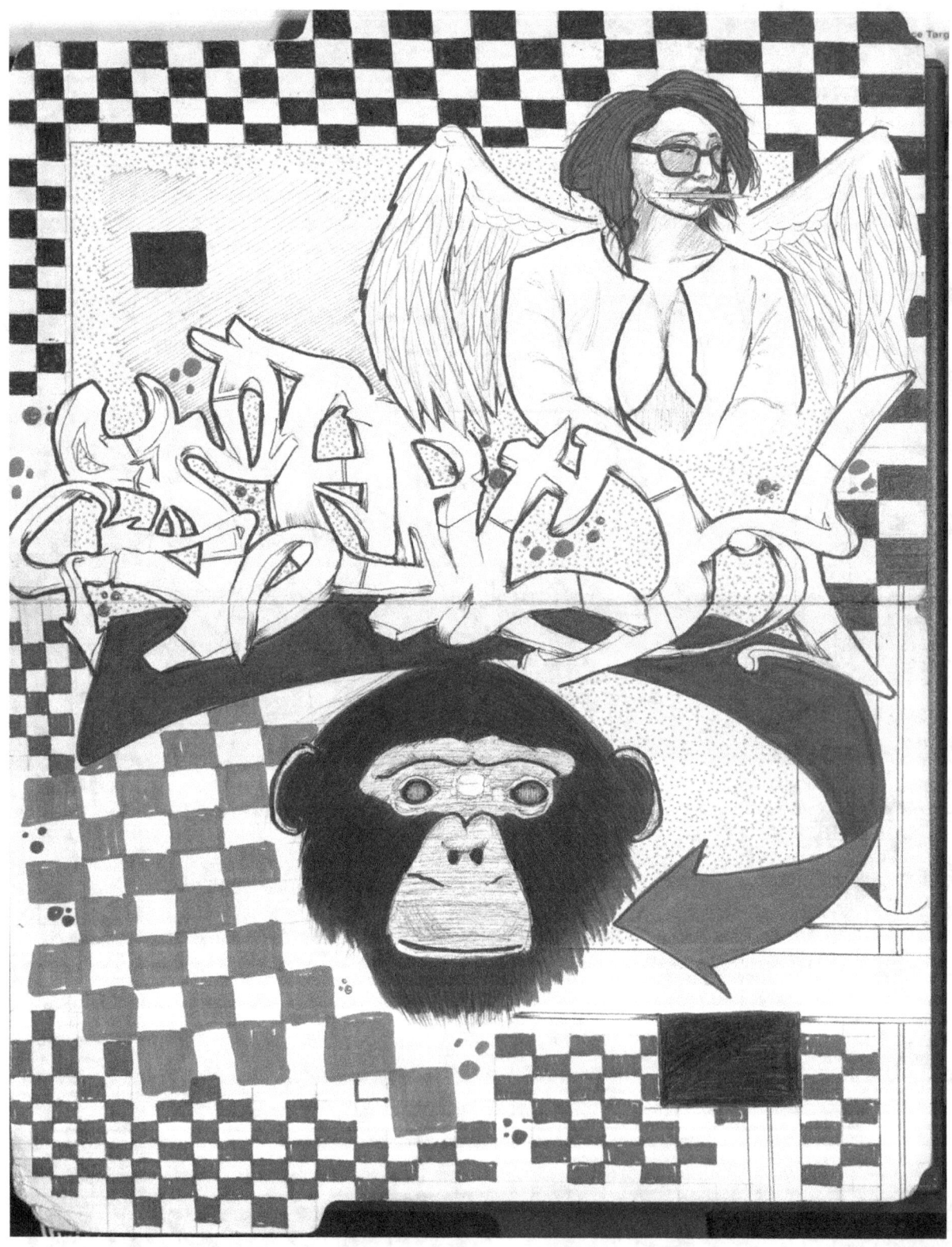

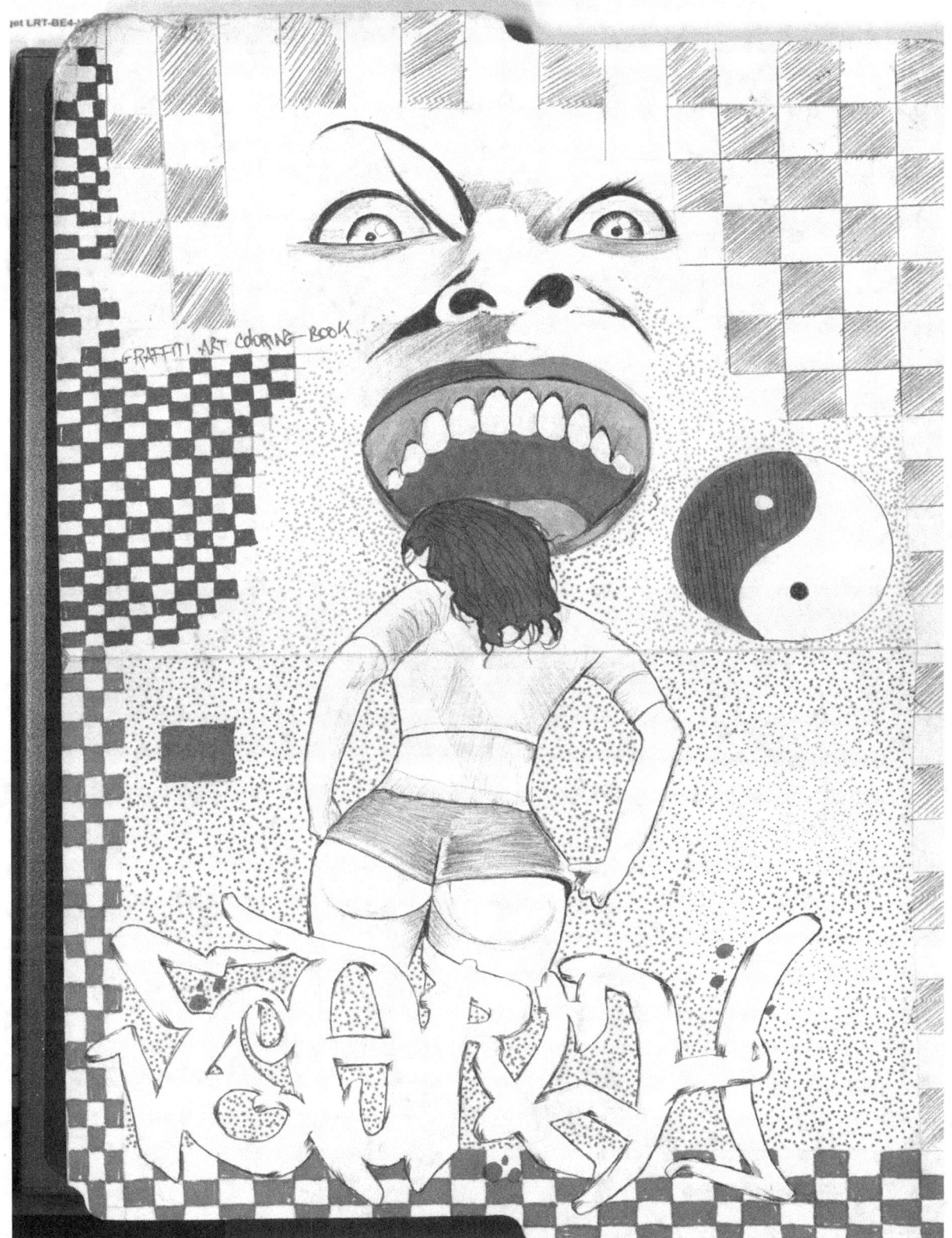

GRAFFITI ART COLORING BOOK

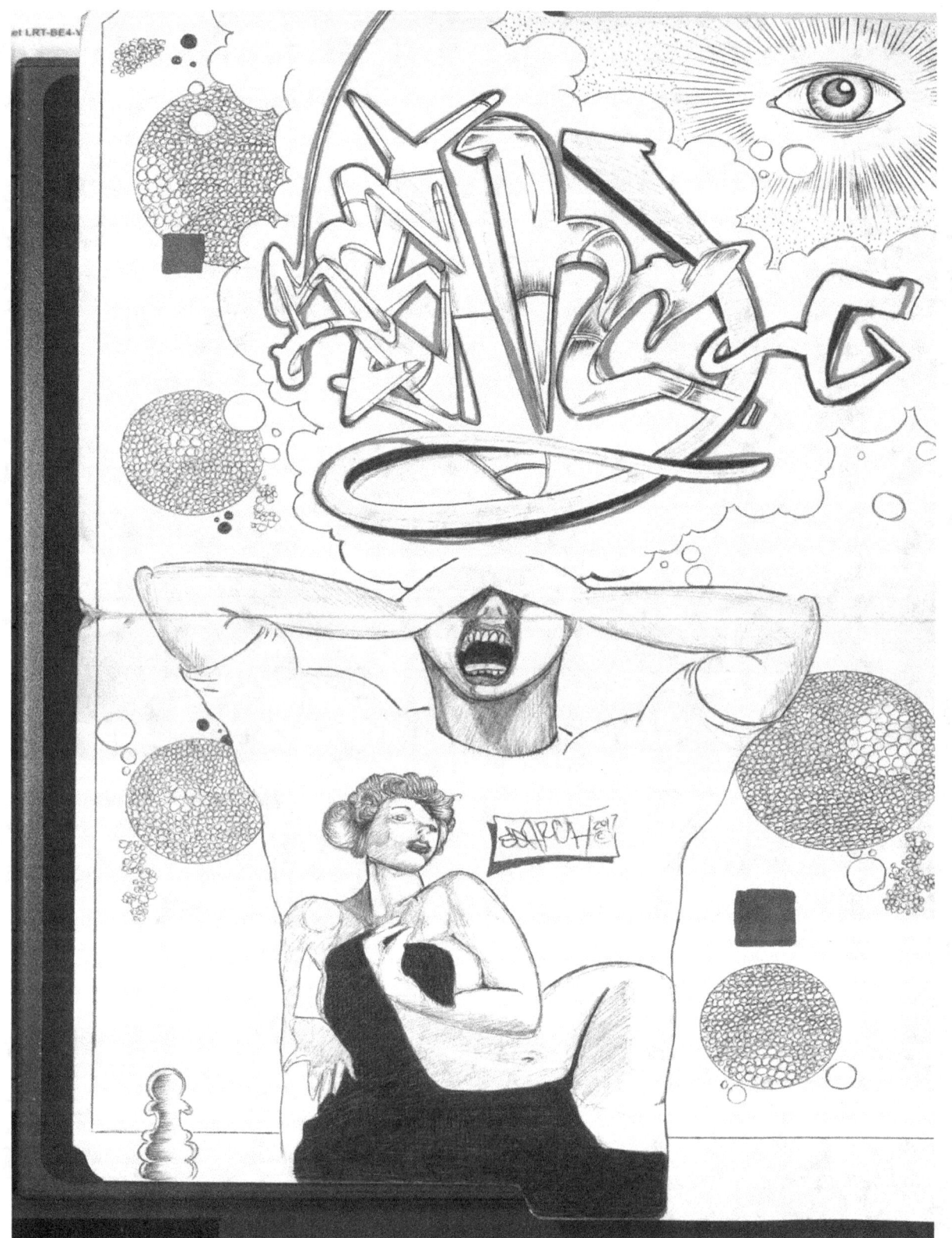

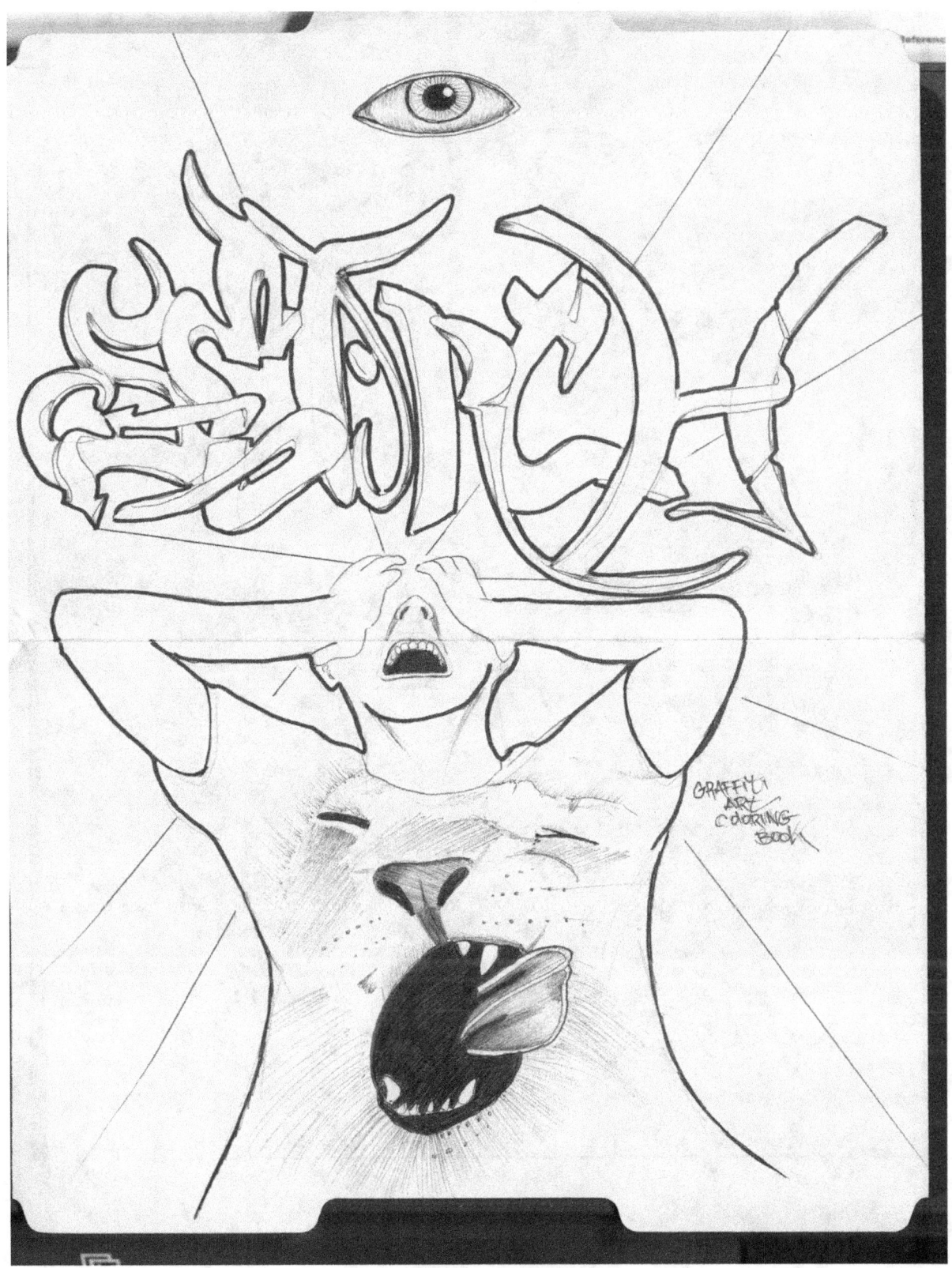

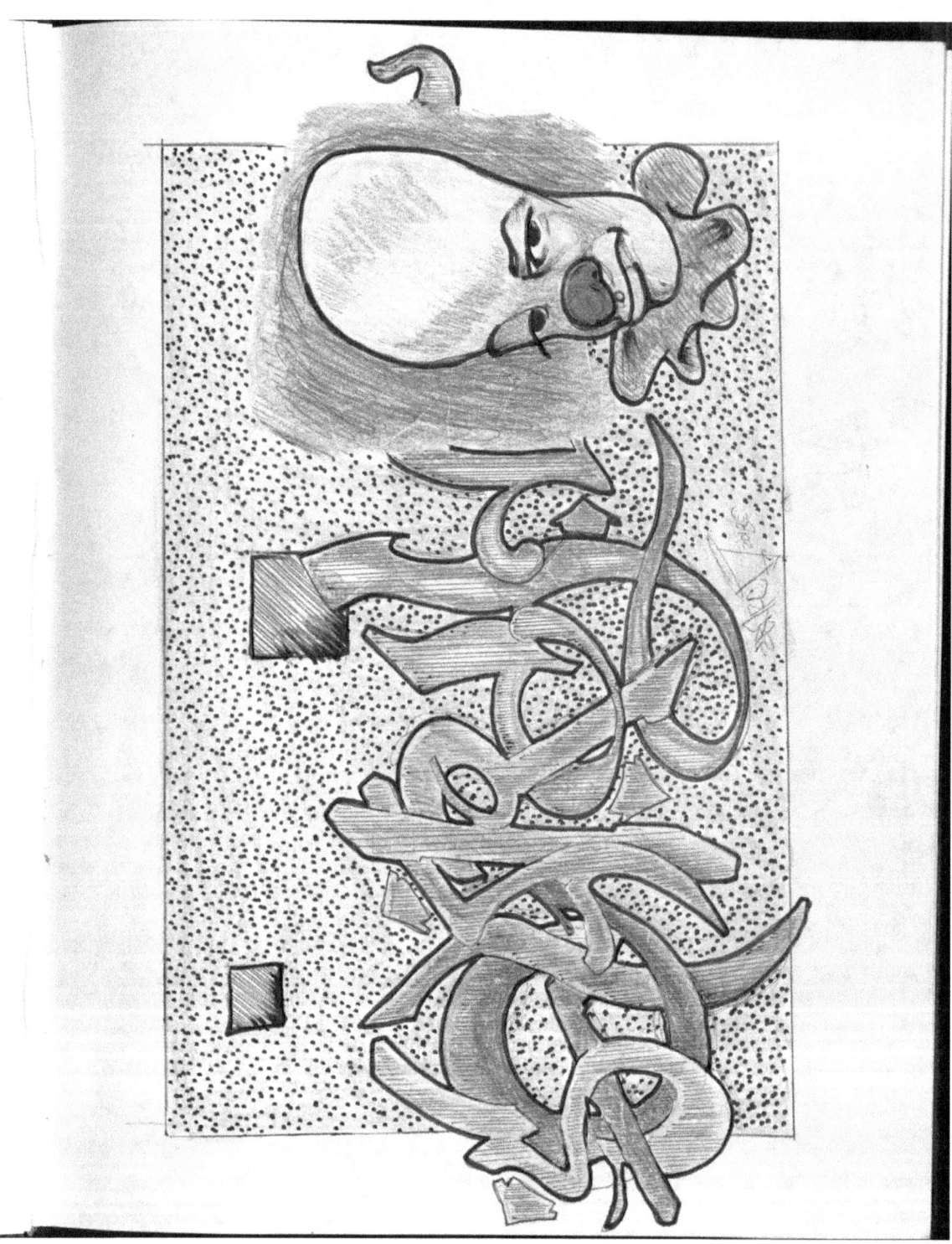

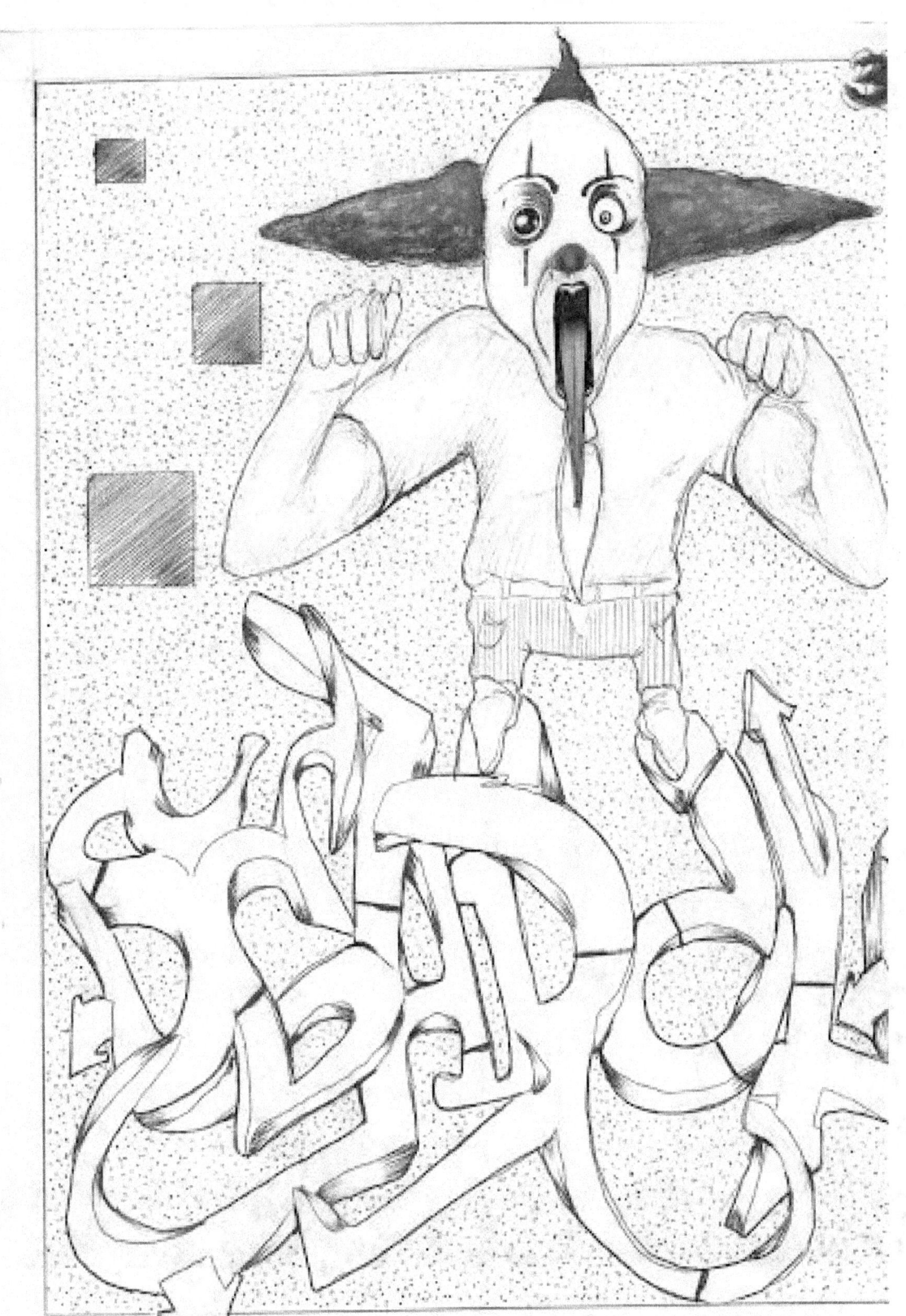

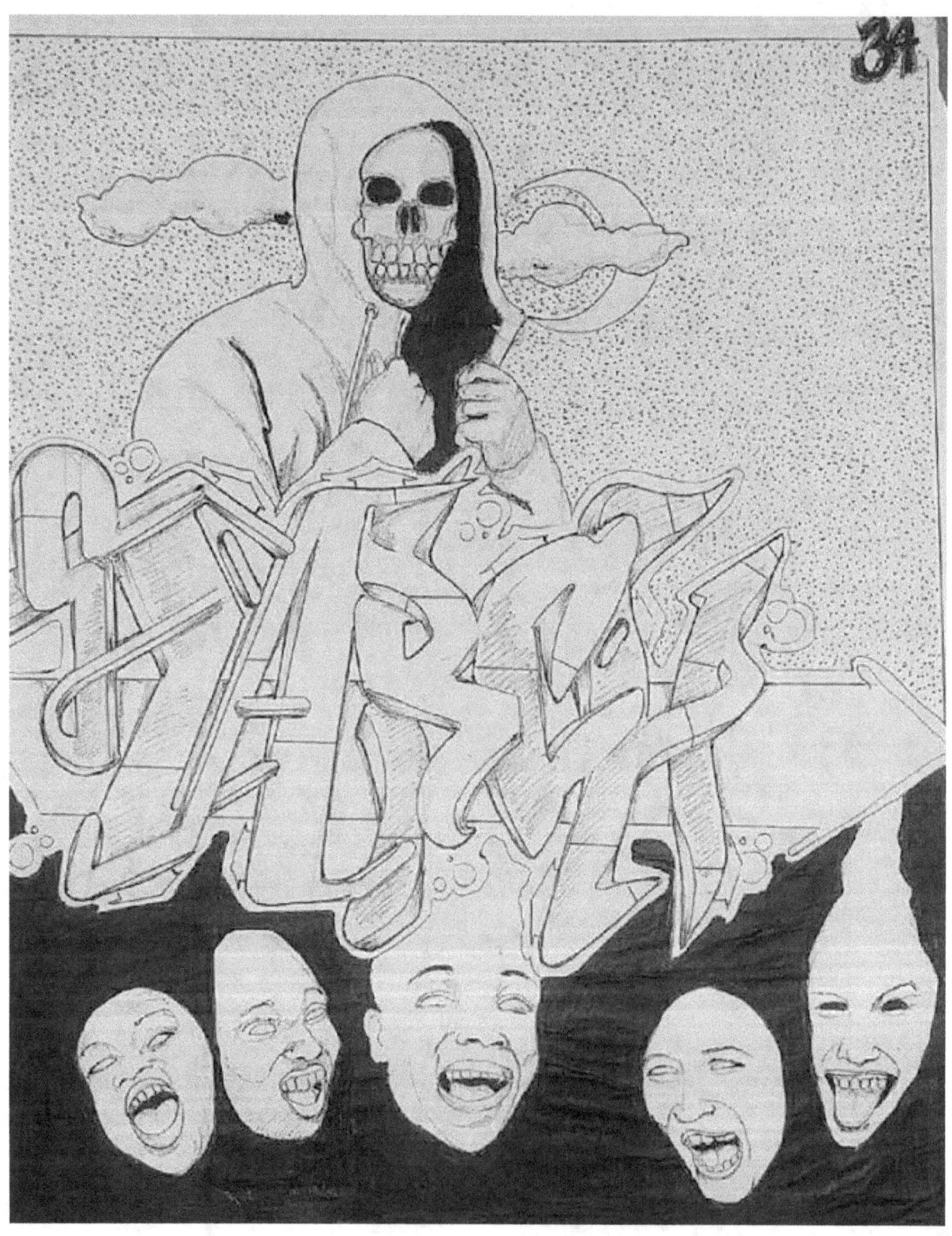

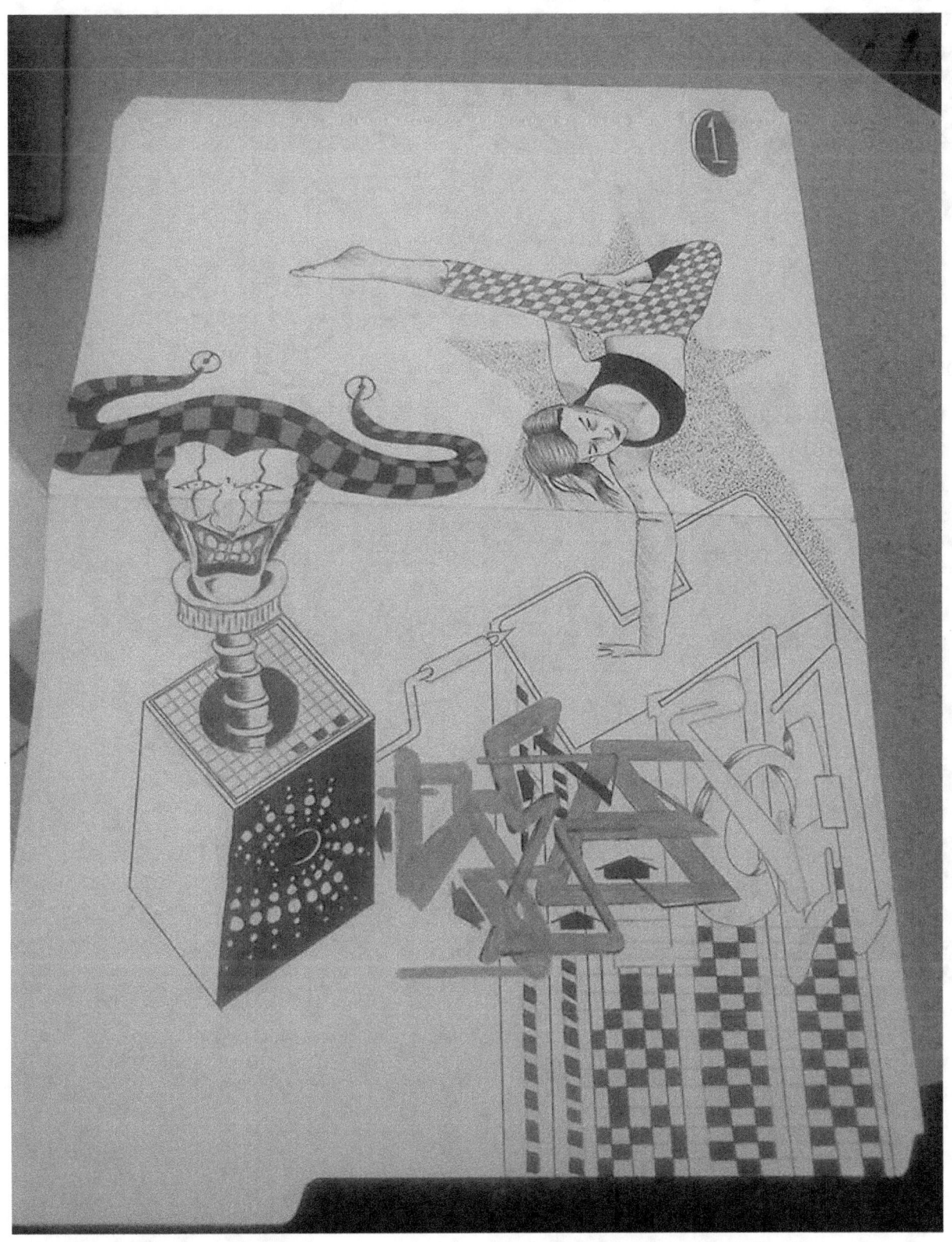

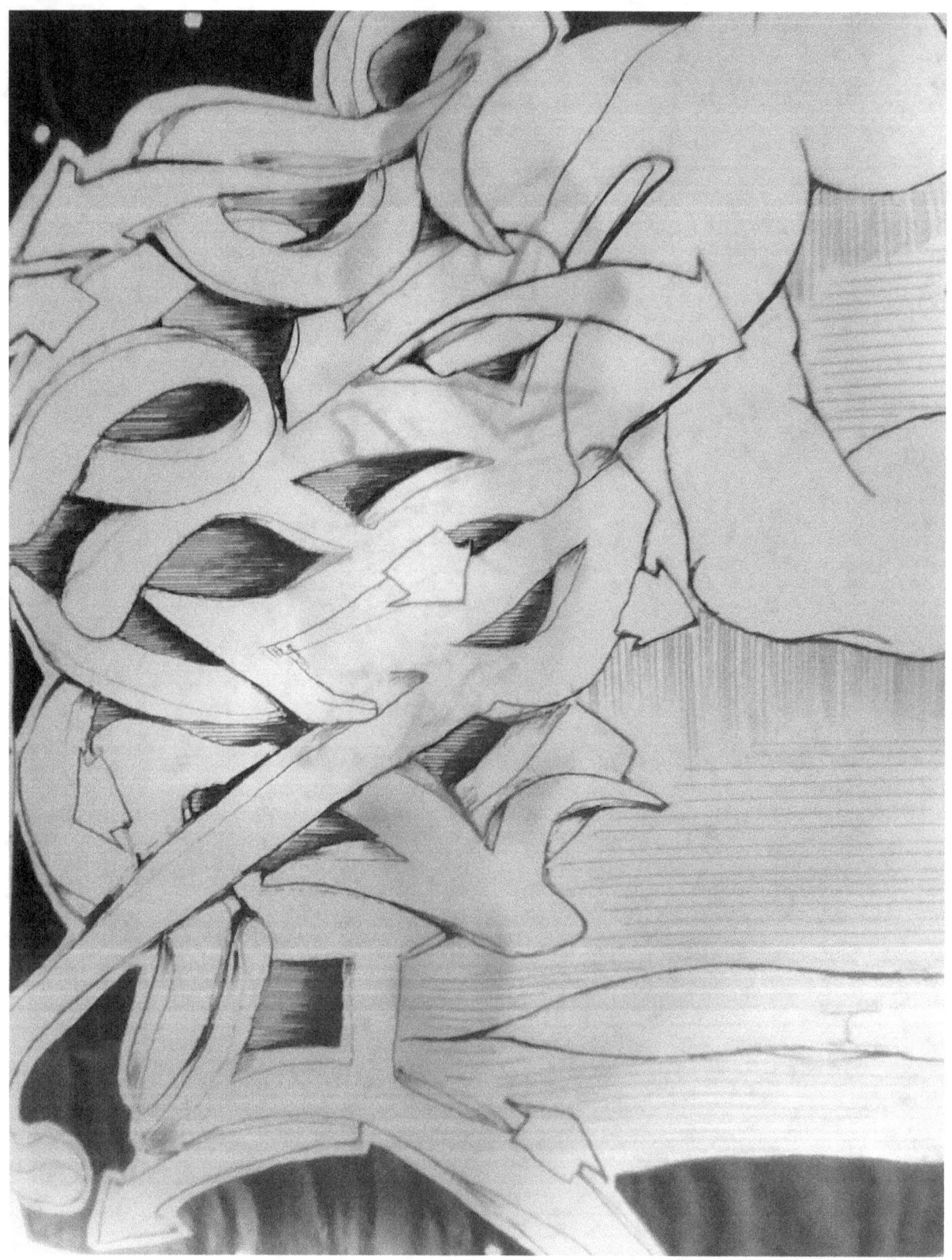

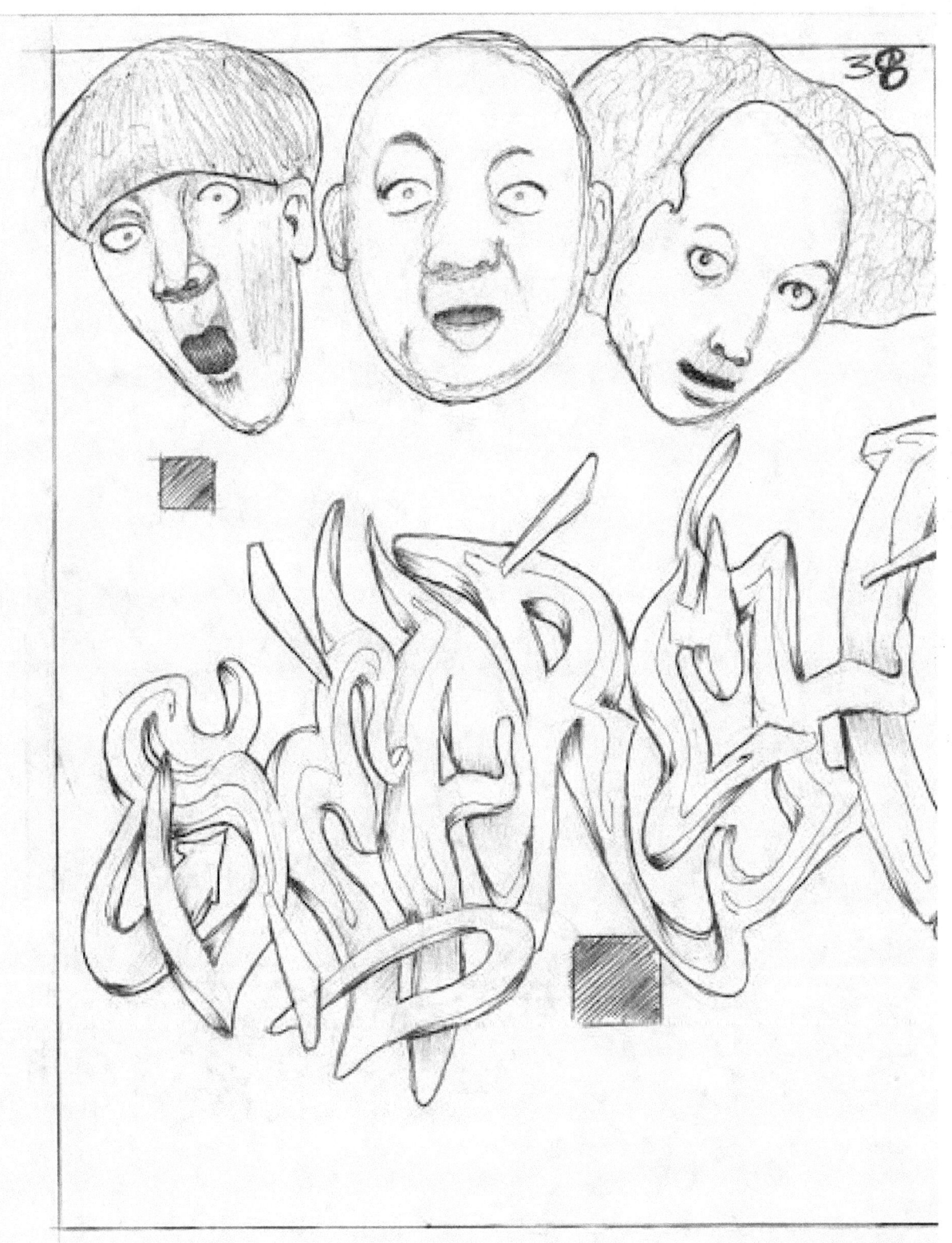

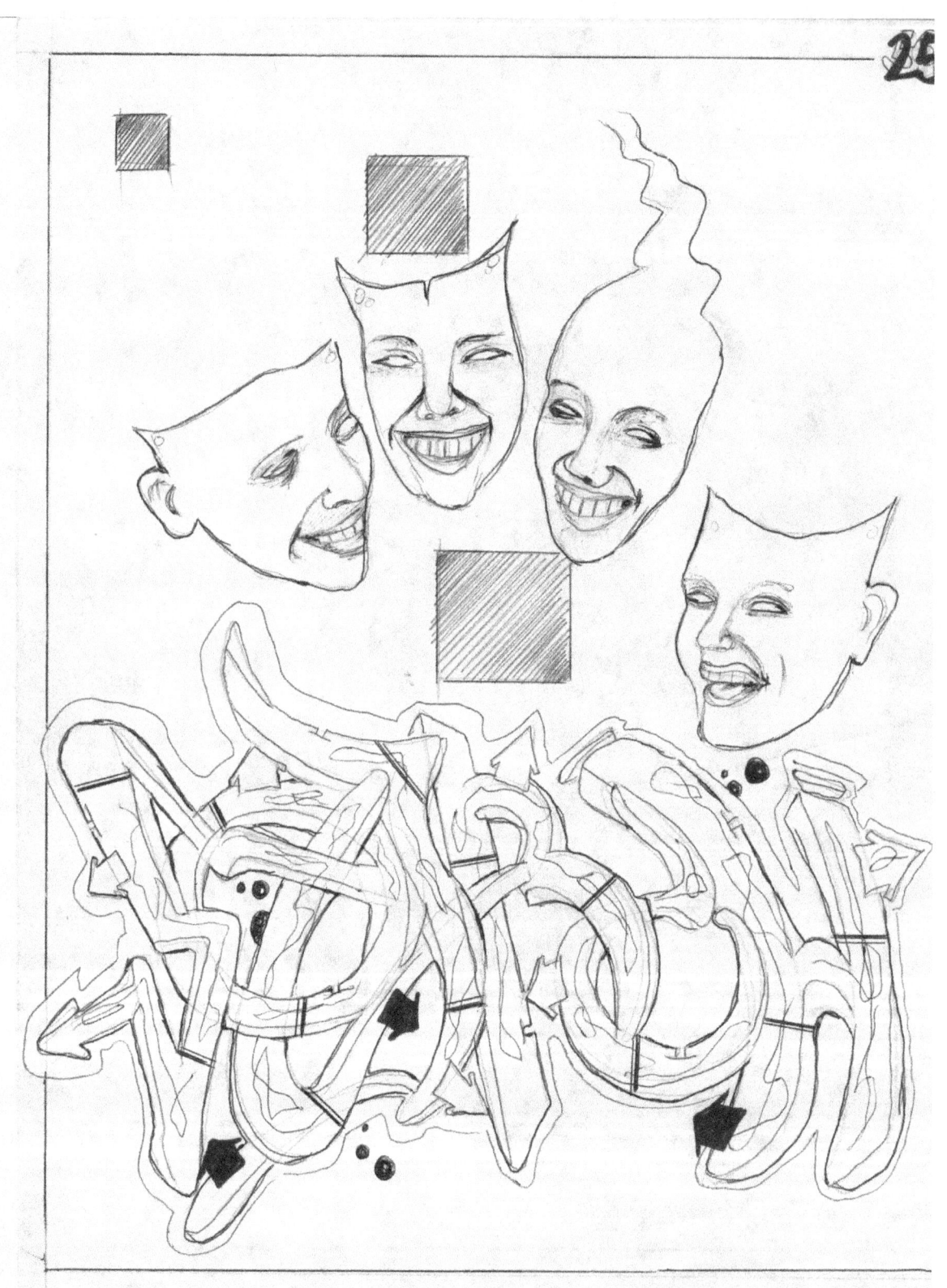

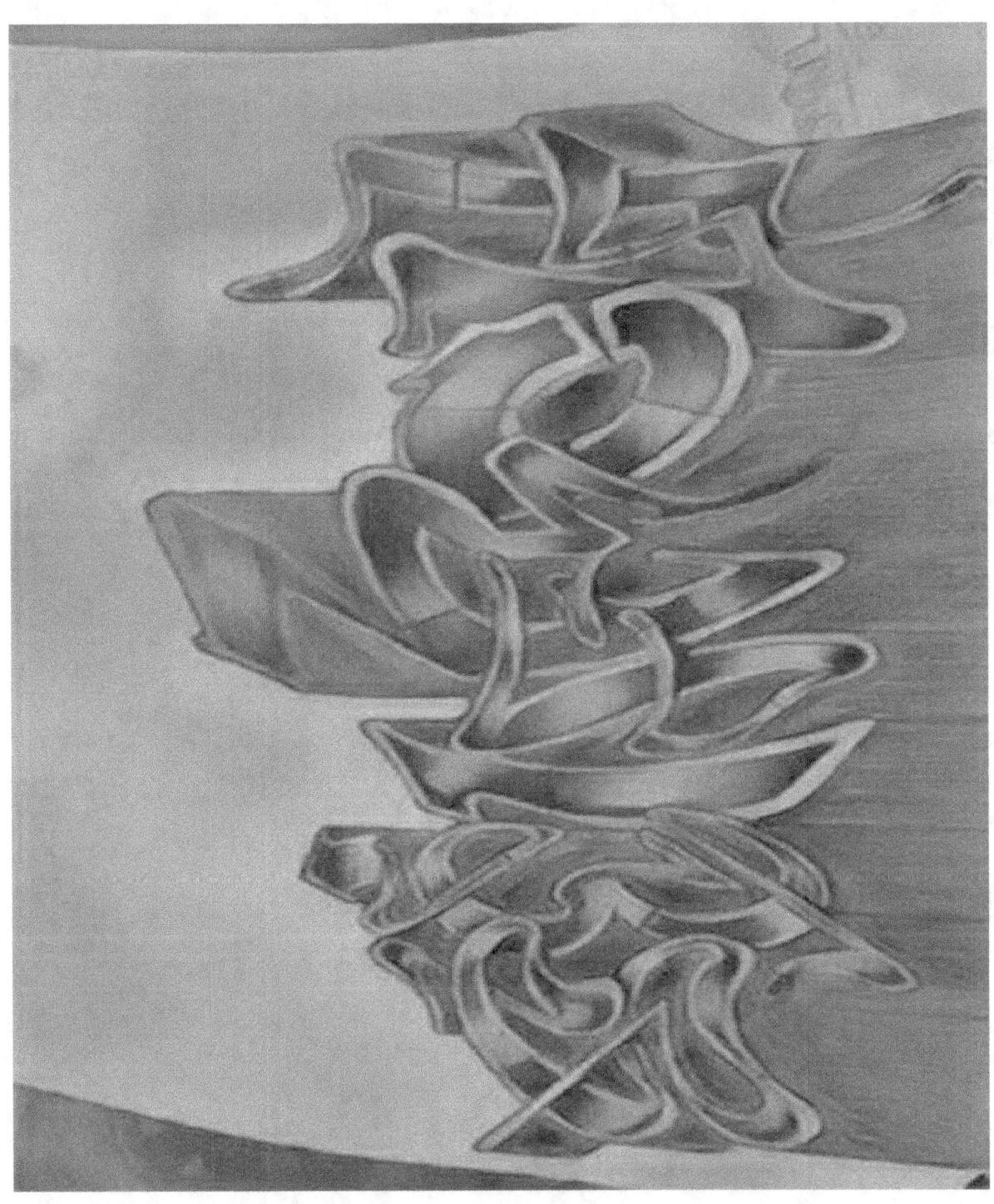

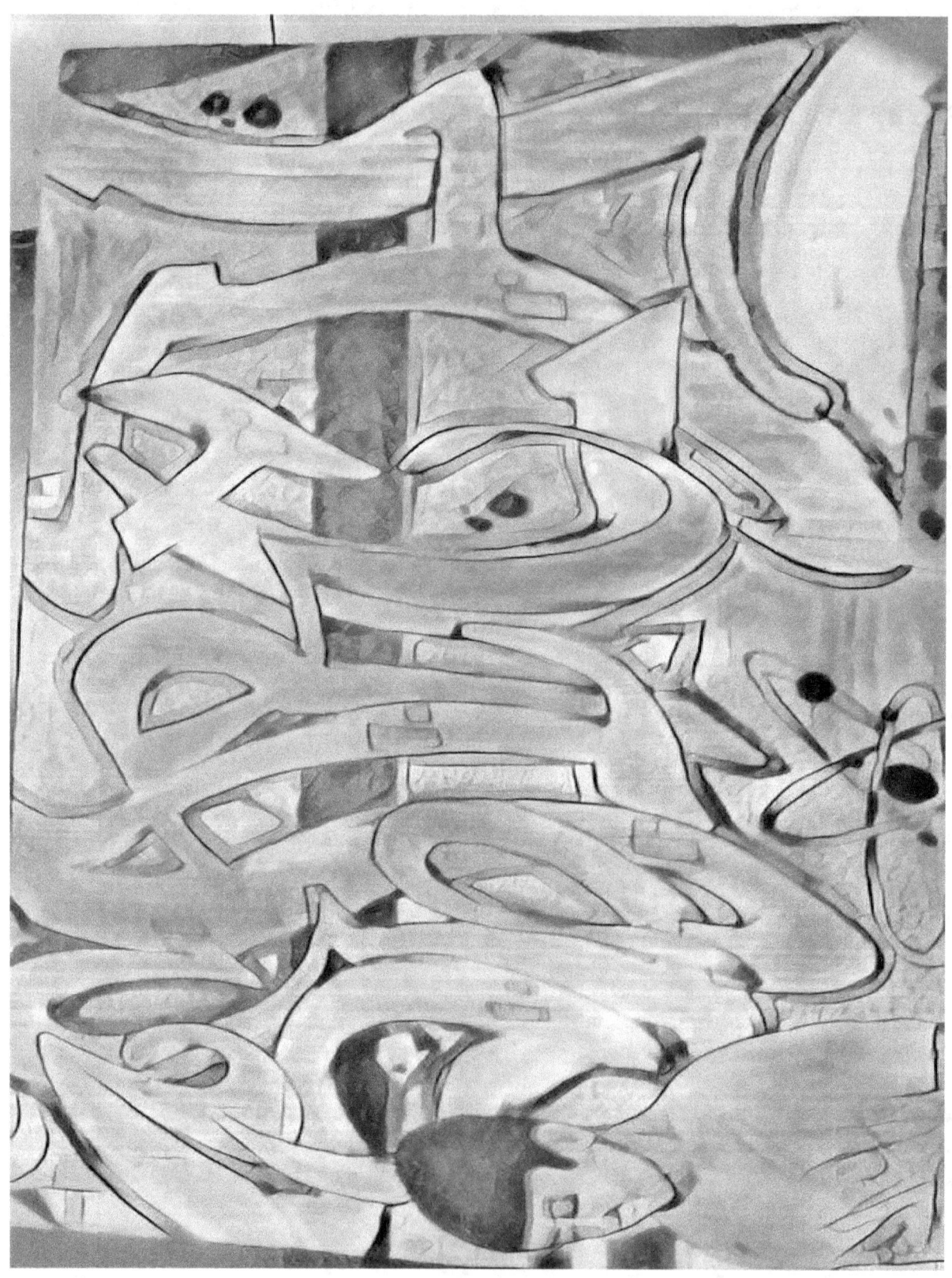

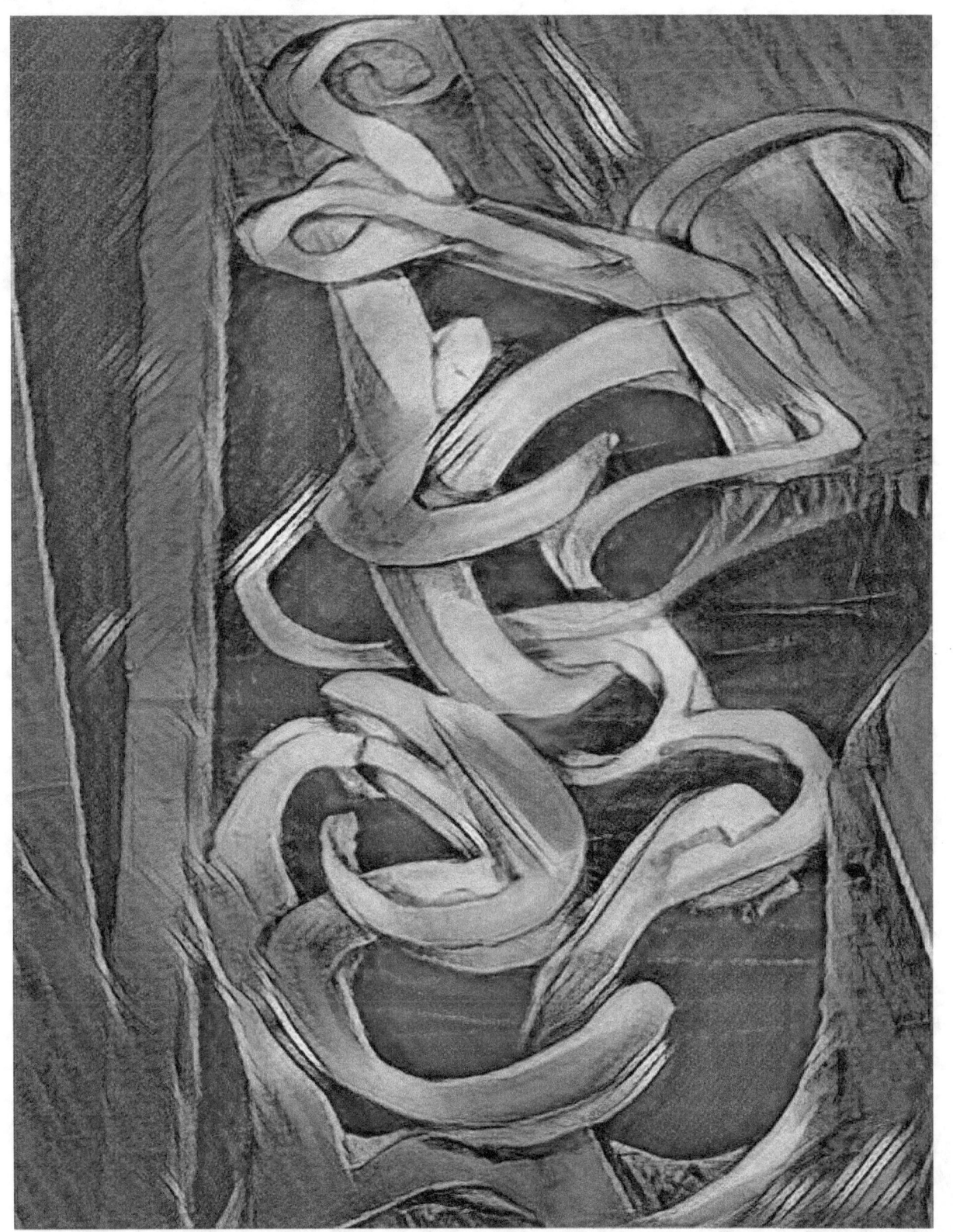

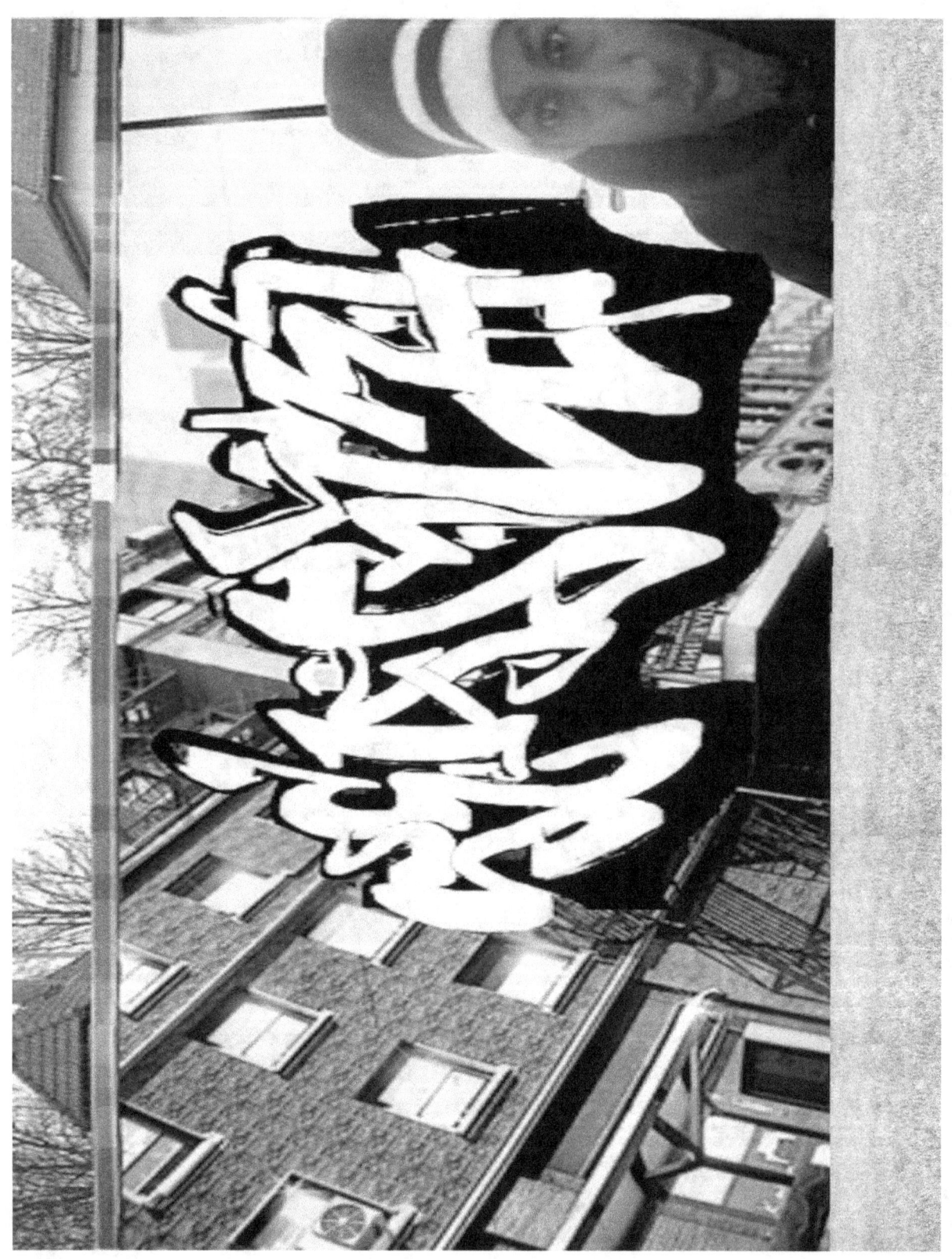

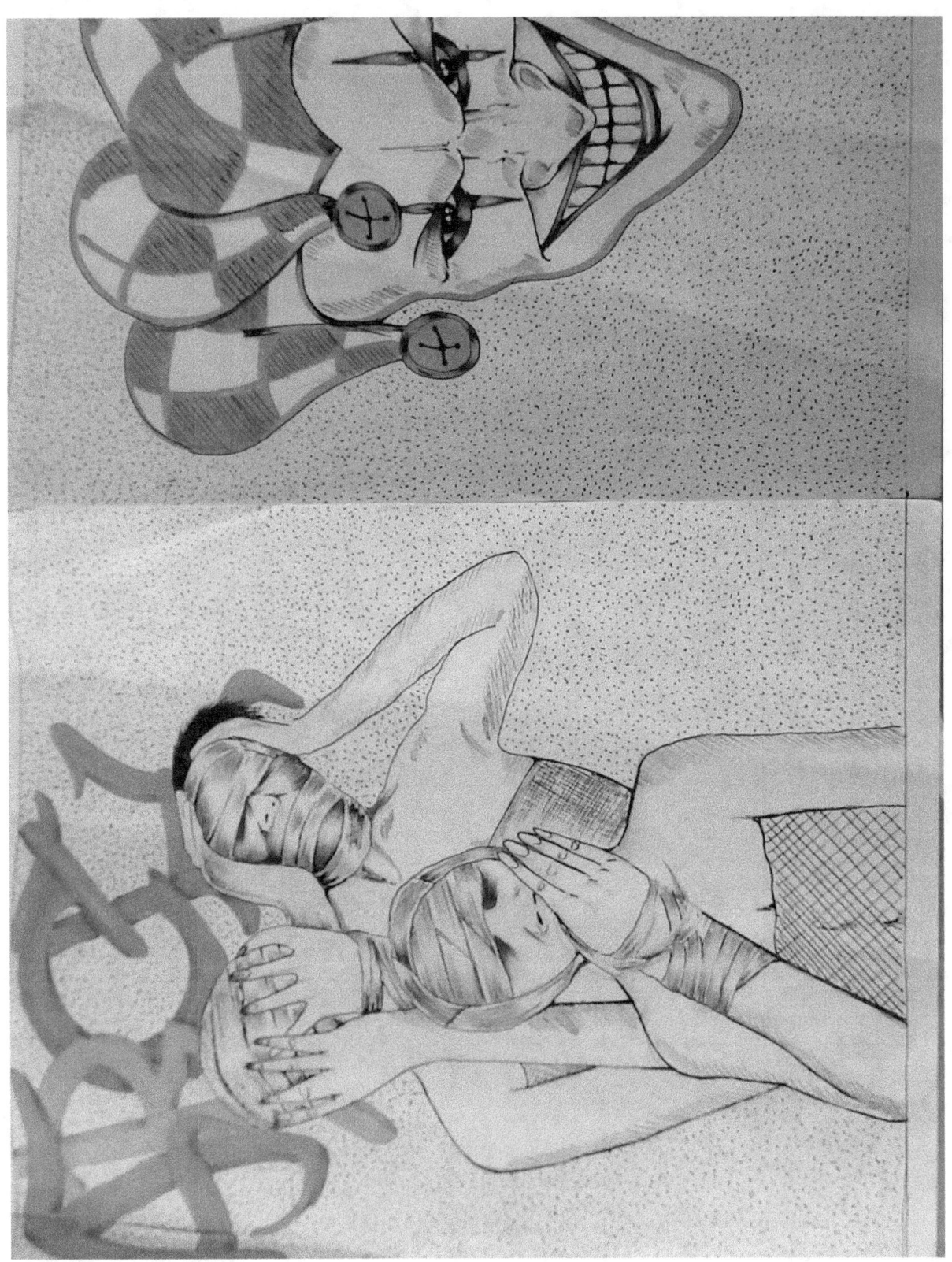

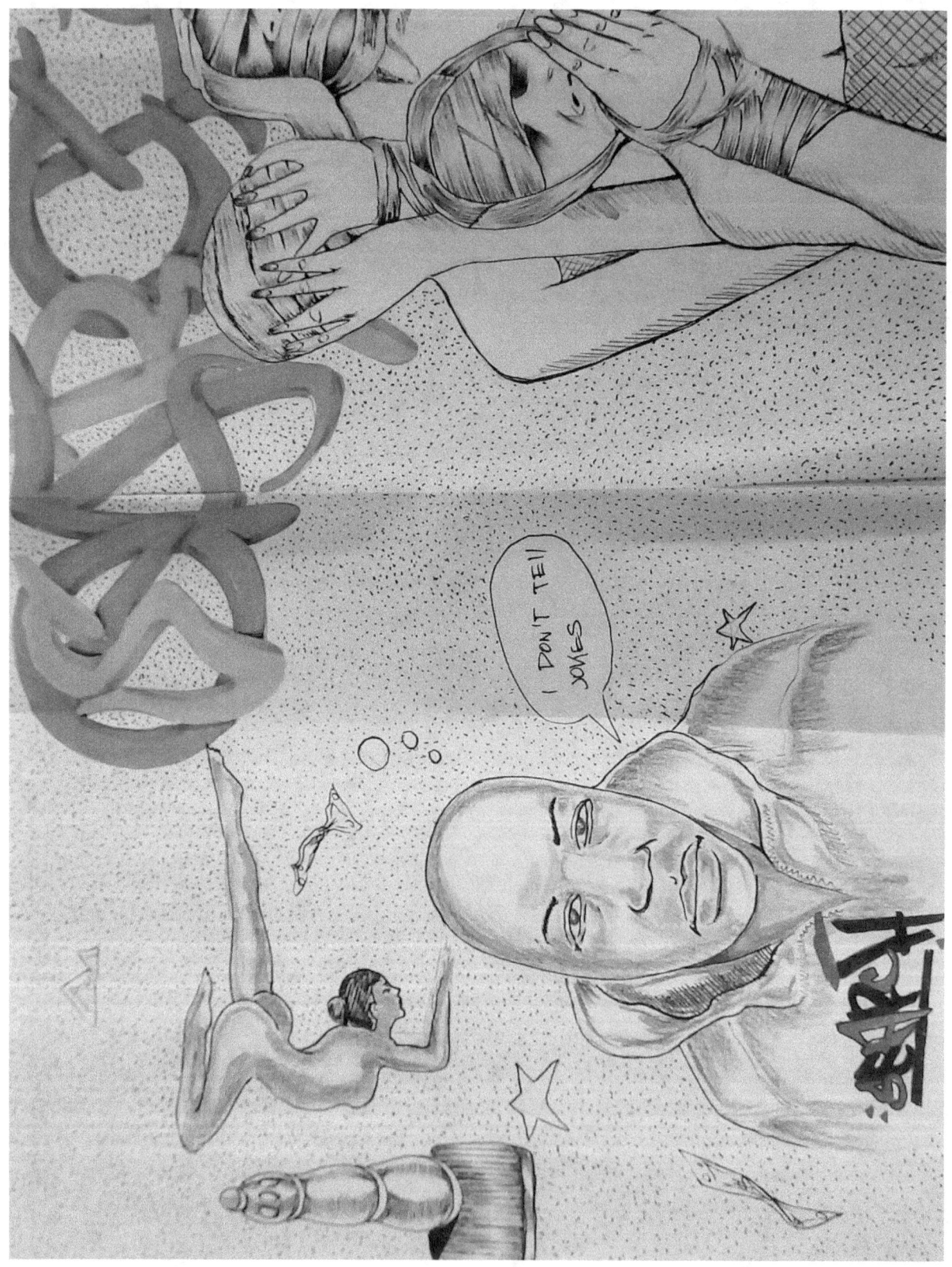

115

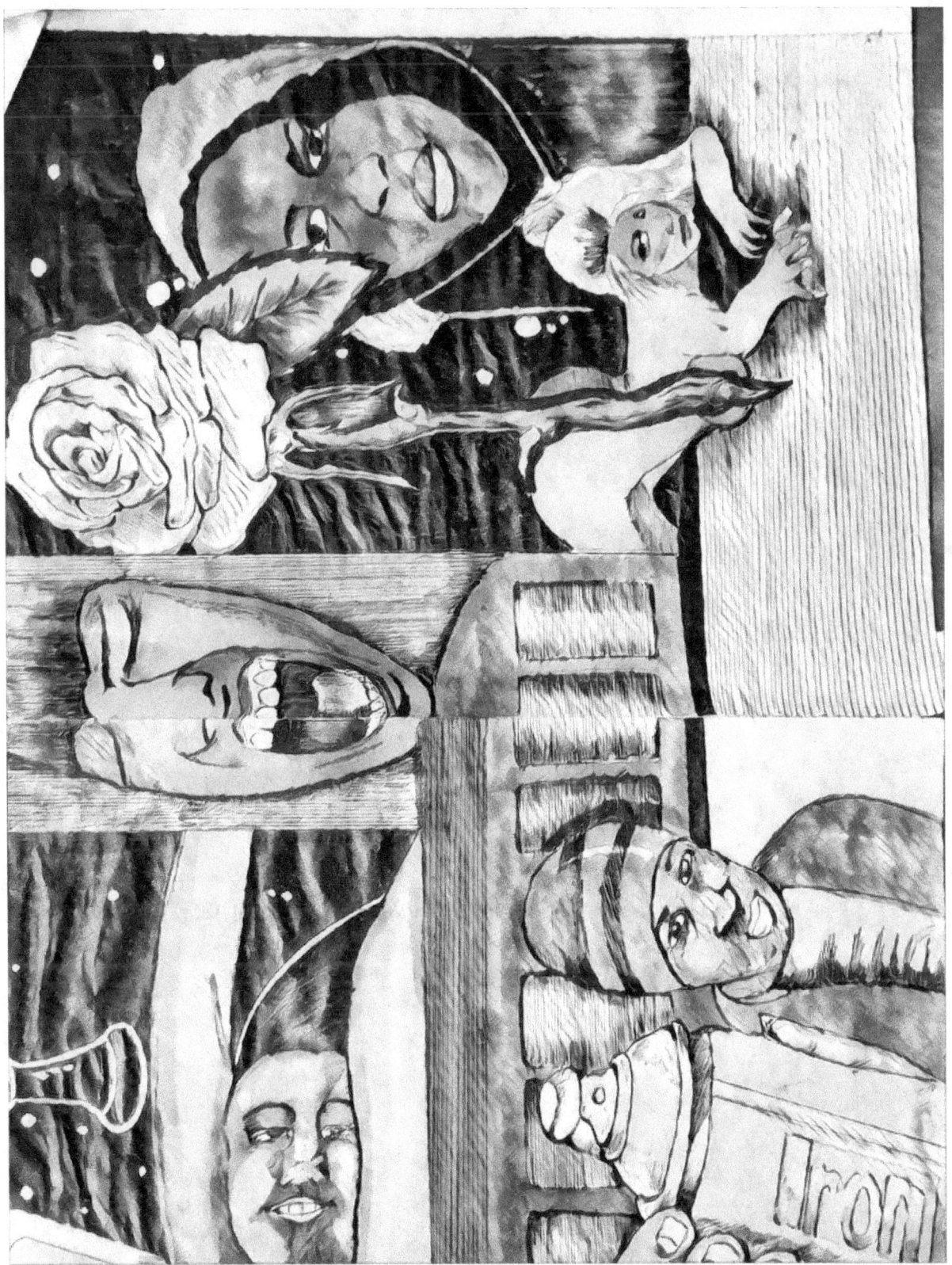

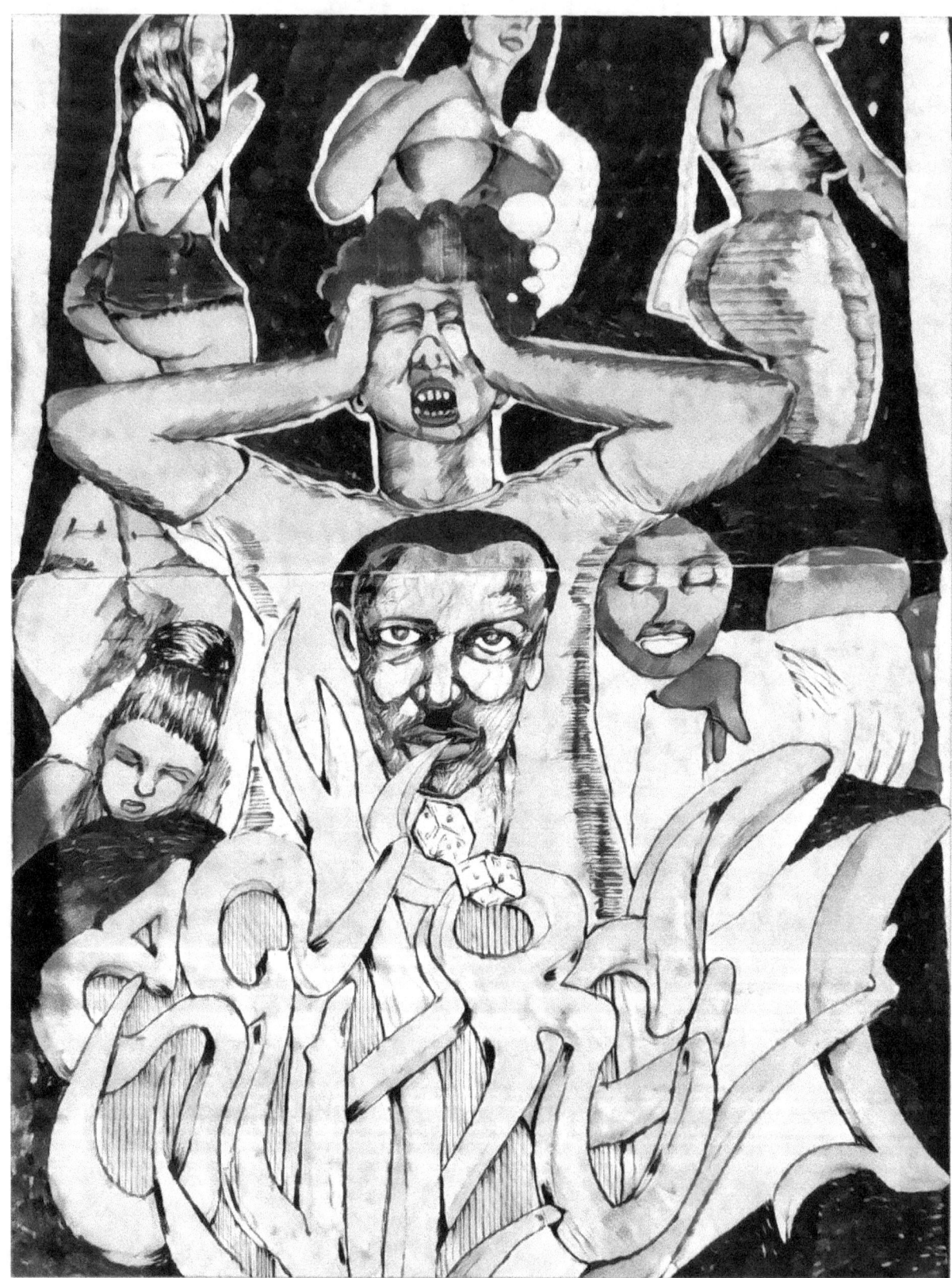

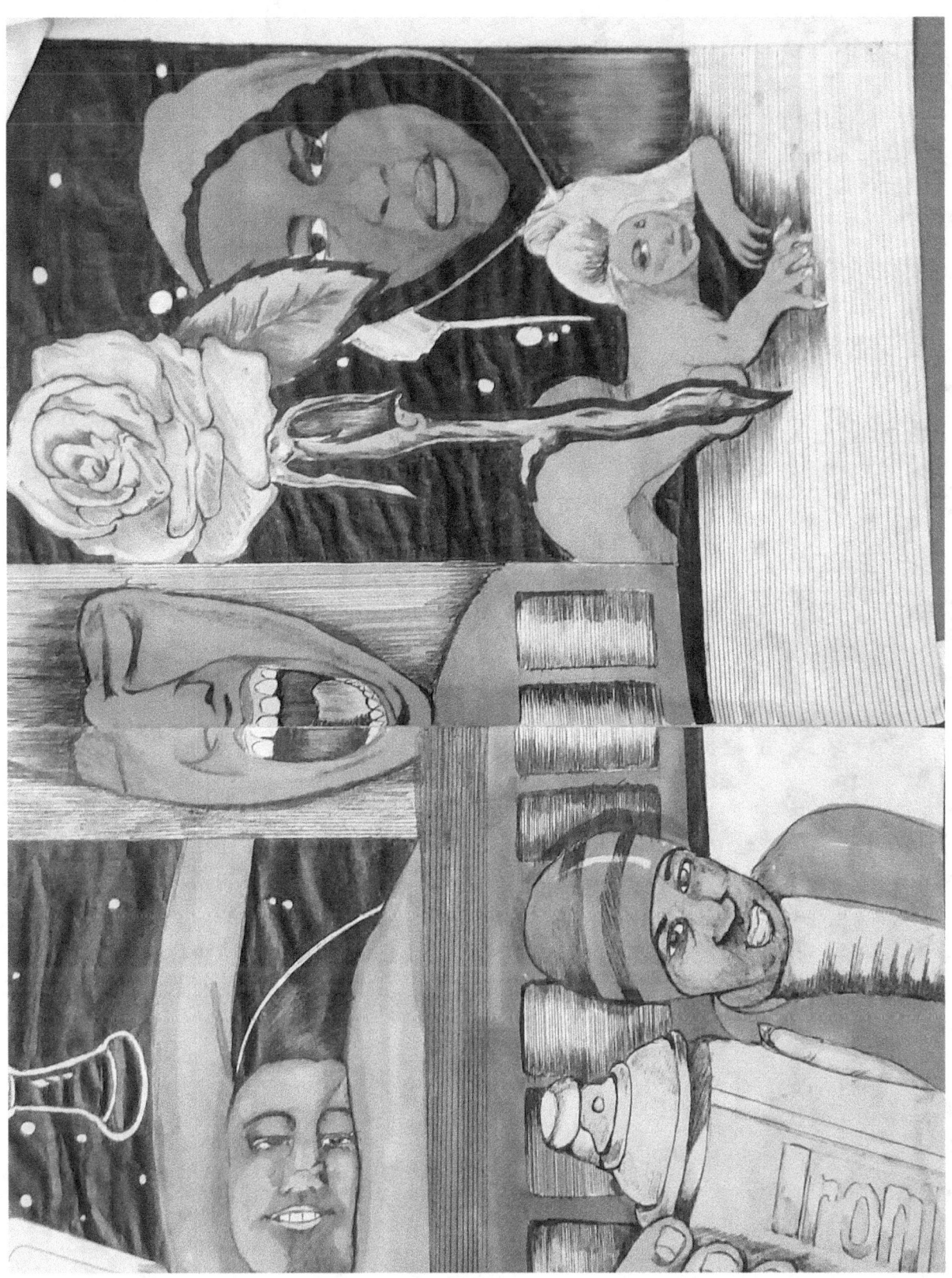

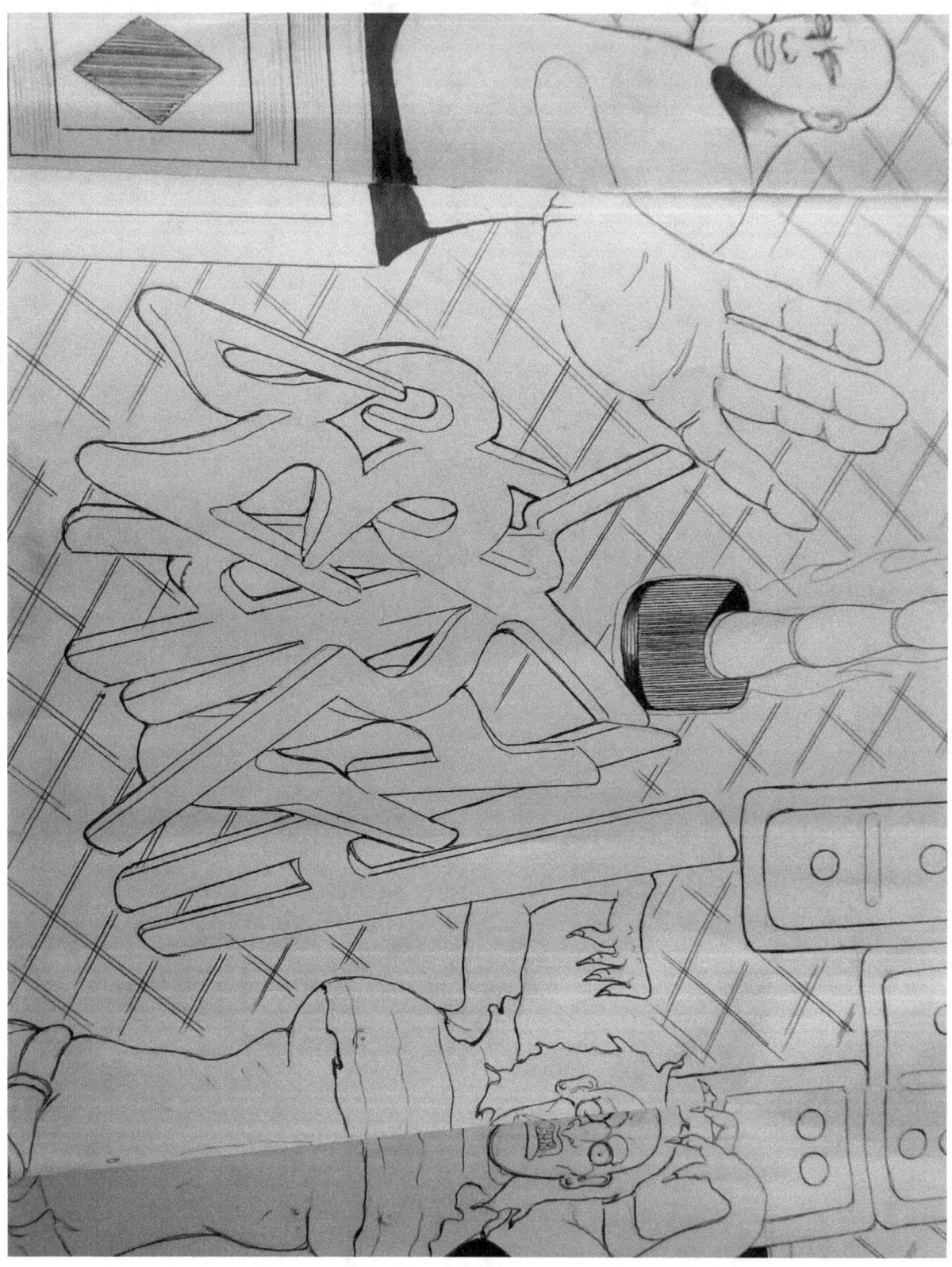

119

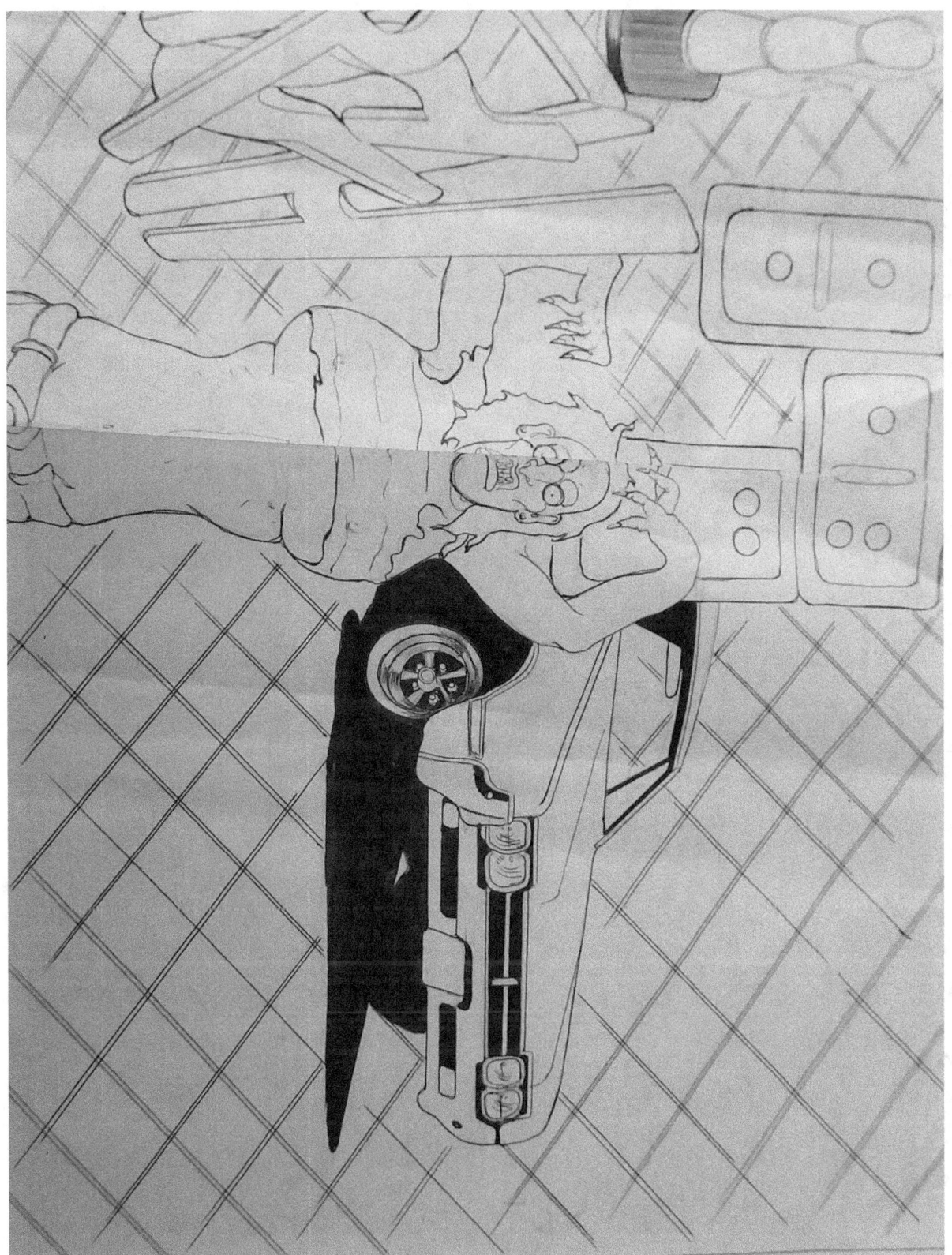

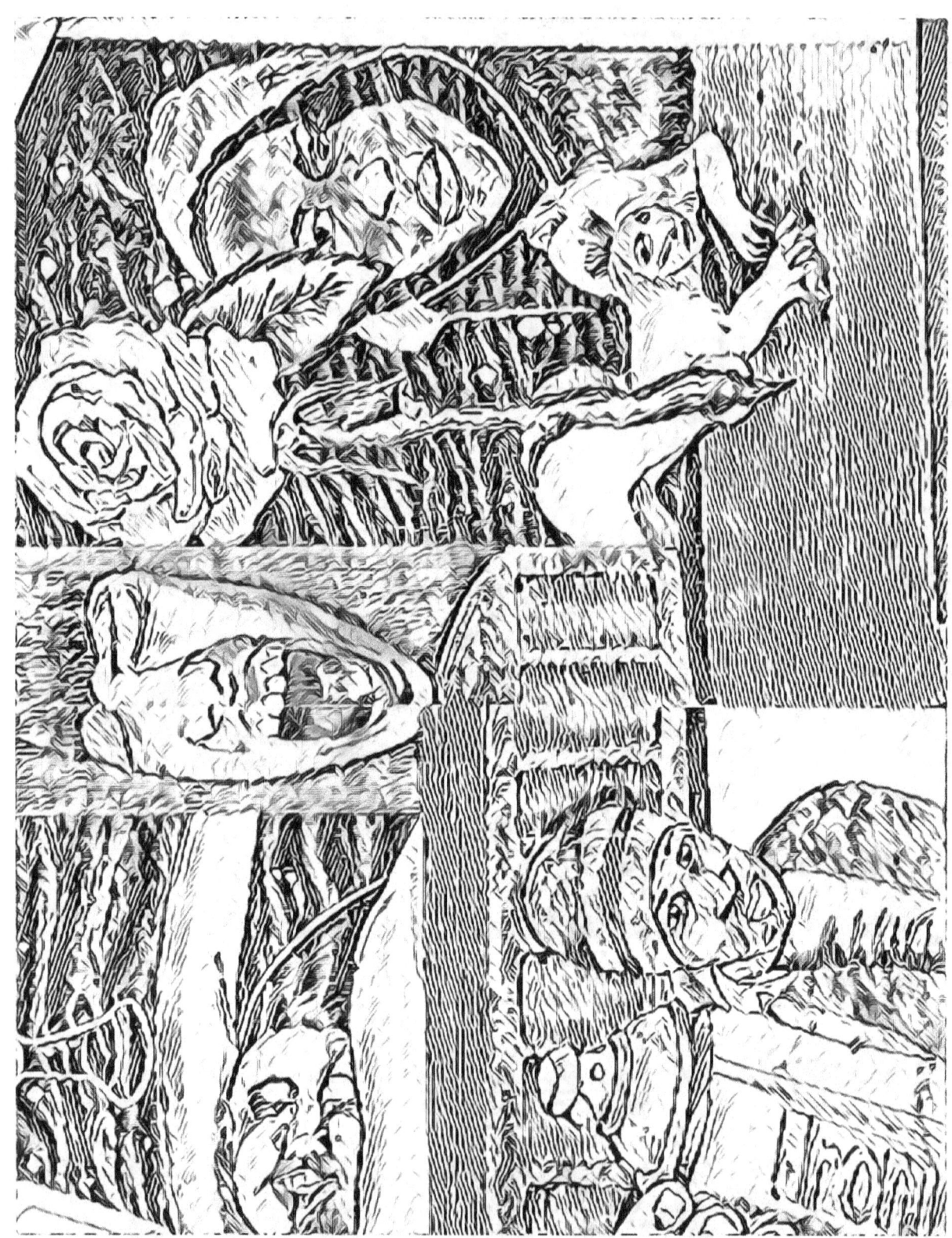

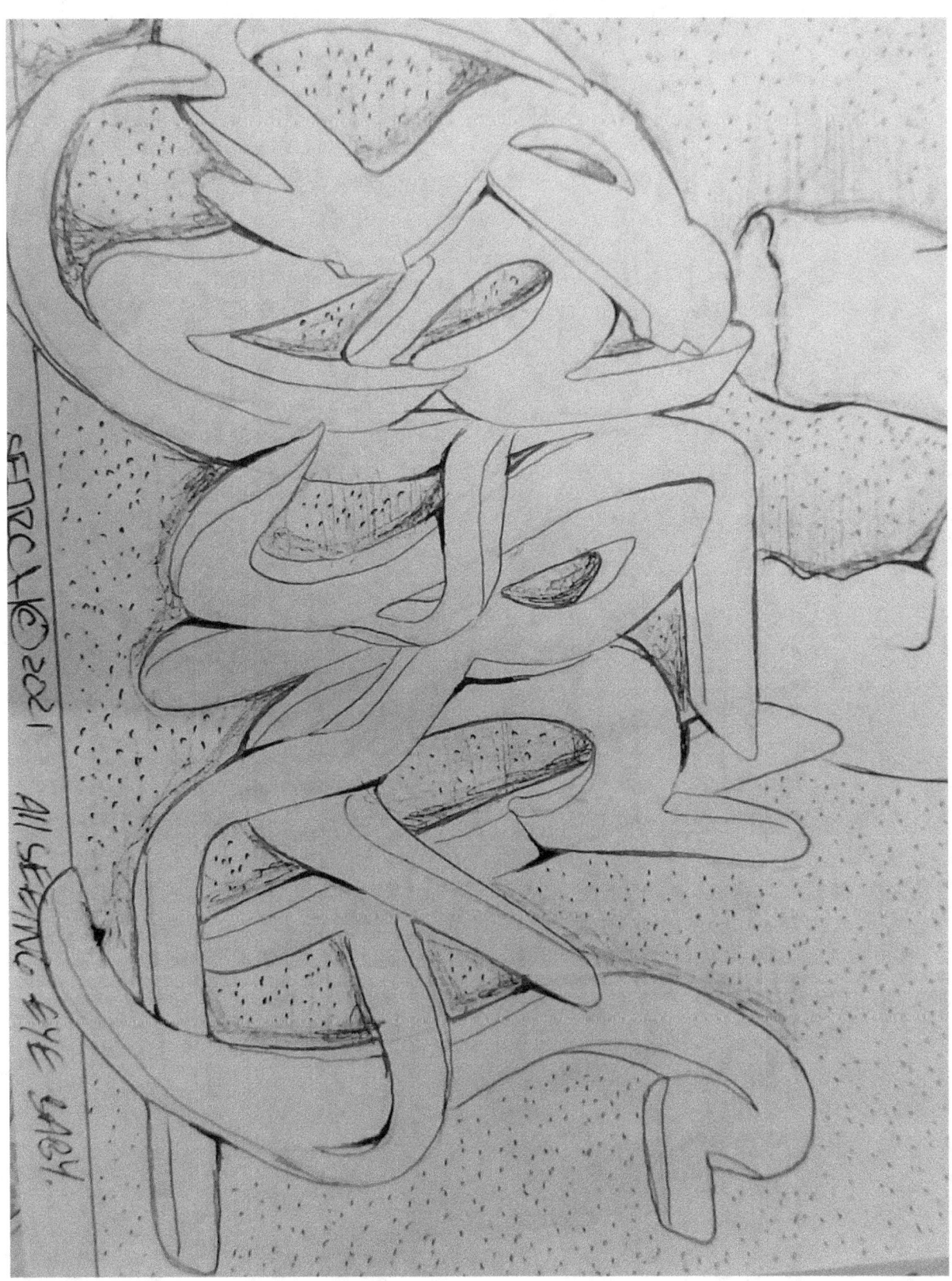

SEEROY©2021 All SEEING EYE BABY.

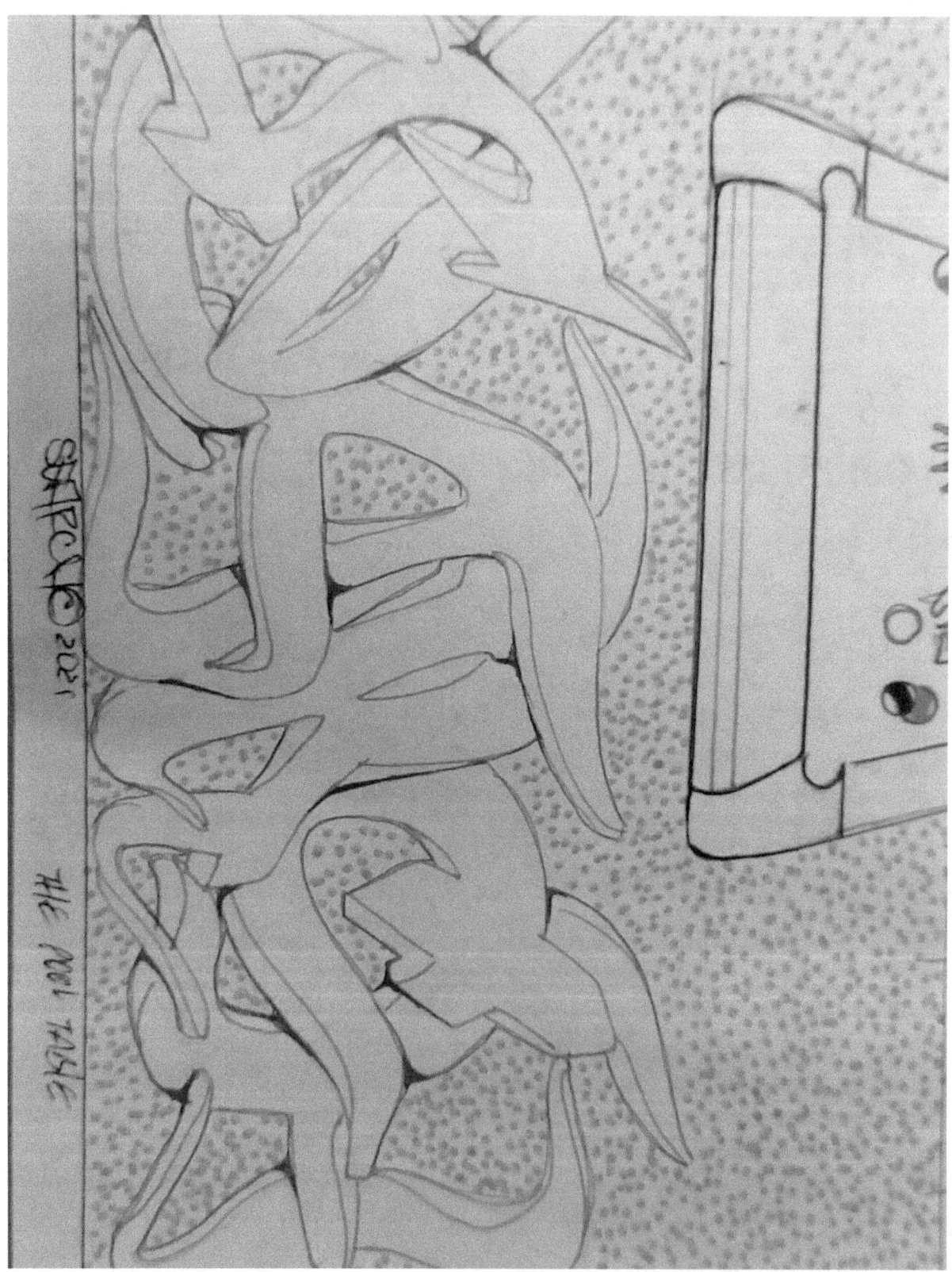

123

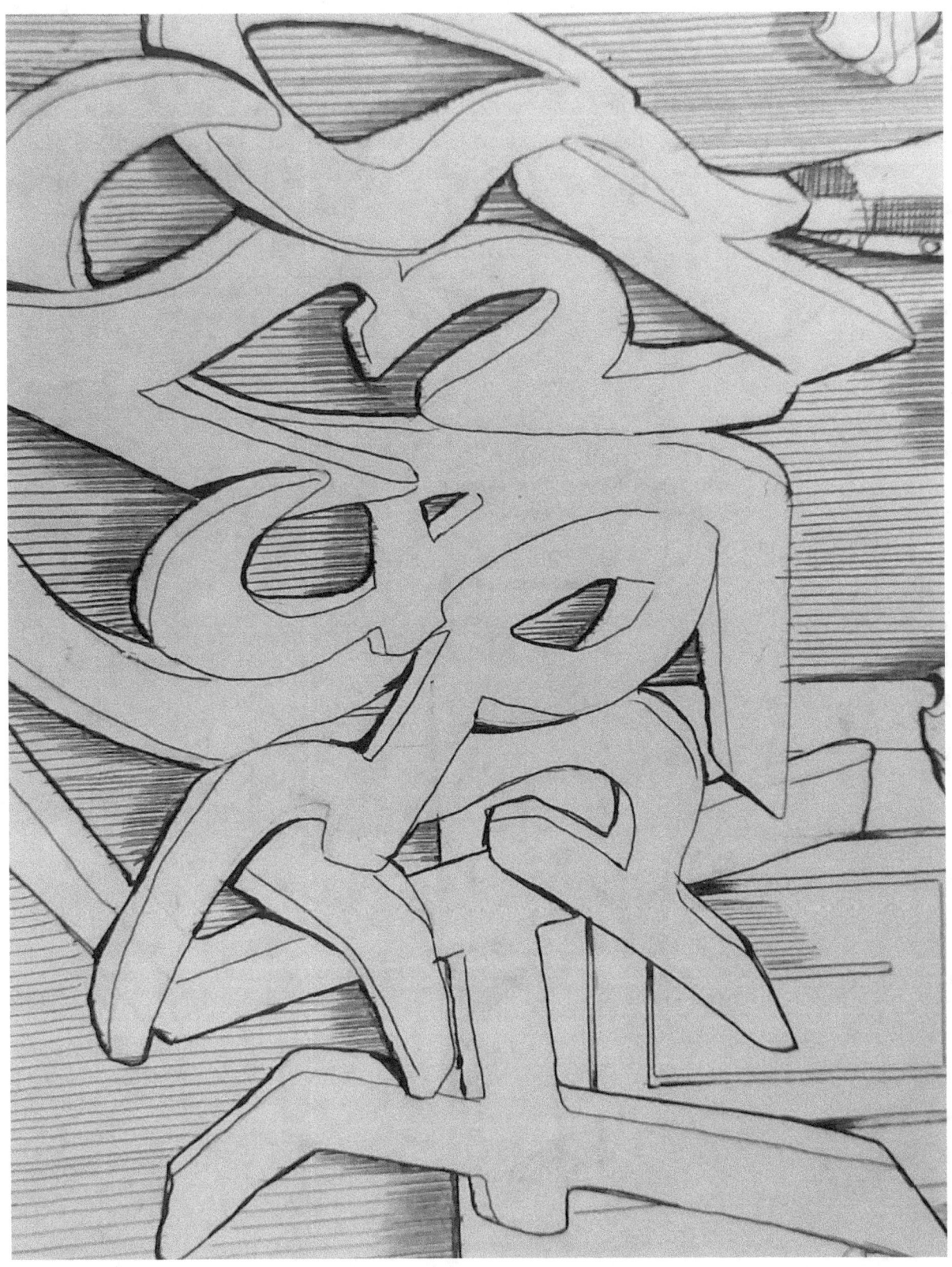

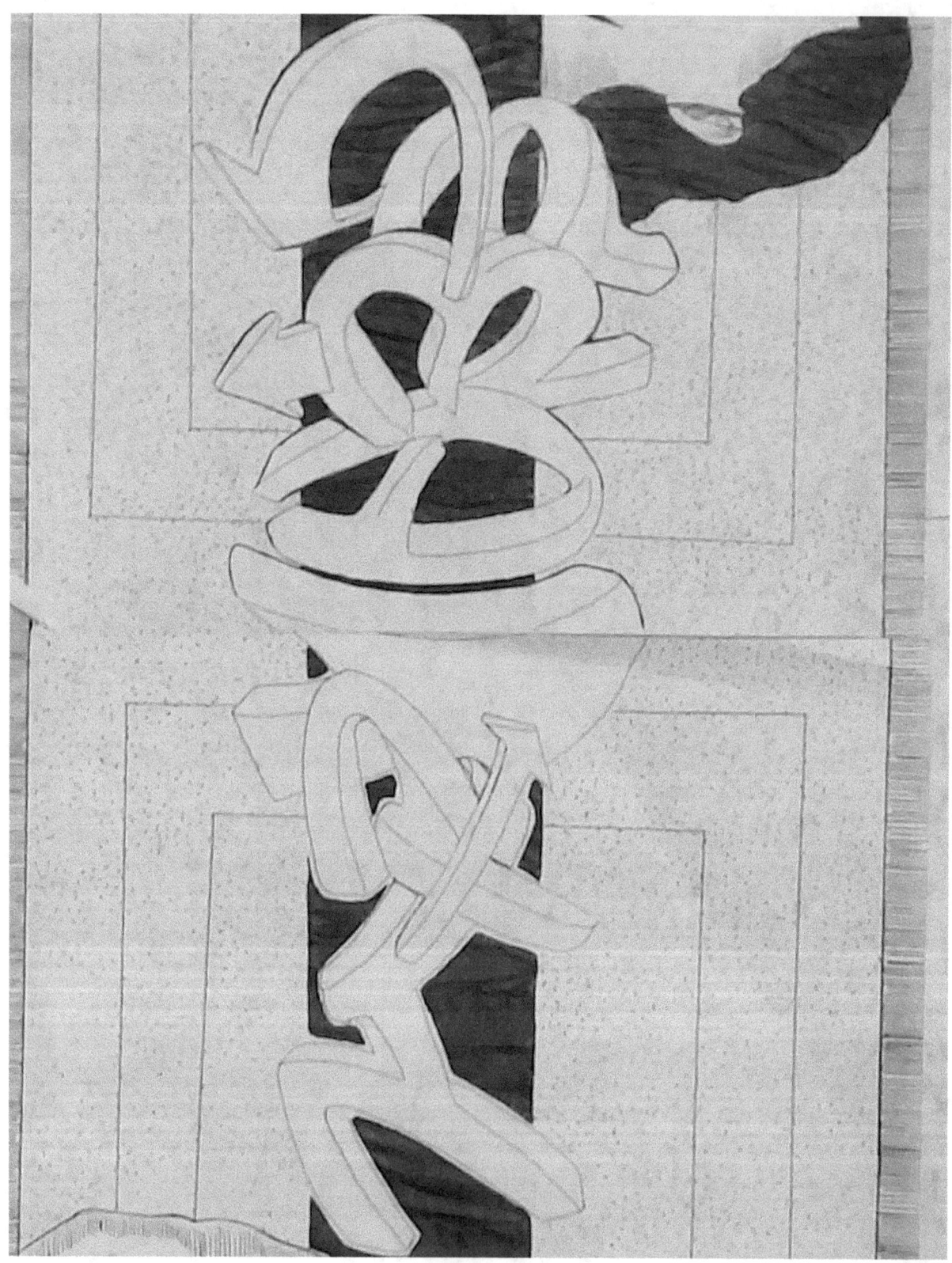

125

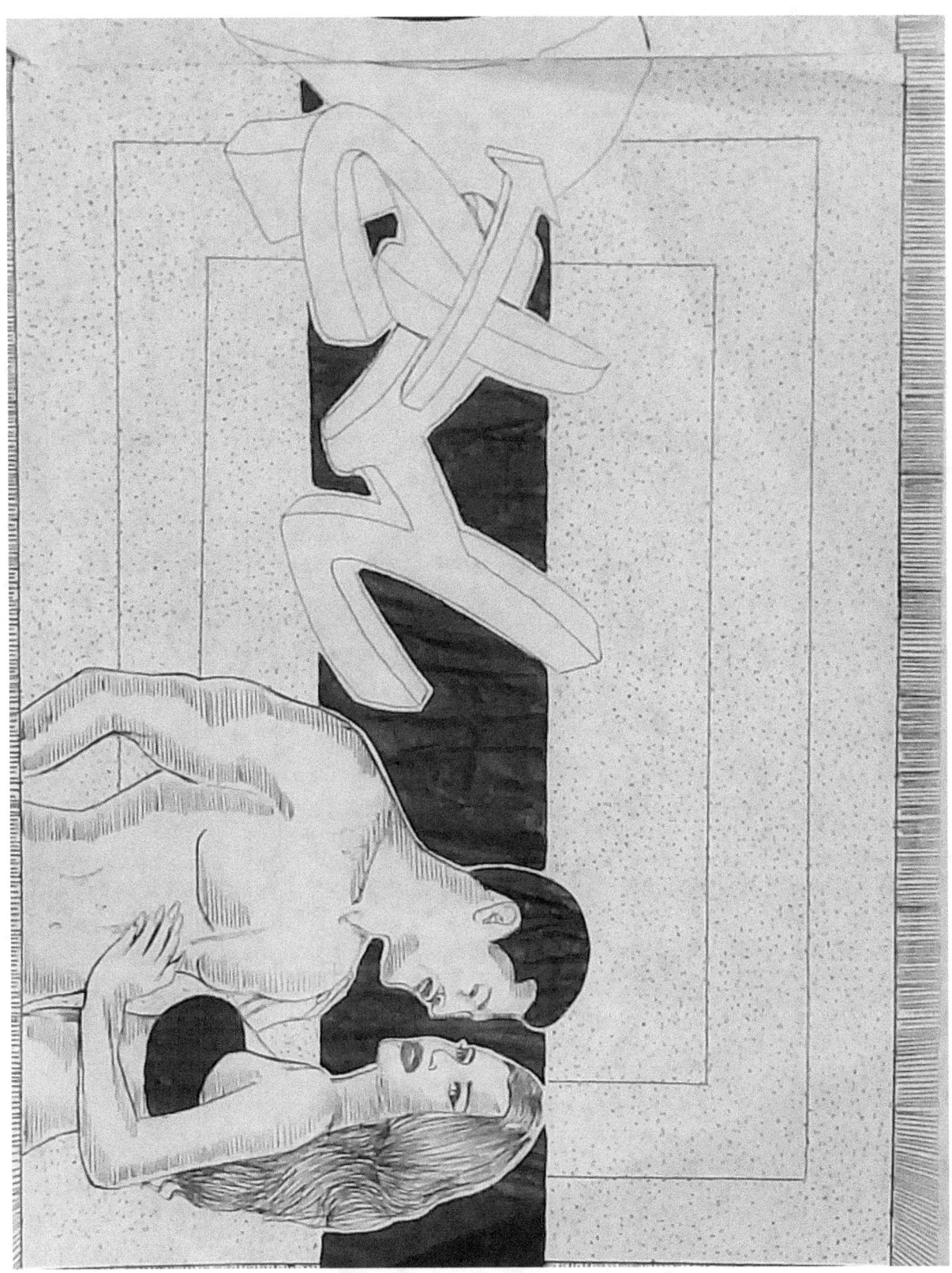

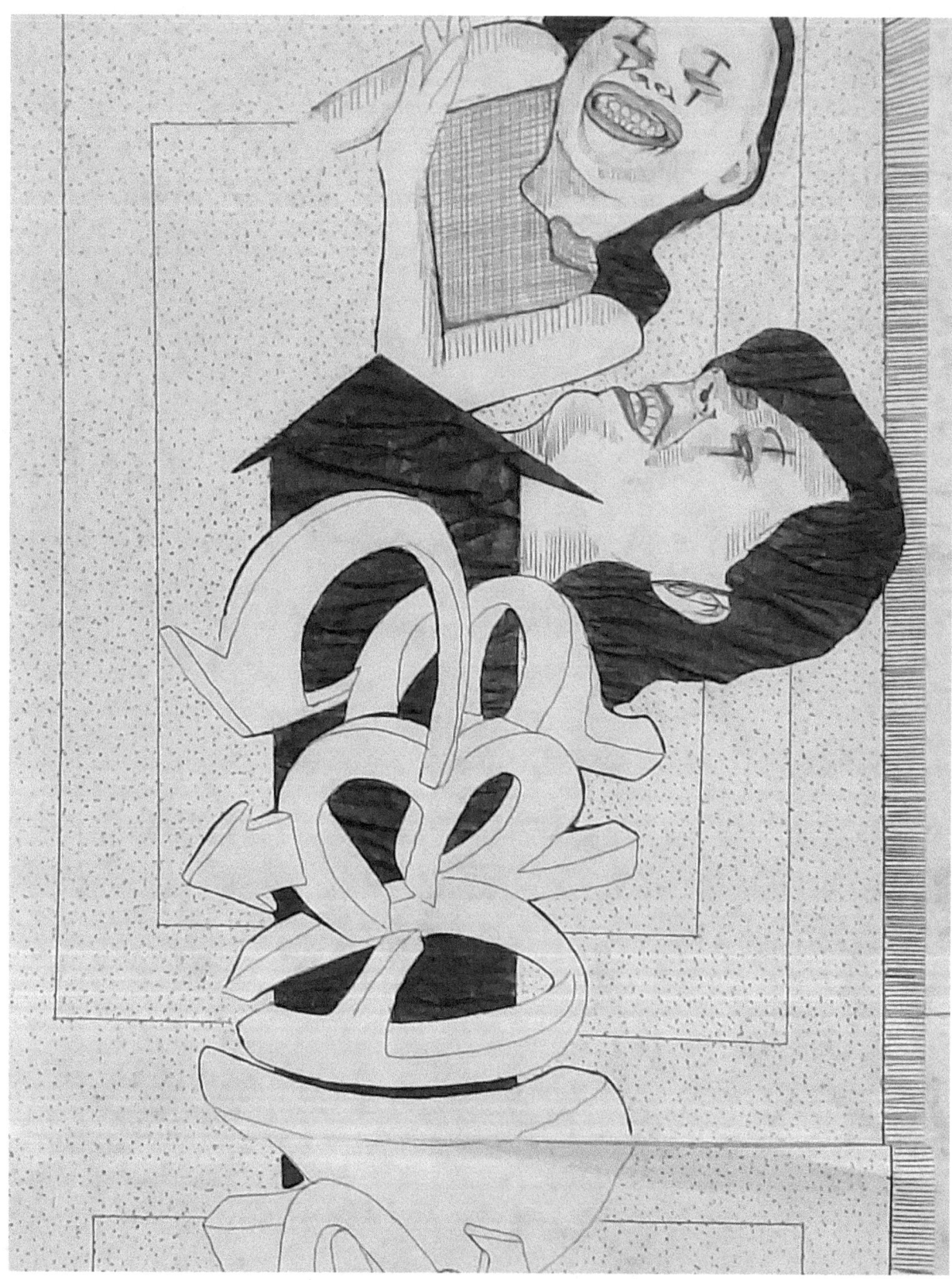

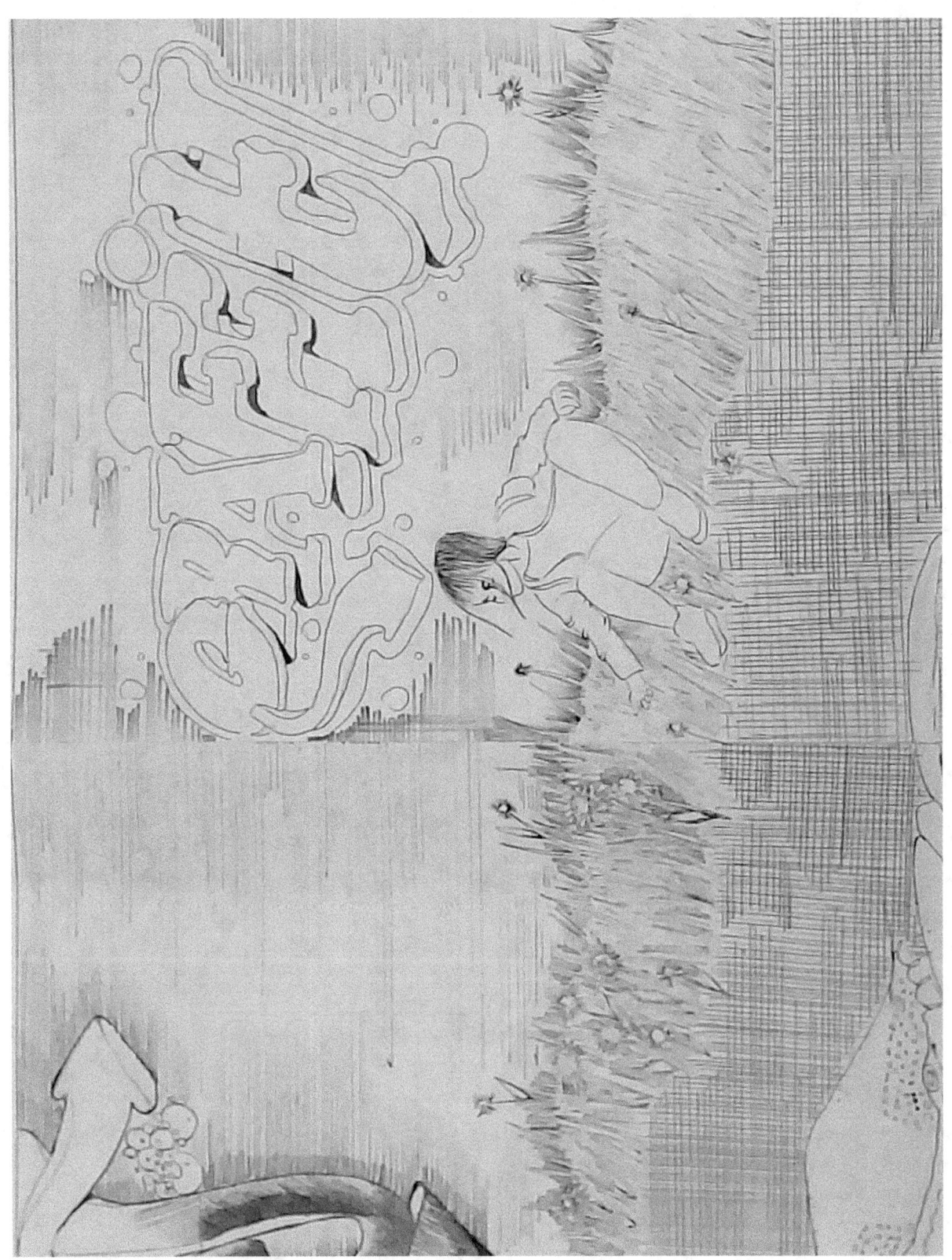

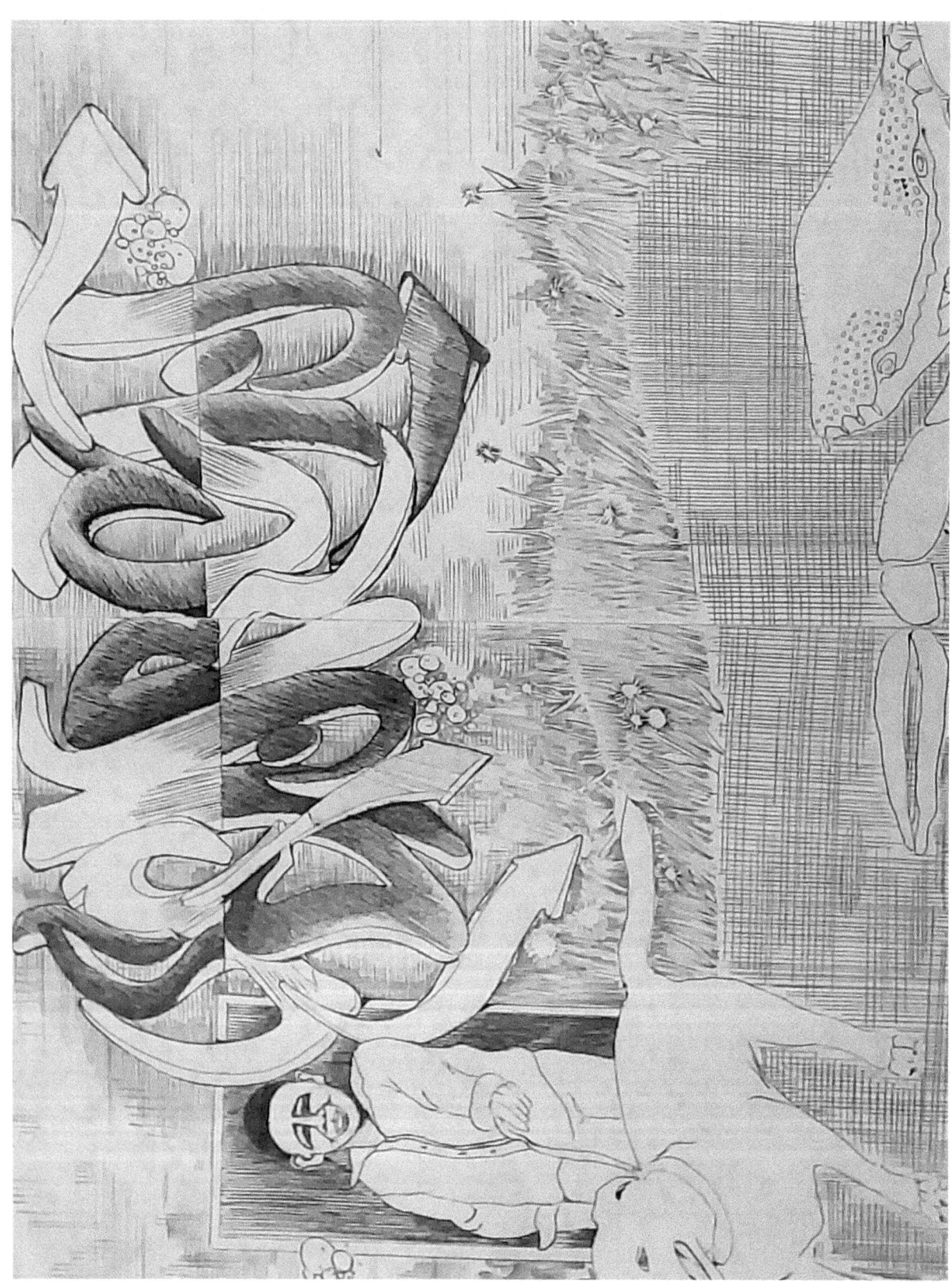

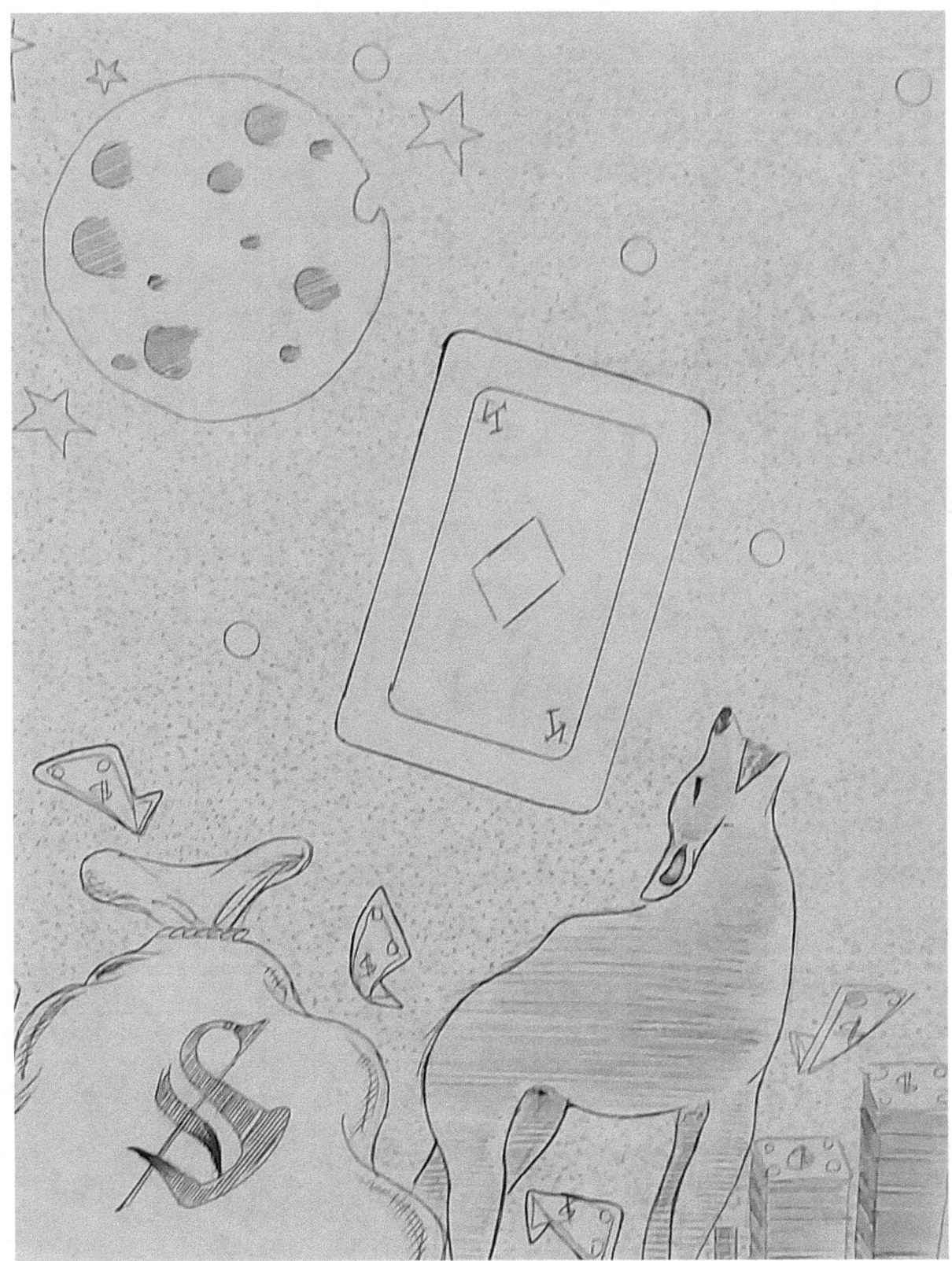

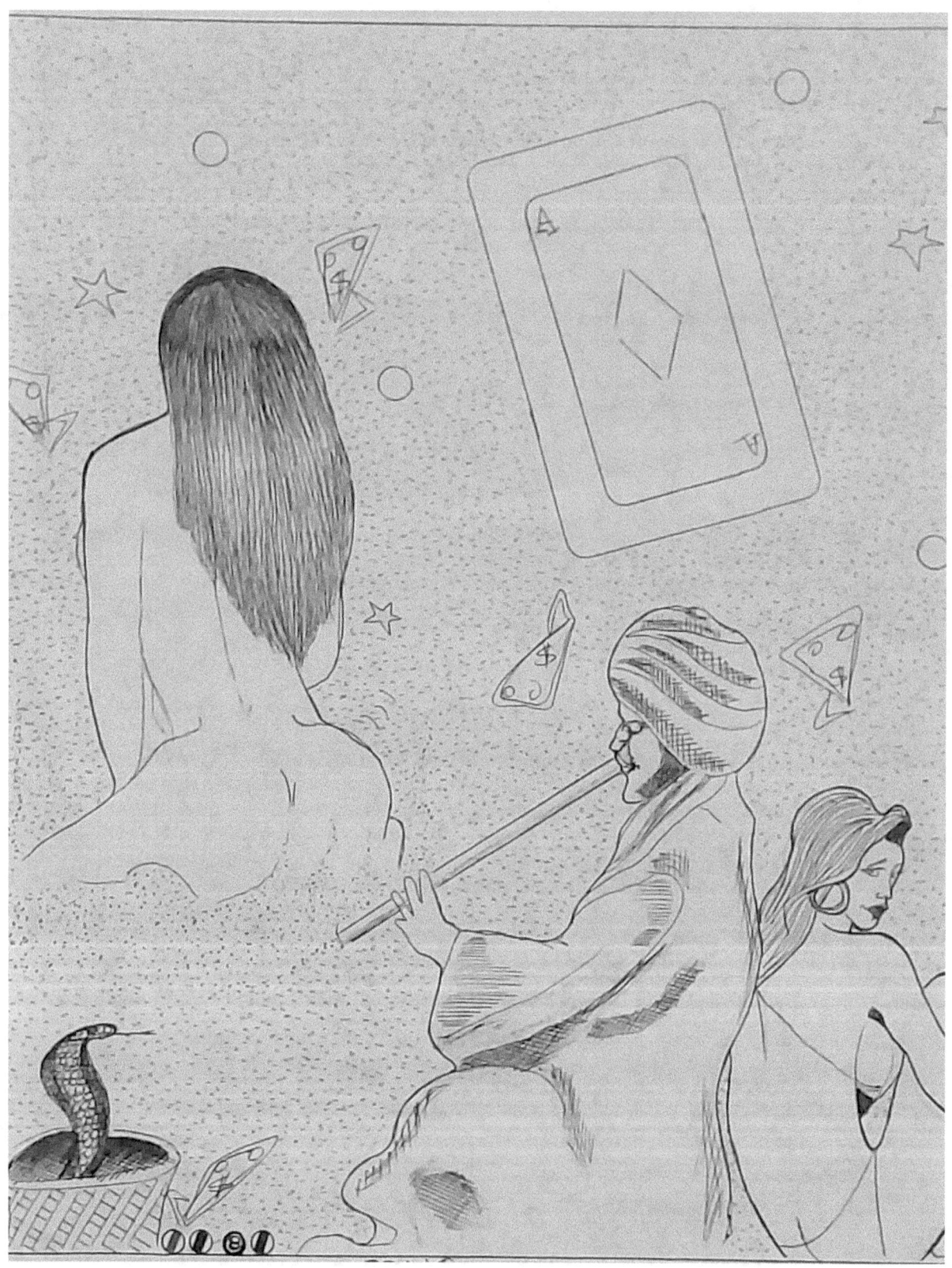

131

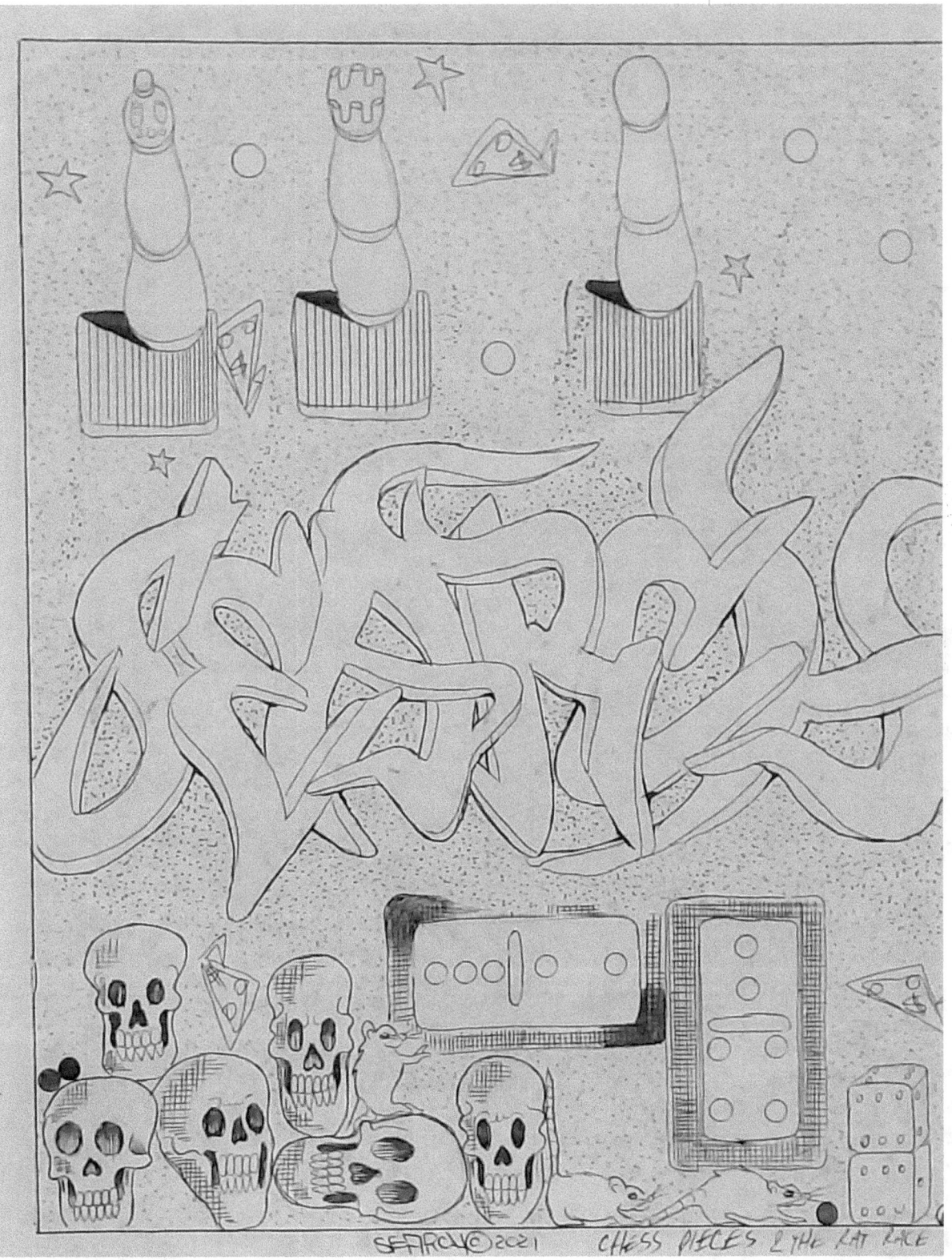

SEFIROV © 2021   CHESS PIECES & THE RAT RACE

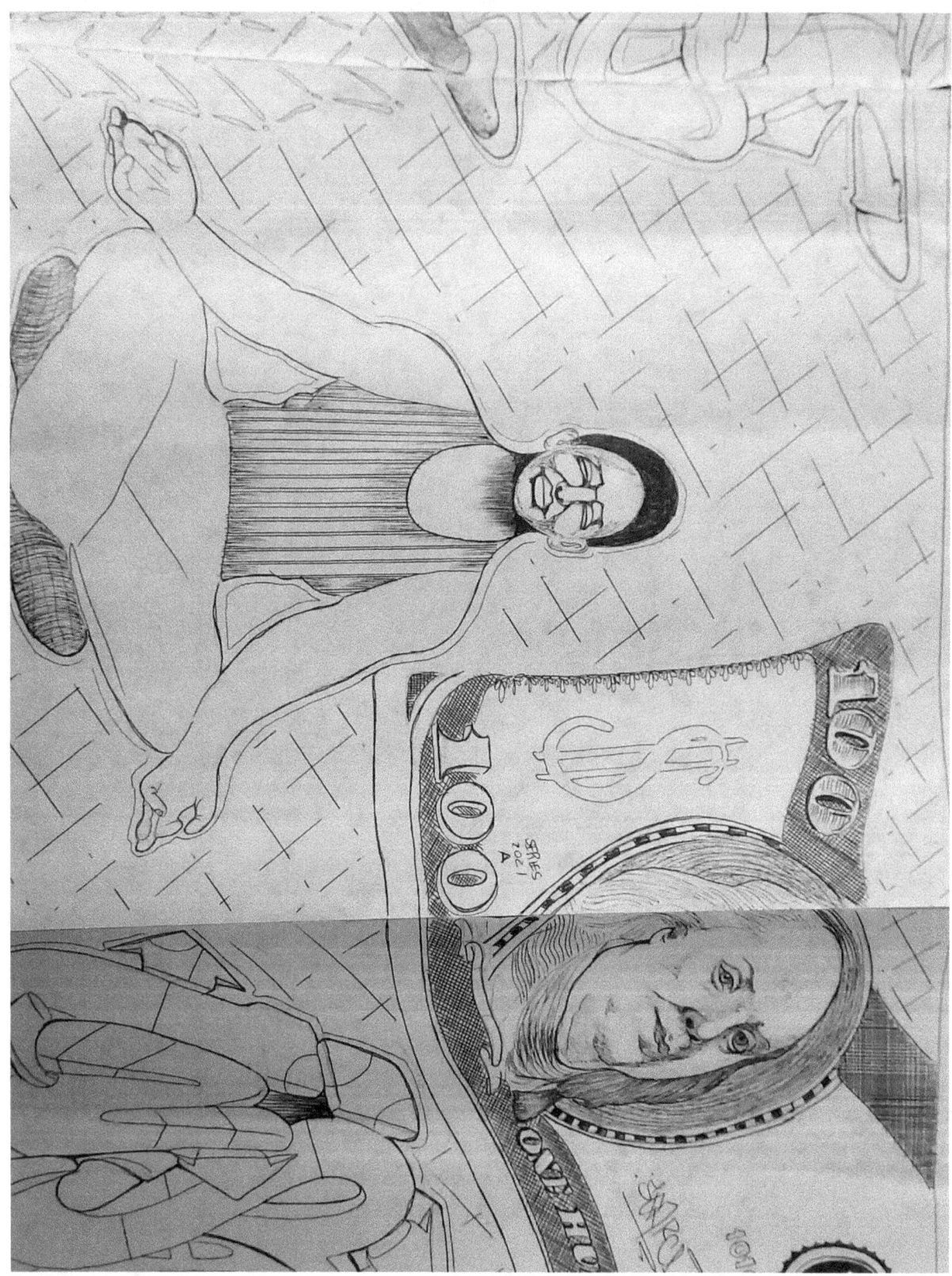

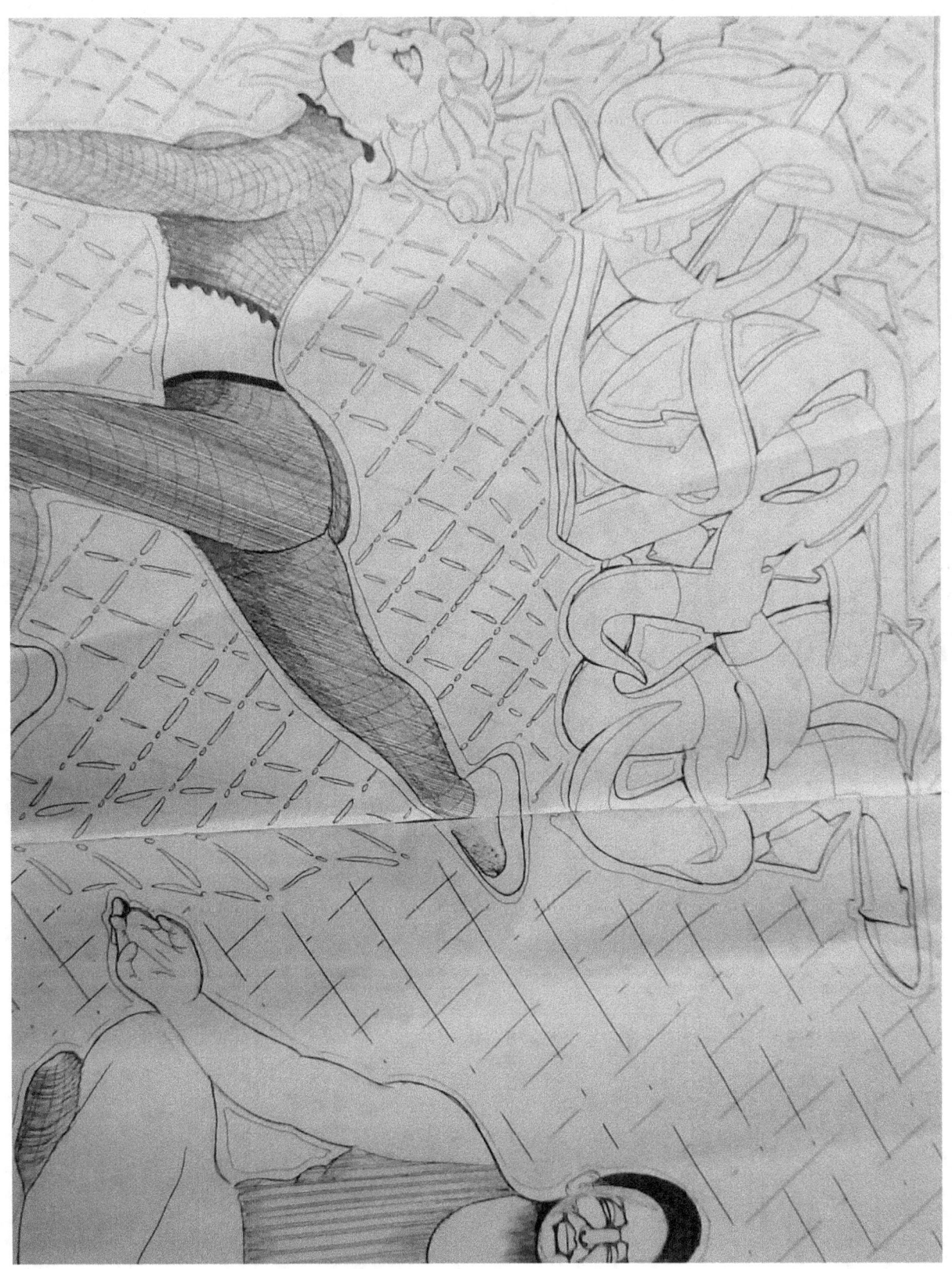

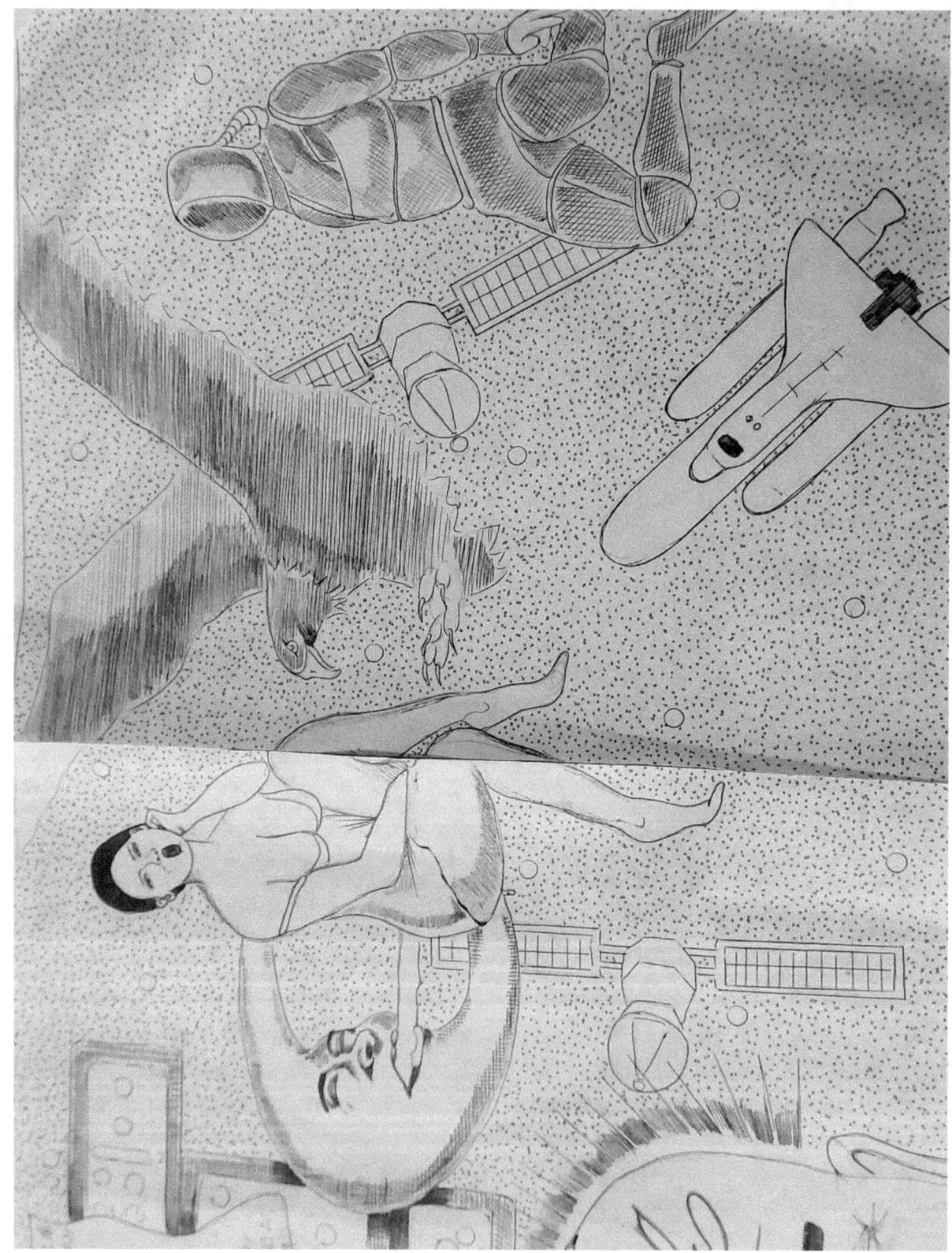

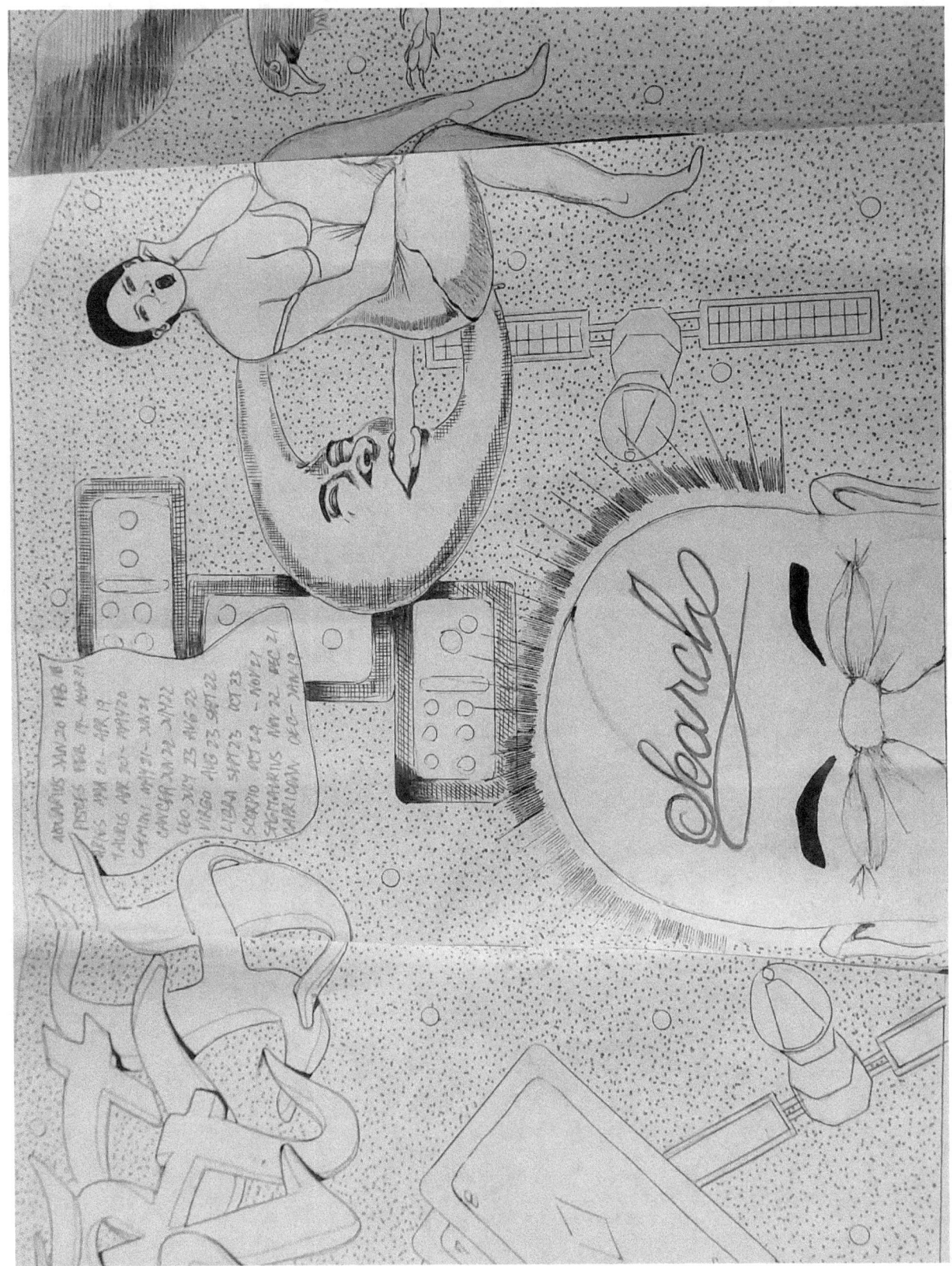

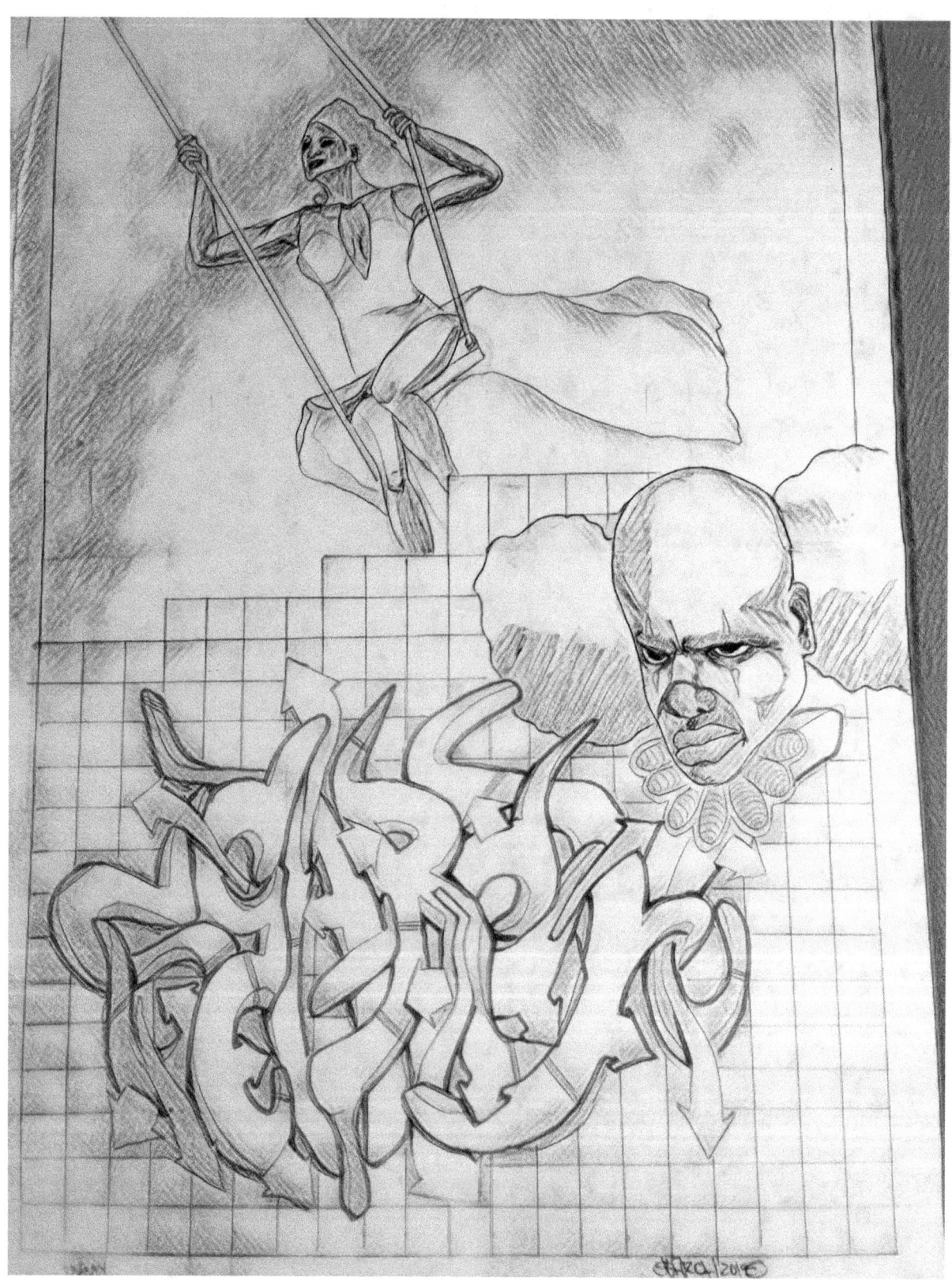

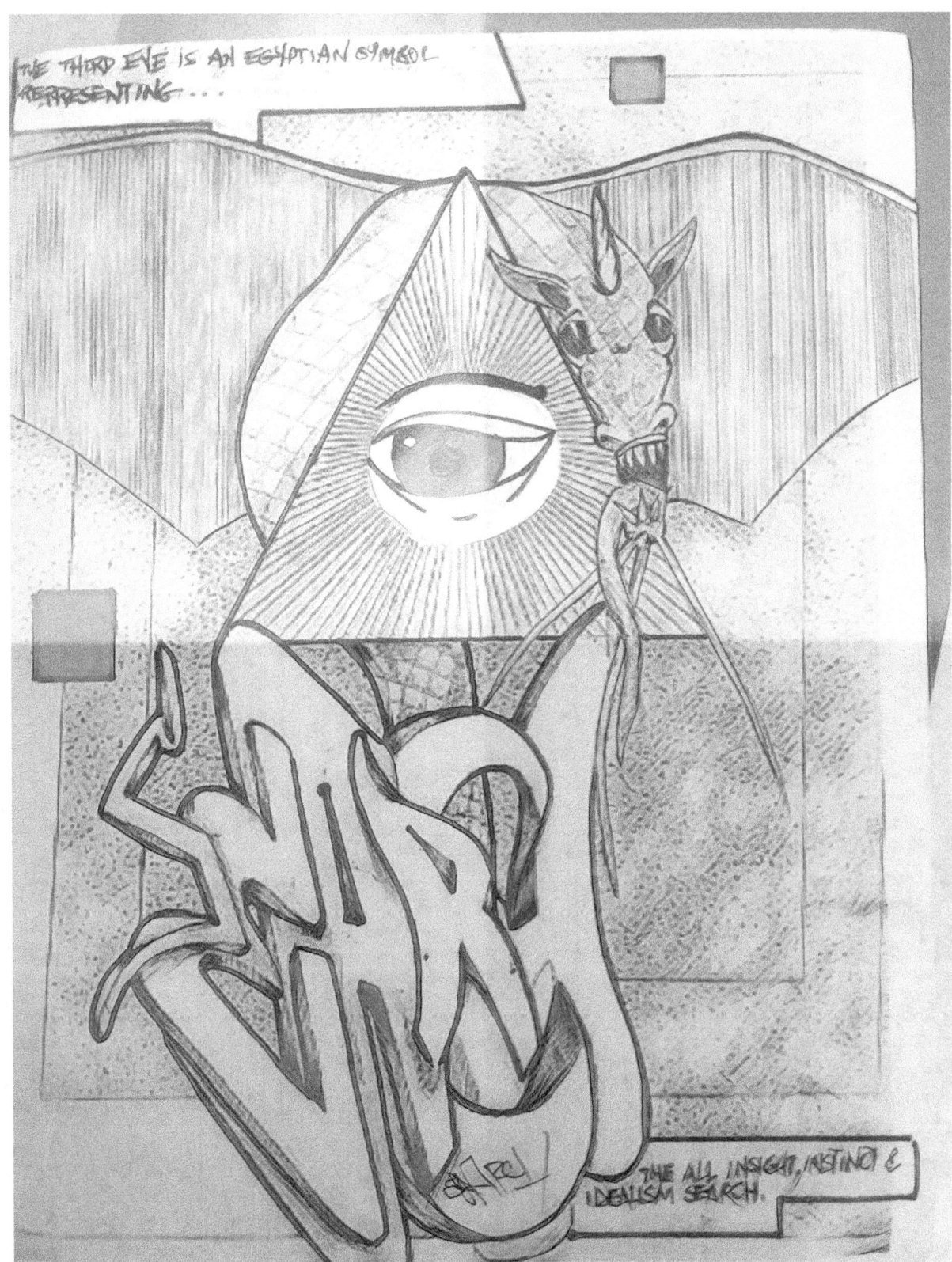

138

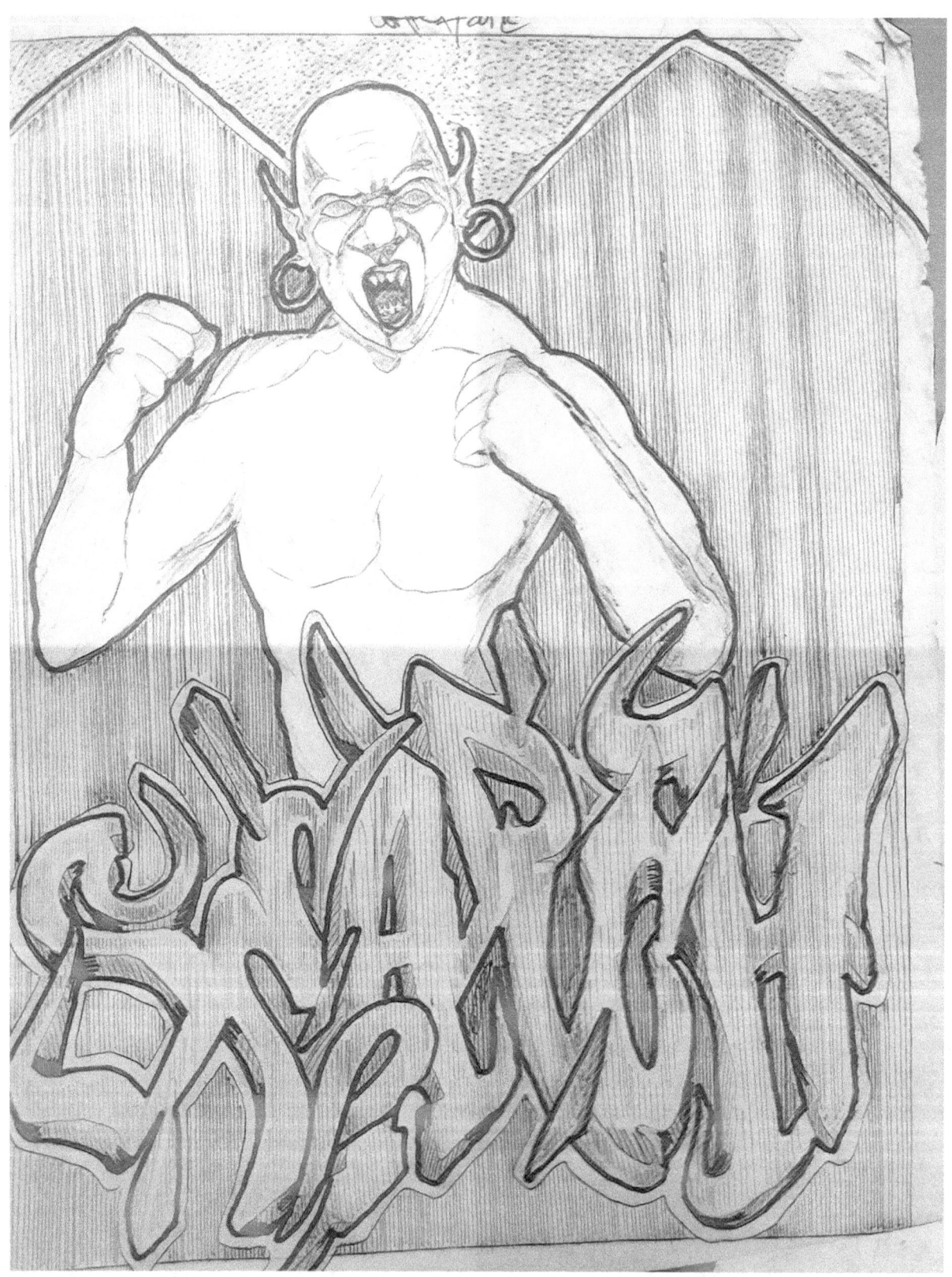

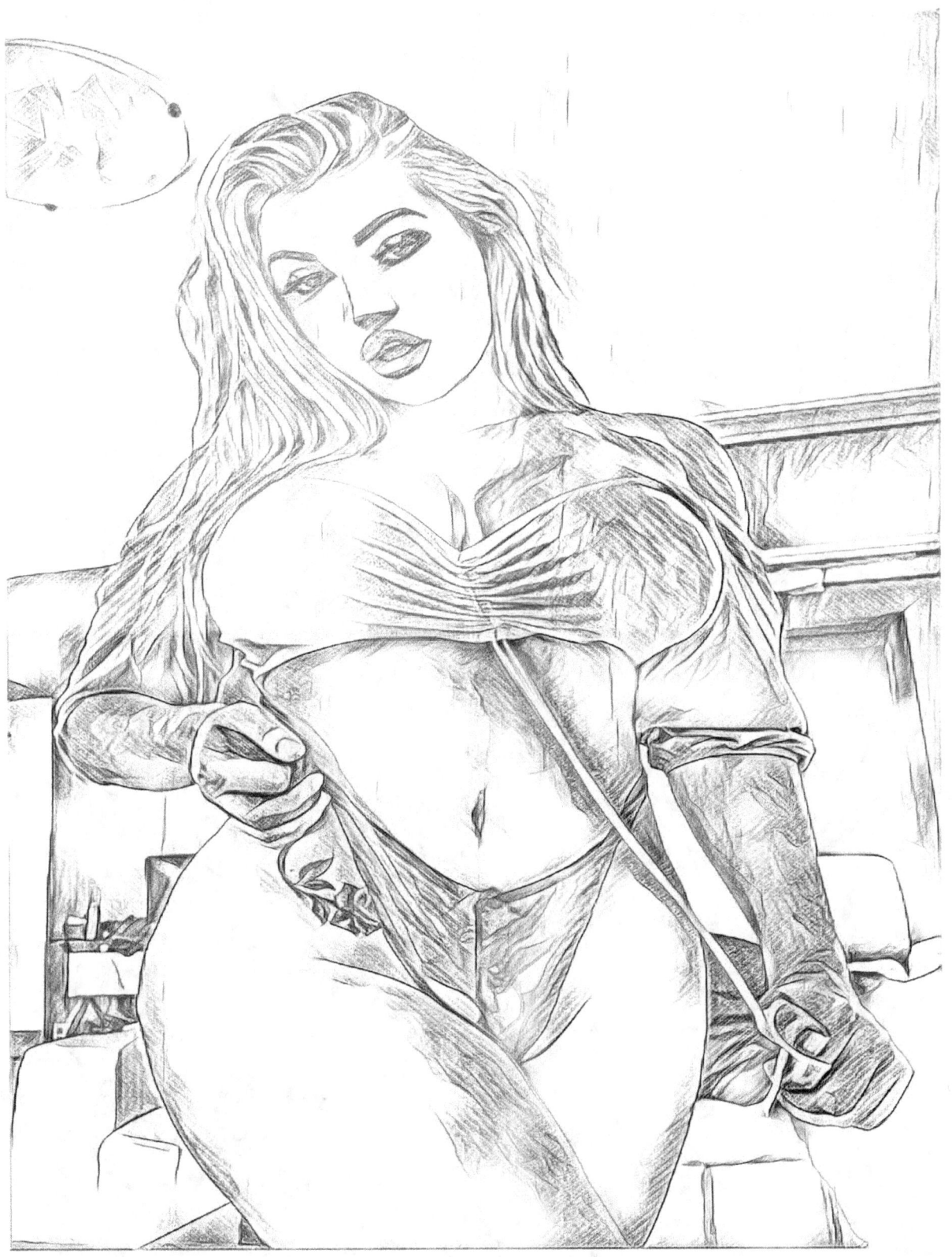

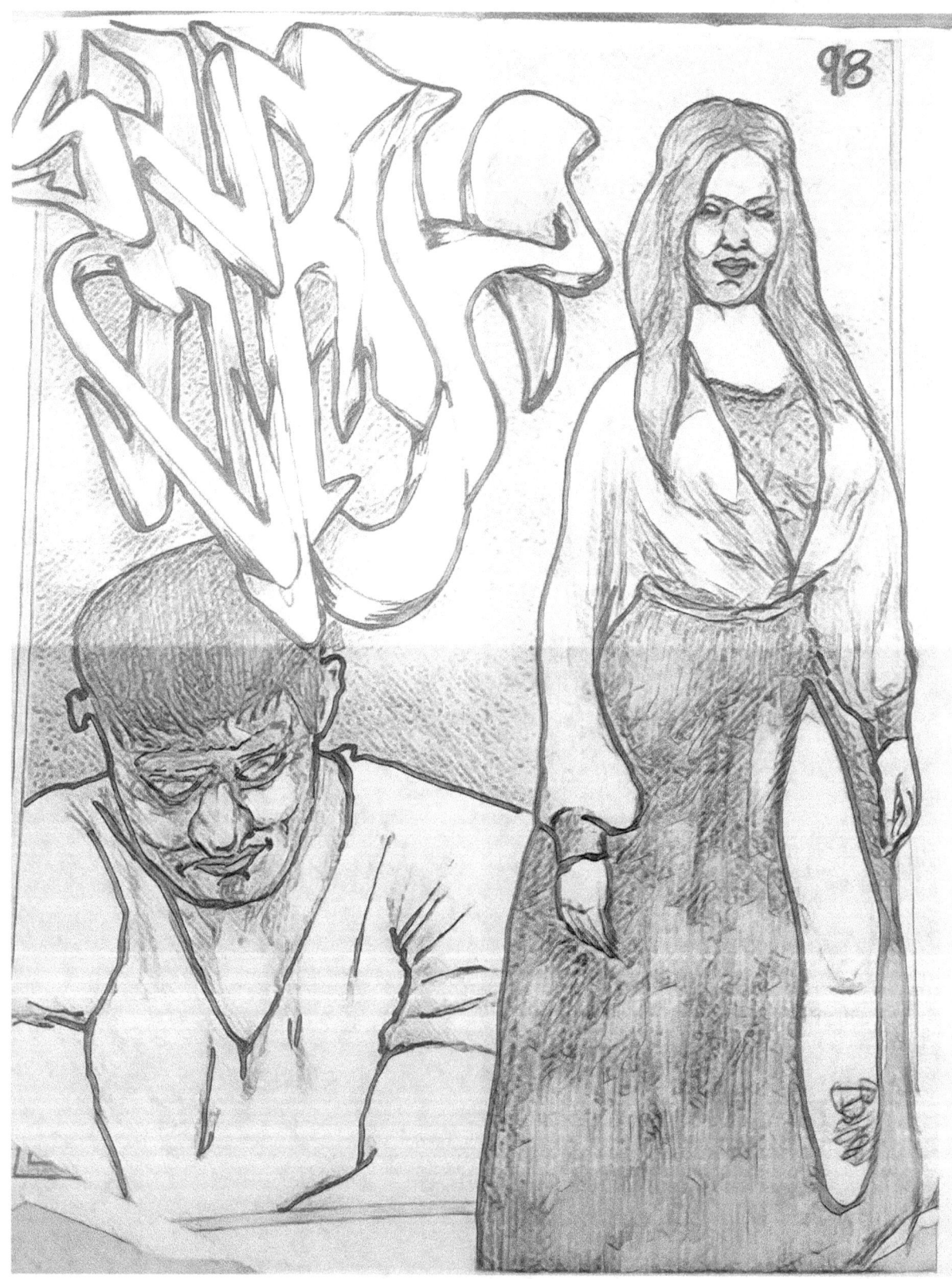

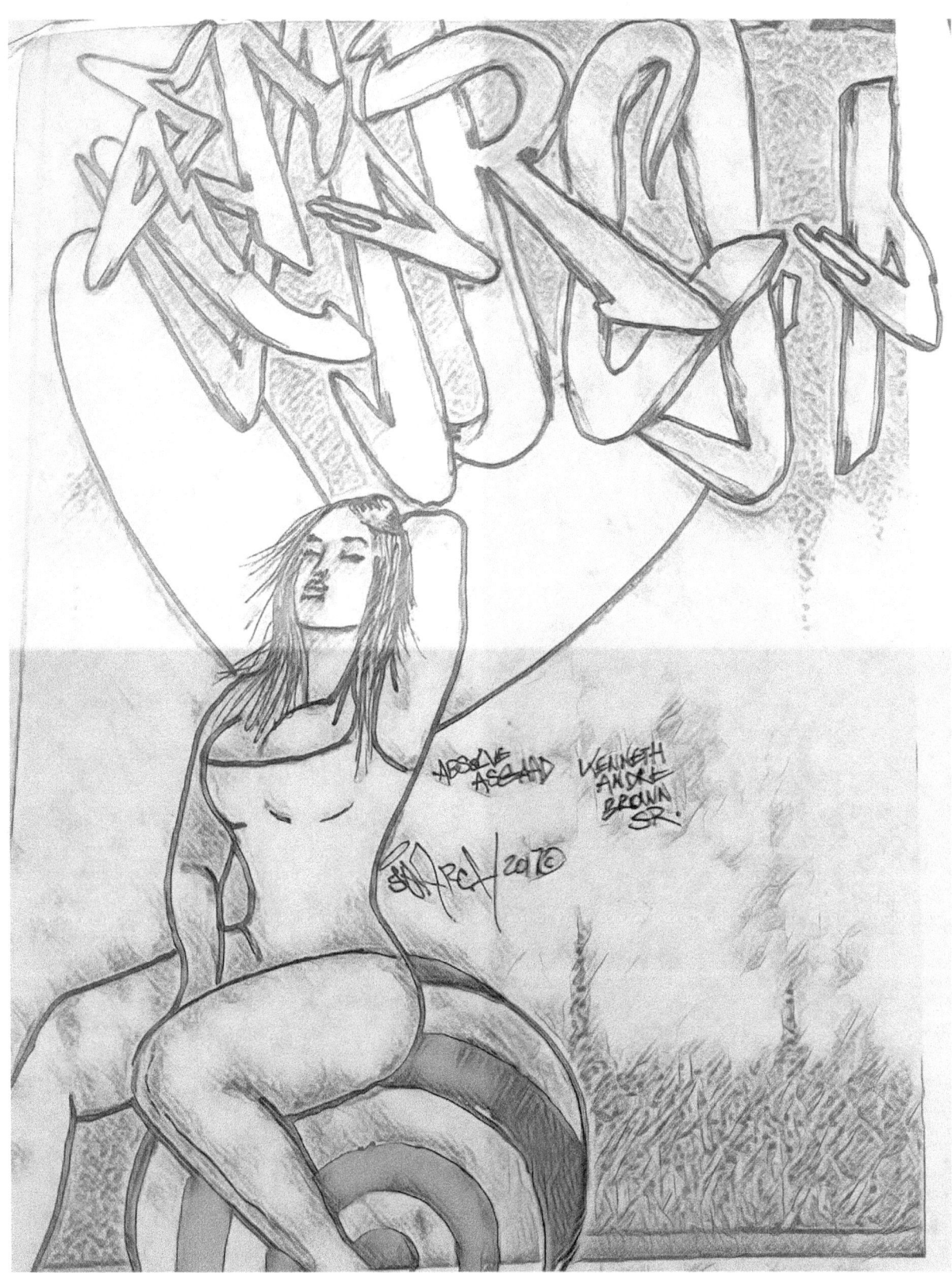

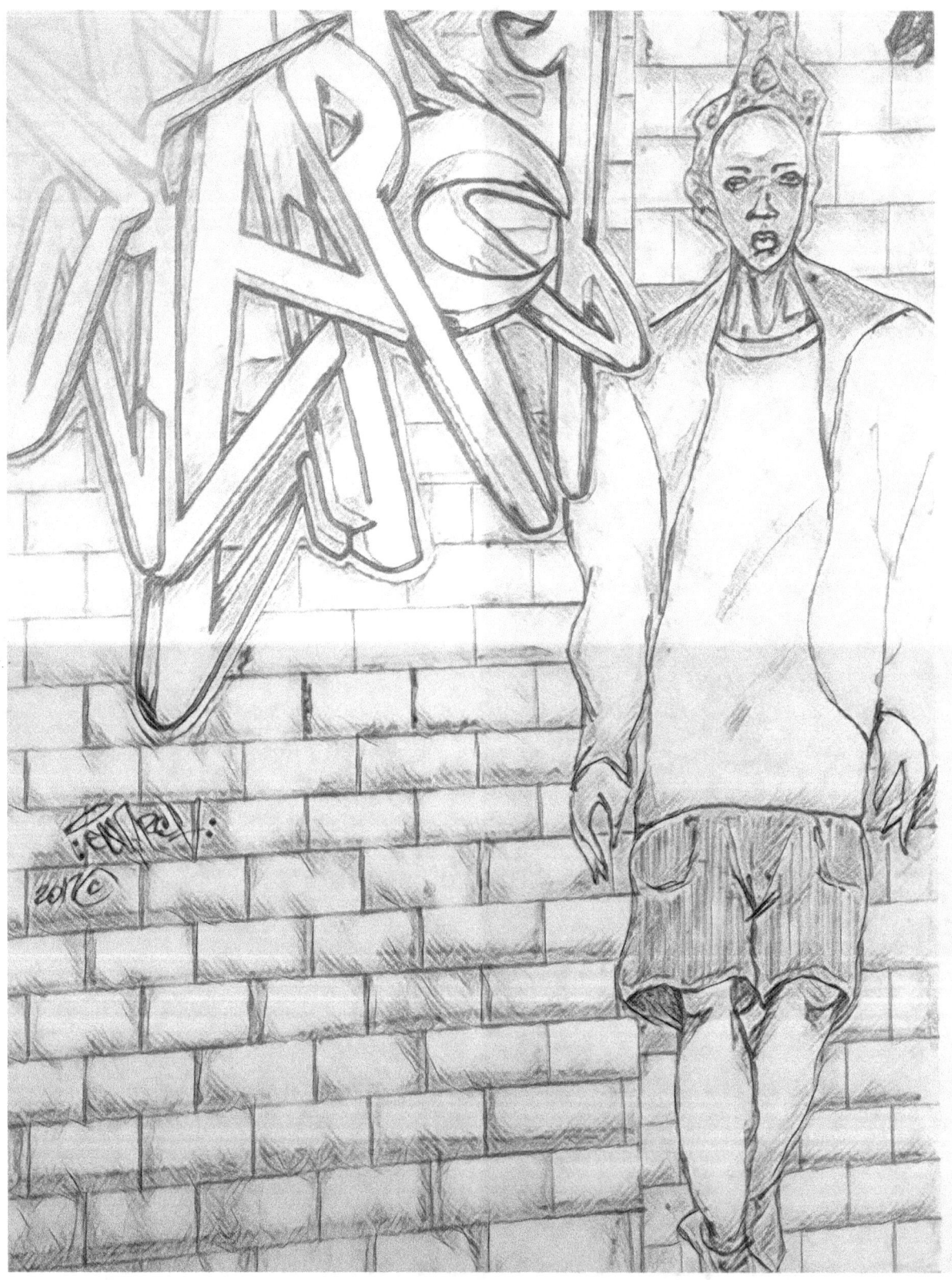

143

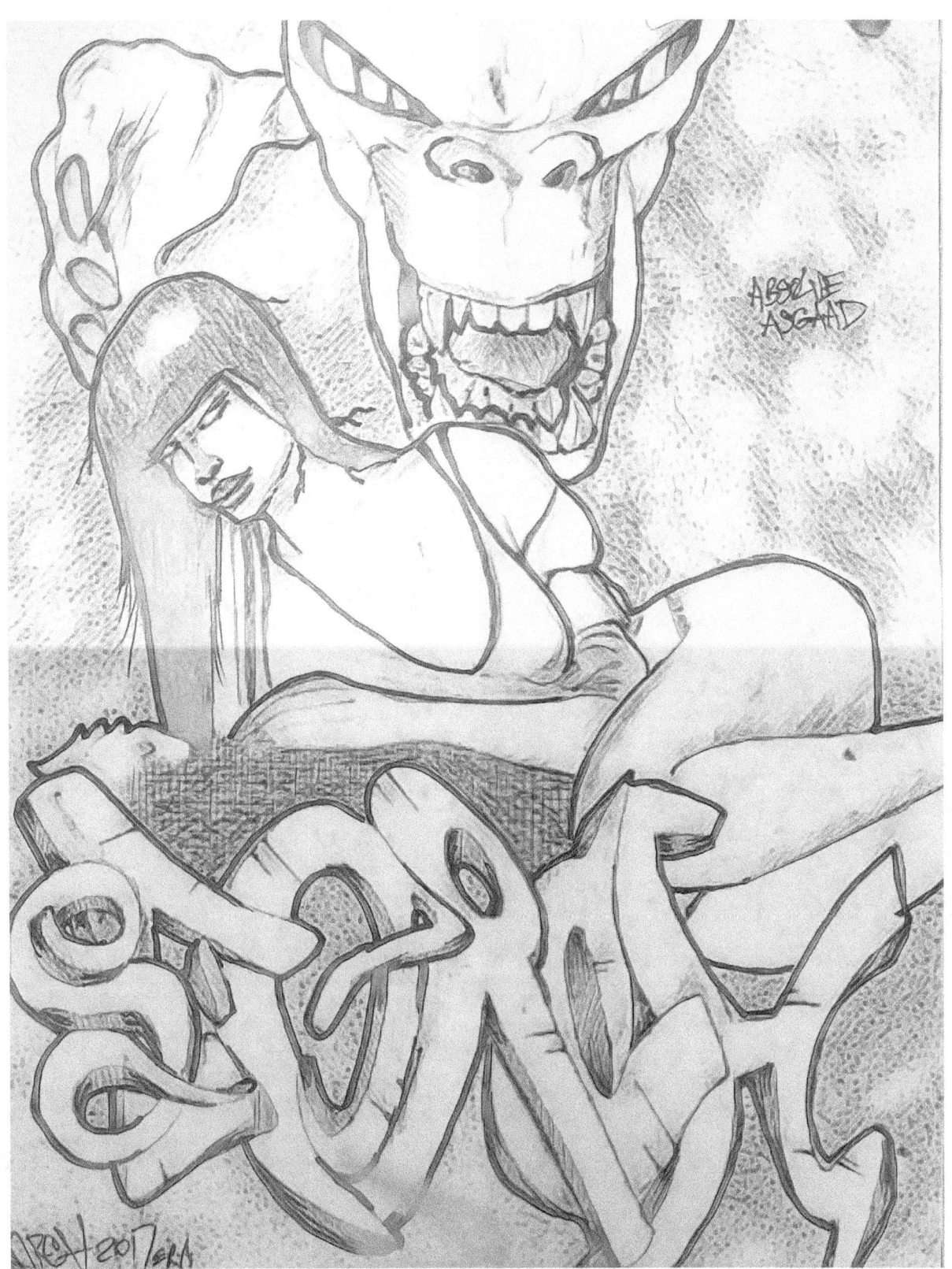

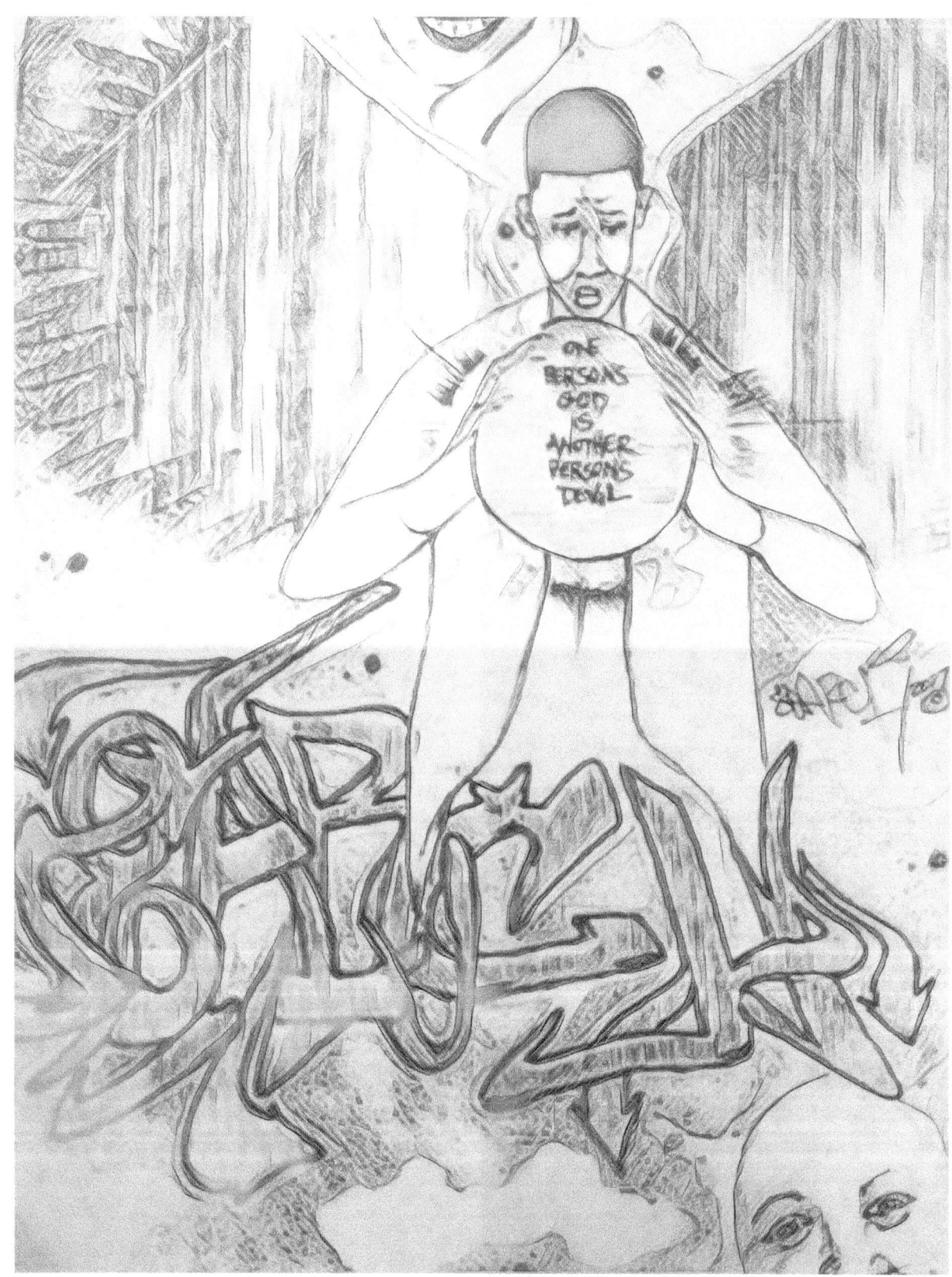

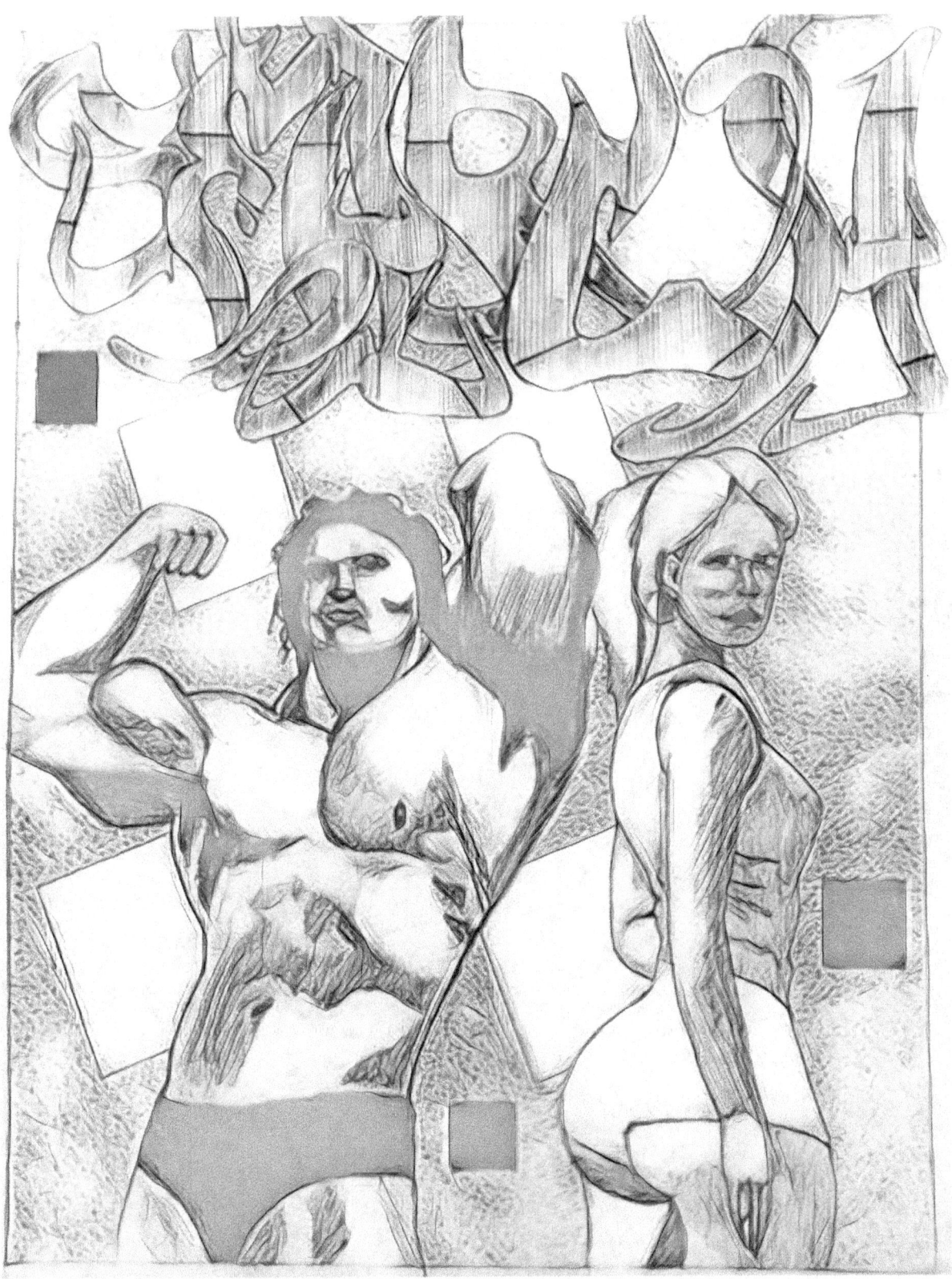

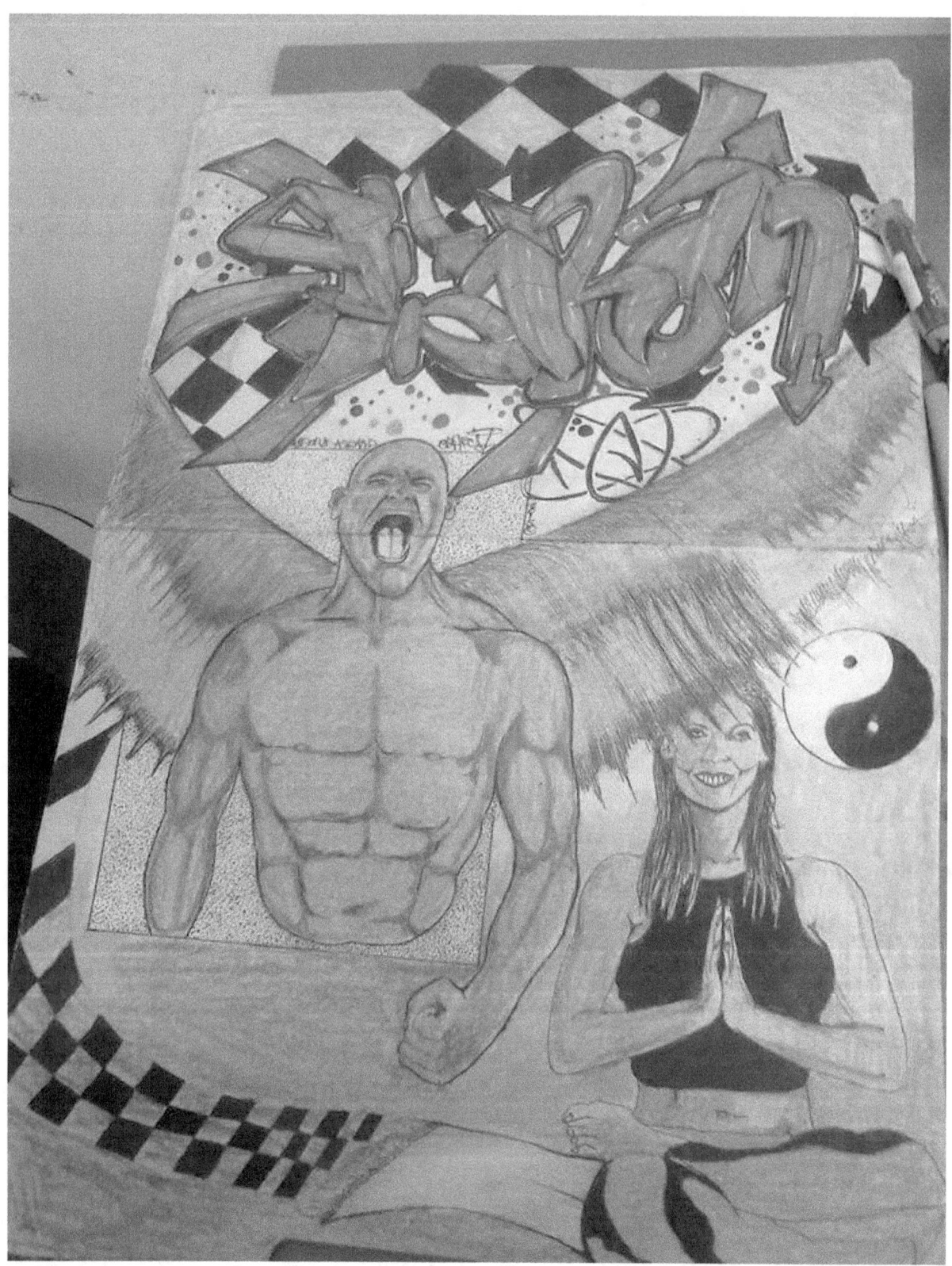

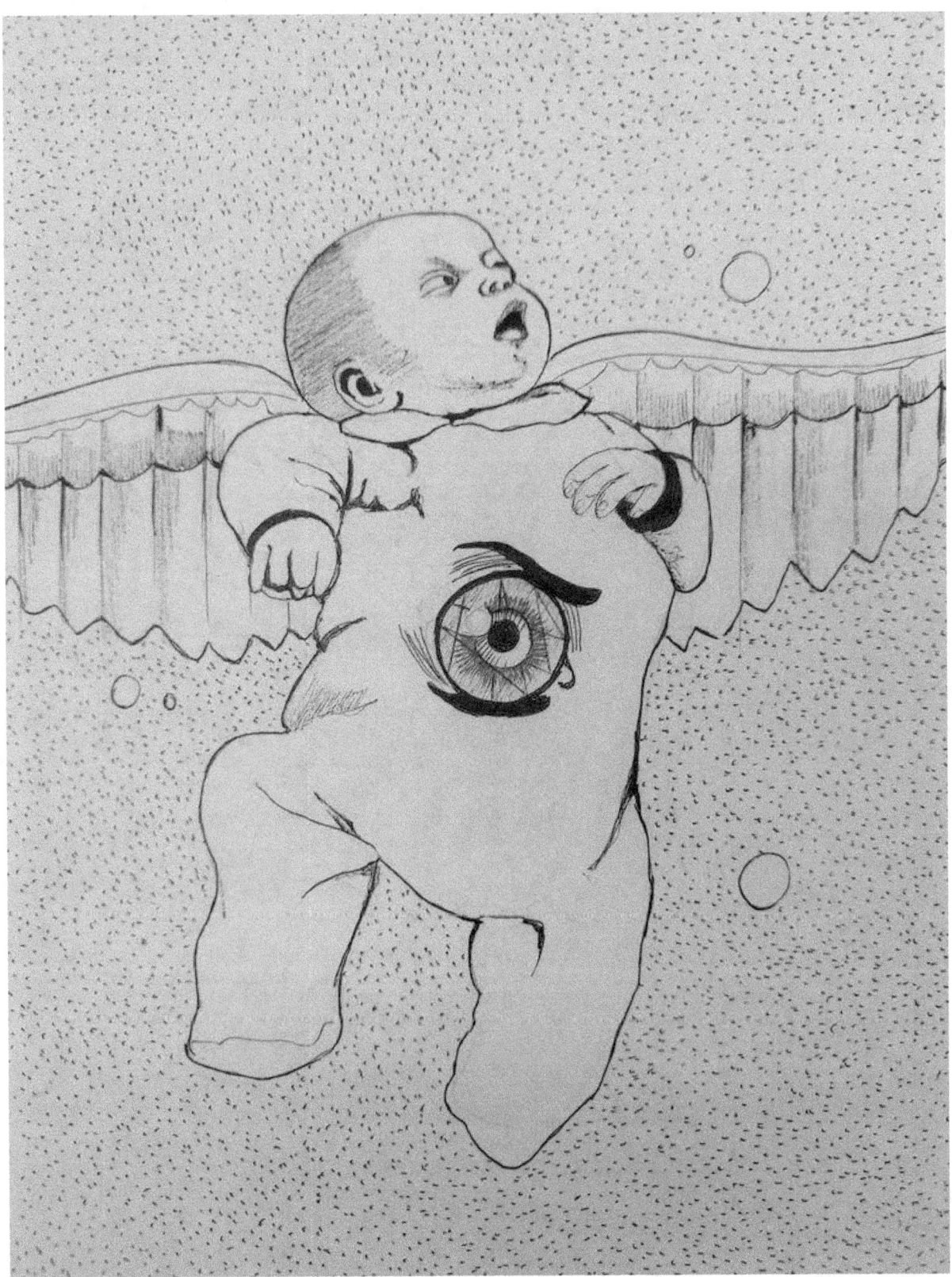

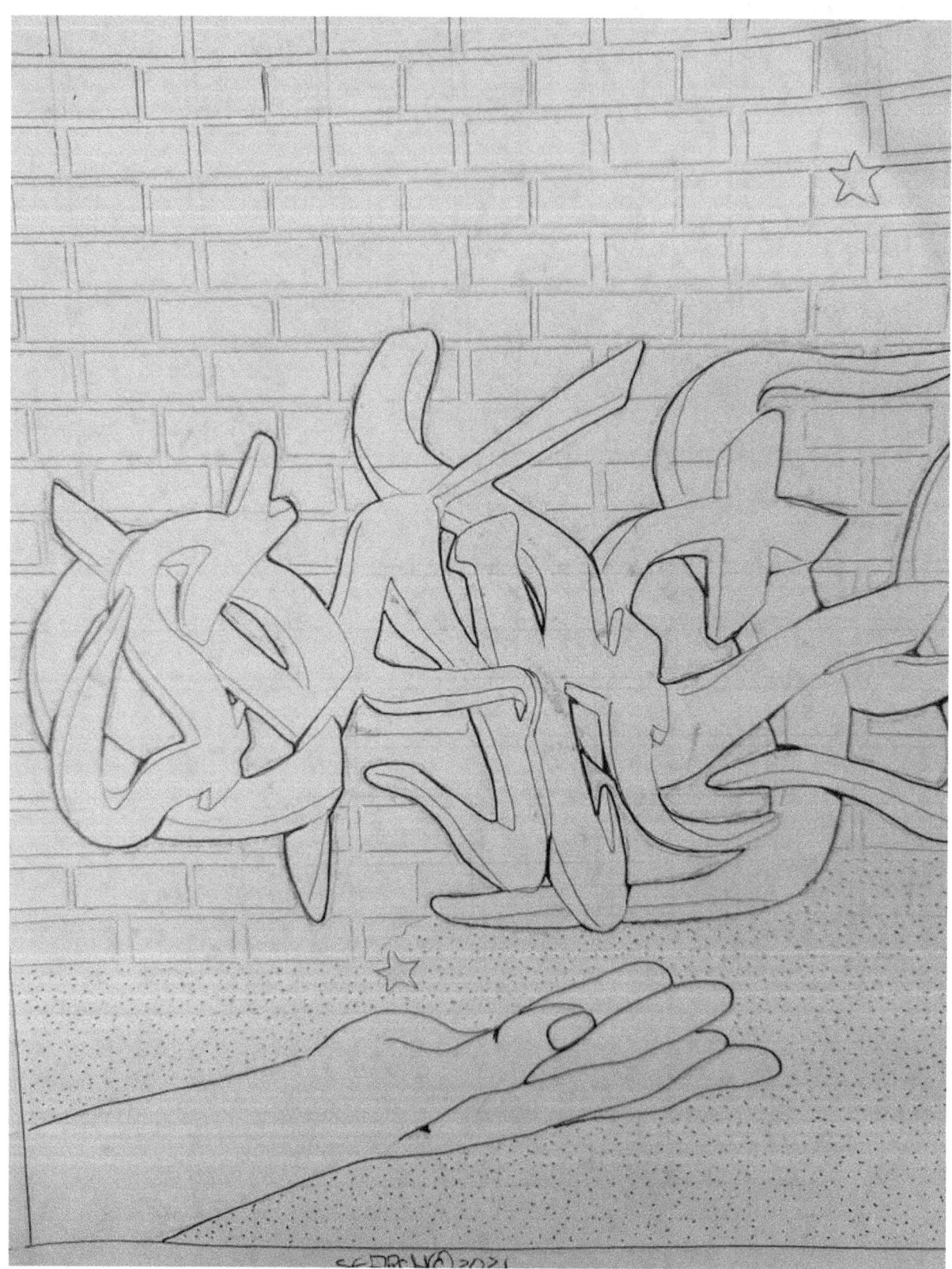

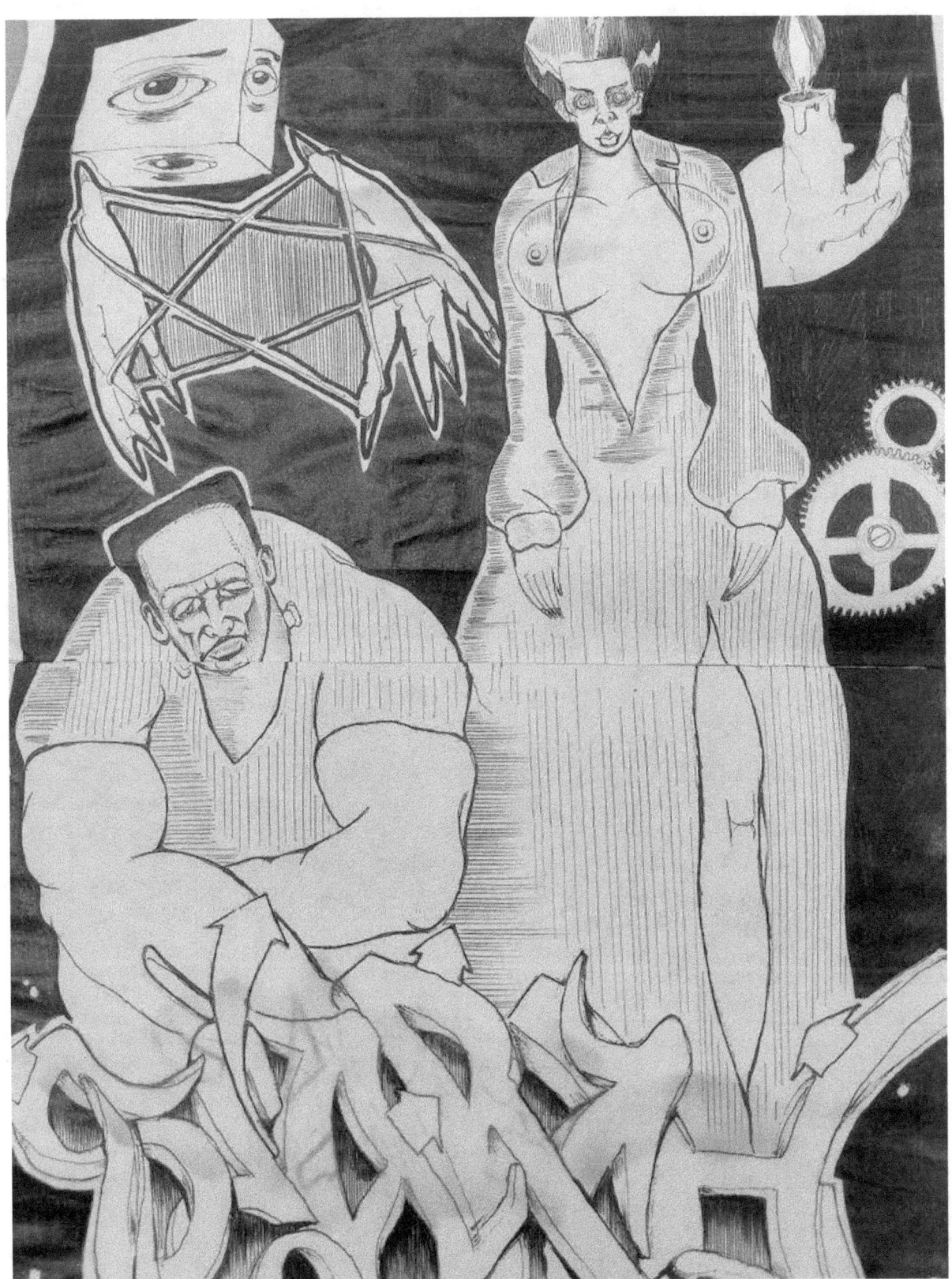

www.ingramcontent.com/pod-product-compliance
Lightning Source LLC
Chambersburg PA
CBHW081259170526
45165CB00011B/3348